Congregation Shaare Shamayim-G.N.J.C.

## In Memory of

### Jessica Katzin

Dedicated By

**Steve, Barbara & Spencer Sussman**

Congregation Shaare Shamayim-G.N.J.C.

## In Memory of

### Jessica Katzin

Dedicated By

**Ronnie & Harvey Meyer**

*Hasidic Tales of the Holocaust*

# Hasidic Tales of the Holocaust

Yaffa Eliach

2816

New York
OXFORD UNIVERSITY PRESS
1982

Library of Congress Cataloging in Publication Data
Main entry under title:
Hasidic Tales of the Holocaust.
Includes bibliogrraphical references and index.
1. Holocaust, Jewish (1939–1945)—Personal narratives.
2. Hasidim—Biography. 3. Tales, Hasidic. I. Eliach, Yaffa.
D810.J4H354 1982   940.53'15'03924   82-7928
ISBN 0-19-503199-7   AACR2

Printing (last digit): 9 8 7 6 5

Printed in the United States of America

When Pharaoh restored the chief butler to his position as foretold by Joseph in his interpretation of the butler's dream, he forgot Joseph. "Yet did not the chief butler remember Joseph, but forgot him" (Genesis 40:23). Why does the Bible use this repetitive language? It is obvious that if the butler forgot Joseph, he did not remember him. Yet, both verbs are used, *remembering* and *forgetting*. "The Bible, in using this language, is teaching us a very important lesson," said the Rabbi of Bluzhov, Rabbi Israel Spira, to his Hasidim. "There are events of such overbearing magnitude that one ought not to remember them all the time, but one must not forget them either. Such an event is the Holocaust."

*The Rabbi of Bluzhov, Rabbi Israel Spira*

For David
and our children Yotav, Rachel, and Smadar

# Contents

TWO
FRIENDSHIP

THREE
THE SPIRIT ALONE

FOUR
AT THE GATES OF FREEDOM

# Acknowledgments

SOME BOOKS ARE BORN IN SOLITUDE, OTHERS AMONG PEOPLE. THIS book resulted from an ongoing dialogue and exchange of ideas with many people. I would like to acknowledge a few among the many: My students at Brooklyn College, for their enthusiasm and interviews; the many Holocaust survivors who were willing to share the accounts of their most painful and lonely years; the Rebbetzin Bronia Spira for her advice, moral courage, and marvelous tales; Dina Spira and Baruch Singer for their time and their dedication to Hasidic stories; Oscar Rosenthal and Harold Zlotnik for their advice at the very initial stages of the book; the City University of New York, PSC-BHE Research Award Program, for funding the first stage of the project; Mollie Fried for typing parts of the manuscript; Uri Assaf for his advice since the inception of the book; Bonnie Gurewitsch for reading the manuscript as it was written and offering many linguistic suggestions; Miriam Hurewitz for doing the copyediting with such thoroughness and care; Beth Rashbaum for making it a labor of love and for her genuine interest in the material and her perceptive insight, which greatly enhanced this book; my children, Yotav and Smadar, for their moral support, offered with good humor; and most of all my husband, David, my teacher and friend, for his patience, wisdom, and knowledge. You all made this book possible. Needless to say, its shortcomings are all mine.

# Foreword

HASIDISM, A POPULAR JEWISH REVIVALIST-PIETISTIC MOVEMENT, made its appearance during the first half of the eighteenth century in Podolia and Volhynia, in the Ukraine. It emerged in the aftermath of the Cossack Bogdan Chmielnicki's massacres in the previous century; the disillusionment with the false Messiah Sabbetai Zevi, who had proclaimed that the year 1666 would be the millennium; and with the decline of Jewish institutions, chiefly the Council of the Four Lands, the central organization of Jewish autonomous life in Eastern Europe.

Hasidism was founded by Israel ben Eliezer, the Baal Shem Tov (1700–1760), "Master of the Good Name," who recognized the need for new patterns of life, leadership, and literature to revitalize the Jewish community of Eastern Europe.

The new movement reshuffled the existing scale of values within the Jewish community. It placed prayer, ecstasy, storytelling, and sanctification of daily life on a par with Talmudic studies. The merit of scholarship was no longer to be the only major avenue to communion and closeness with God.

The new patterns of leadership, likewise, were no longer based solely on scholastic achievements. Charismatic individuals became leaders in various locales in Poland and the Ukraine. Hasidism eventually evolved into a leader-devotee relationship, where allegiance to a leader (zaddik) was established and handed down from generation to generation, giving rise to dynasties of zaddikim and their Hasidic followers. The various sects were always named after places in Eastern Europe (and later in other countries) which were associated with crucial events in the zaddik's life; the name could be that of the zaddik's birthplace, or it could be where he established his court or where he died. By the turn of the eighteenth century, Hasidism had

grown from a minority group facing strong opposition, particularly
from the Lithuanian scholarly community, to a wide-ranging popular
movement. Eventually, it was to become one of the major movements in Eastern Europe, with a strong following in the Jewish
communities of the Austro-Hungarian Empire.

One of the movement's most important contributions was its literature, particularly the tales and anecdotes. The main themes of Ha-
sidic tales are love of humanity, optimism, and a boundless belief in
God and the goodness of mankind. The typical Hasidic tale is charac-
terized by a unique blend of folkish elements and sophisticated wit.
The first collection of Hasidic tales, *Shivhei-ha Besht (In Praise of the
Baal Shem Tov)*, consisted of anecdotes about the life of the founder,
and was published in 1814. A year later *Sippuri Maasiyyot*, by Rabbi
Nachman of Bratslav (1772–1811), the great-grandson of the Baal
Shem Tov, was published posthumously. These thirteen stories,
which first appeared in a bilingual edition of Yiddish and Hebrew,
are among the classic masterpieces of Hasidic literature. Their alle-
gorical themes are a continuing source of inspiration and scholarly research. These first collections were followed by an outpouring of
anthologies of Hasidic tales, most of them focusing on the lives of the
early masters and their devoted Hasidim. Since most of the tales were
written in Yiddish, which was the vernacular, as opposed to Hebrew,
the language of scholarship, they attracted many women to Hasidism
and made Hasidic tales "best sellers" of their time.

Since its emergence as a prominent literary genre, the Hasidic tale
has stimulated and inspired many distinguished men of letters such
as Franz Kafka, I. L. Peretz, Martin Buber, and S. Y. Agnon (Israel's Nobel Laureate in Literature), and countless others less well
known who have also found in the Hasidic tale a traditional and a the-
matic content which suited their particular philosophy, world out-
look, and temperament. Peretz imposed on the Hasidic folktales and
material that he collected his own aesthetic imprint. He discovered in
the tales an expression of moral beauty and grandeur, and a deep
mystical truth in the lives of the poor and the simple. Like Peretz,
Buber, one of the pioneers in bringing Hasidic literature to the world

at large, was deeply moved by the religious message of Hasidism, and he considered it his duty to convey that message to the world. His fascination with Hasidic literature was to last a lifetime. In 1906, Buber attempted to translate the tales of Rabbi Nachman into German, but later decided to retell them in German in a free adaptation; in 1908 he translated the *Legends of the Baal Shem Tov*. He also engaged in a collaboration with S. Y. Agnon, who came from a Hasidic home in Galicia. Agnon's father was a follower of the Tchortkover Rebbe (see "Grandfather Avrumche Backenroth's Table" in Part Four). Much of Agnon's work is an artistic attempt to recapture the waning tradition of pious Jews and the love and life of Hasidim.

During the Holocaust, when European Jews were systematically destroyed and the cultural achievements of western civilization were fragmented, Hasidism continued to create its magnificent tales in ghettos, hiding places, and camps. Despite the unprecedented scope of the mechanized destruction of human lives, Hasidism did not lose its values, its belief in humanity. In fact, it seems that the very nature of the Hasidic tale made it a most appropriate literary form through which to come to terms with the Holocaust and its aftermath. The overwhelming number of dead, the anonymity of the victims, the scope of the destruction, seemed to leave other genres of the literary tradition of Europe at a loss for words. The Polish poet Tadeusz Rozewicz may well have been a spokesman for an entire post-Holocaust generation when he wrote that after the war he fashioned his poems "out of a remnant of words, salvaged words, out of uninteresting words, words from the great rubbish dump, the great cemetery." Others, like the critic George Steiner, in the face of the unspeakable, simply recommended silence. The British critic Stephen Spender has suggested that this inability of western literature to cope with the Holocaust stems from the traditional preoccupation of Greek and Christian literature with the fate of the solitary sacrificial victim—Oedipus, Christ, or Lear—and that such a literature is inevitably ill equipped to confront a disaster that affected millions of people, to create tragedy from that disaster.

The Jewish poet, on the other hand, beginning in biblical times, may be better prepared to deal with tragedies that affect the lives of millions of anonymous victims. Traditionally, the biblical poet/ prophet gave voice to the sufferings of an entire people in the face of calamity. Thus, the Scroll of Lamentations is the cry in unison for a desolate city, a nation, a motherland laid to waste, as well as a plea for redemption. In the Bible, time loses its everyday chronological significance. It is moments in the history of a people, rather than the experience of an individual (no matter how exalted), that are the subject matter of the biblical poet. Aesthetic and artistic forms exist to express the people's collective consciousness.

The Hasidic tale draws from both European literary tradition and from a variety of Jewish sources—Bible, Midrash, Kabbalah, and others. Central to many Hasidic tales is the singular, almost mythological, charismatic personality of the zaddik, the saint. Unlike the Greek or Christian hero, the zaddik possesses a larger-than-life personality and mystical powers which enable him to transcend the historical reality of his surroundings. He can endow the pain and the suffering of his Hasidim (his followers, literally "the Pious"), as individuals or as a multitude, with personal hope, with national and universal meaning. The zaddik struggles to remain optimistic even in the valley of death. His concept of eternal time enables him to surmount the brutal reality of his temporal surroundings. He is determined to believe that evil is transient and good must ultimately triumph. Faith becomes an optimistic link, providing the structural continuity between past and future, while endowing the wretchedness of the present with dignity.

In "Good Morning, Herr Müller," in Part Three, the S.S. man in charge of the selection line recognizes a rabbi, an acquaintance from before the war. Müller, who is sending thousands to their deaths with a single motion of his index finger, sends the rabbi to the right, to life. Even in this murderer, Hasidism is able to see a spark, a glimmer of hope, if only for a brief moment, for the split second when Müller lapses into humanity. As for the rabbi, now a Holocaust survivor, he can still bring himself to conclude, despite all the unspeakable atrocities he has witnessed, that greeting another human being is a worthwhile human practice. He ends his tale by saying: "This is the power of a 'good morning' greeting. A man must always greet his fellow man."

Thus the rabbi's faith and tradition provide him with historical and normative links with the pre-Holocaust past and the post-Holocaust world.

The anonymous, ordinary Hasid, whose only distinction is his unlimited faith in his zaddik, also finds it easier because of that faith to come to terms with the Holocaust. He is sure that his zaddik's supernatural powers can carry him over the abyss (see the first tale, "Hovering above the Pit"). He believes that a blessing uttered in the distant past promises survival, that because of the zaddik's blessing, even the Auschwitz number tatooed on his forearm may assume a mystical message of life (Part One, "Number 145053"). The naked lad in Mauthausen is saved from freezing in the subzero Austrian weather when he remembers his beloved zaddik's melody ("A Bobov Melody," Part Three).

These tales are not merely the personal stories of a particular Hasidic rabbi or of individual Hasidim; because of the conditions that gave birth to them, they assume the dimensions of moral and social reflections and commentary. At a time when human beings were stripped naked of everything, even of their names, the only resource remaining to them was their inner spiritual strength. This was the very essence of their existence, and it is this that the tales record. For the zaddik, this resource was his faith; for the Hasid, it was often his faith in his zaddik. It alone could provide a continuum of history and humanity amidst a distorted, chaotic new order.

From its very beginnings, dating back to the movement's founder, the Baal Shem Tov, the function of the Hasidic tale was to restore order and to mend the broken lines of communication between man and his fellow man, and between heaven and earth, at a time and place when faith and prayer failed:

But the truth is that in the stories that the world is telling are many concentrated lofty ideas. . . . The Baal Shem Tov, may the mem-

ory of a Zaddik be blessed . . . when he saw the lines of communication with heaven were broken and it was impossible to mend
them with prayer, he used to mend them and restore them by telling a tale.

These words were written by Rabbi Nachman of Bratslav in the foreword to his magnificent tales, which inspired many writers, including Franz Kafka.

The Hasidic tale is by its very nature capable of coming to terms
with the reality of the concentration-camp universe and its aftermath. When, as Rabbi Nachman said—long before the Holocaust—lines of communication between man and his fellow man are
broken, when men of faith are lonely, lost, solitary figures and the familiar social order is shattered, the Hasidic tale can offer solace to
those whose faith has failed them, whose prayers seem not to be
heard. The tales can restore the vital communication link between
man and man, between heaven and earth. The optimistic power
vested in the Hasidic tale defies the burning furnaces and glowing
chimneys of the concentration-camp universe.

Despite the bleak reality of his surroundings, the Hasidic storyteller has unlimited options open to him, including sources based in
folklore and humor. Hasidism imposes no restrictions on its
storytellers. For a creative mind within a religious movement, this is
an extraordinary and very welcome freedom, almost without parallel
in the literature of other religious movements. Because of its "holiness," the Hasidic tale enjoys a unique status, a concept discussed at
length by Yoseph Dan of the Hebrew University in his book *The Hasidic Tale*. The tale is the agent entrusted with the mission of spread-
ing the movement's ideas; it instructs, without any restrictions on
structure, protagonist, or content. Because of its mission, the tale
must never become the exclusive domain of the few or the initiated,
as happens in other groups and cultures where storytelling is central.
Such unlimited literary freedom was instrumental in the flourishing
of Hasidic literature and gave rise to many outstanding creative personalities, such as Nachman of Bratslav, Elimelekh of Lyzhansk

(Lezajsk), and Levi Yitzhak of Berdichev, to name a few in the first decades of the movement's development in Eastern Europe.

This supreme, unquestioned literary freedom of the Hasidic tale enables and encourages the teller to probe dangerous, problematic, and otherwise forbidden topics. The Hasidic tale created during the Holocaust enjoys the same freedom. It can and does discuss any topic without restrictions and restraint. It provides a platform for the airing of conscious and subconscious issues, for theological, historical, and social issues that would otherwise be taboo.

The Hasidic tale of the Holocaust raises a wide range of questions regarding the scope and impact of the Holocaust and its aftermath. It deals with national consciousness, with universalism, with good and evil, crime and punishment, and with the cruel, meaningless deaths of millions of innocent victims. It does not shun questions of faith, of losing faith in men and God. It documents man's cruel struggle for survival and the high price he must pay for it. The tale can even examine the zaddik's performance critically: he too could fail his Hasidim, as in "No Time for Advice," in Part One.

The tale describes the intricate, complicated relations between man and man, man and God, victim and executioner, Jew and non-Jew. Man, at the lowest ebb of his humanity, is not denied his human image; there are still sparks of redemption and restoration. The mystical cosmic concept of the restoration of the "broken vessels," the hope that the cosmos can be restored to its original pure state, persists even in the concentration-camp universe. Despite the scope of human destruction, the Hasidic tale believes that there is a way out of the inferno, not just a way into it. The normal and physical struggle against evil provides man with a normative and historical link with a pre-Holocaust past and a post-Holocaust future.

The collection of tales in this volume is original and of a pioneering nature. It is the first major collection of original Hasidic tales in over a hundred years, the only major collection of Hasidic tales and anecdotes to have been compiled from the Holocaust experience, and the first collection in which not only Hasidic men, but Hasidic women, too, are often protagonists. The women play a major role here, not merely because they are the daughters, sisters, or wives of Hasidic personalities but because of their own faith, convictions, and moral courage.

The tales recounted here are based on interviews and oral histories that I have conducted during the past six years with the help and enthusiasm of my Brooklyn College students. Brooklyn College was the ideal place for such a project. The Borough of Brooklyn has the largest concentration of Hasidic Holocaust survivors anywhere in the world. This is strongly reflected in the student population of my classes. The students in the courses on Hasidism and the Holocaust are primarily children of Holocaust survivors, or survivors themselves. Many are from Hasidic families, with strong ties to most of the outstanding Hasidic rebbes, and the various Hasidic communities. Only in America, and perhaps only in Brooklyn College, can one find college students from such a background. The students' own interviews with their parents, relatives, friends, and neighbors and the contacts they established for me were my primary sources in America, Israel, Europe, and Australia. After the students established my "credentials" I faced no difficulties within the Hasidic community. For a woman, that was an important breakthrough which opened many closed doors, and many hearts filled with faith and suffering.

In many cases, the relationship established in classes and during the course of the interviews continued afterwards, and we formed ongoing personal friendships. I am often invited to weddings and to other family and community gatherings and events at which former students whom I encounter on such occasions are eager for me to meet the subjects of their interviews, in many cases their own fathers and mothers. Many a time, on a New York subway or on an international flight, strangers have walked over to say how grateful they are for the opportunity to tell their children, and posterity, of their suffering during the war. Some speak in torrents, others in a few restrained sentences. More and more, the Hasidic community and its tales, the legends that grow in Brooklyn, have become part of my life, contributing so much both to the academic and literary aims of this collection, and to my personal experience in compiling it.

Once while serving on President Carter's Holocaust Commission I was asked with other members to travel to Eastern Europe on a fact-finding mission to sites of former concentration camps and ghettos. I had personal reservations about returning to the scarred European landscape, especially in front of the eyes of the television and news cameras. I shared my doubts with the wonderful Rebbetzin Bronia Spira. The Grand Rabbi of Bluzhov, Rabbi Israel Spira, was consulted. He responded: "Is one traveling to Eastern Europe for the sake of the dead or for the sake of the living?" And so I went (see Part Four: "Two Funerals," "Hans and I at the Rema's Grave," and "God Does Not Live Here Anymore"). Attending my classes were close relatives of prominent Hasidic personalities from the major Hasidic dynasties in the world. Such an intimate association with the Hasidic community and its personalities has given me a viable, personal tie with the Hasidic storyteller and the movement's unique tradition.

As in many societies with strong oral traditions where storytelling has a prominent place, some events or segments of the tales in this volume have been circulating orally among the various Hasidic communities for years, especially on Saturdays at dusk during the Third Meal (see "The Third Sabbath Meal at Mauthausen" in Part Three) or on Saturday night, a traditional time for storytelling. Others were told by survivors, not necessarily practicing Hasidim, to their family and friends, in private homes and at dinner tables on family occasions, on the Sabbath and on religious holidays, especially during the Passover season.

The original interviews were conducted in more than nine languages and in numerous dialects. When I myself did the interviewing, I have indicated so at the end of the tale, and, depending on whether I tape-recorded it or recalled it from conversation, have written either "Based on my interview with" or "I heard it from, or at the house of . . . ." I translated the stories into English, extracting the raw material of the tale from the mass of the interview and rewriting it in consistent literary style so as to give the tales a cohesive form and structure. But in the process of transforming the material from documentation to art, I made a conscious effort to remain as faithful as possible to both the literary genre of the Hasidic tale as well as the individual storyteller and the particular historical event. As Agnon, in his foreword to a collection of Hasidic tales, *A Hundred and One Tales*, wrote, "Some of the tales I copied from books, some tales I heard, in all of them I retained their ideas and intentions but not their language."

Unlike Agnon, I could not consult written sources, since there were so few of them. Most of these tales have never before been committed to print. It was my intention in writing them down to retain as much as possible the unique expressions and phrases of the original storyteller, the language of the concentration-camp universe, and that of the Hasidic world. I also wanted to preserve something of the painful silence, the anguished pauses of the interviewees, their frequent requests—"Please, let's stop, it is enough for today"—or their remarks at the end of the interviews—"What you just heard is only a fraction of a reality that no words can convey and that no one can understand unless he was there." I wish I could do justice to the single, lonely tear that somehow always made its way down the well-worn furrow from the corner of the eye to the cheek. How much simpler would it be if "letters could talk"—but I am constrained by the inadequacies of language and by my own limitations.

Writing this book was a most difficult task. The thousands of miles traveled to gather these tales were outnumbered only by the miles traveled to verify them and the hours spent listening to accounts of the horrors that man has inflicted upon his fellow man.

At one point, while I was listening to the tape of an oral history account, my tape recorder fell off my desk and broke. I rushed upstairs from my study to tell my family. Our daughter, Smadar, who since grammar school has watched me sit at my desk and listen to tapes, said: "Mother, your tape recorder did not break, it simply jumped off your desk and committed suicide. How could you have expected your tape recorder to function till now? It never played a cheerful sound of music, it never recorded ordinary conversation. Even a machine can't bear it any longer."

My tape recorder "recovered" quickly. I could close it, push a button and silence it. But my mind was rarely "off." Tales would follow me and stay with me. The experience overwhelmed me with a sense of responsibility and left me doubting my abilities to fulfill my mission. I constantly sensed that the tale entrusted to me was a living witness, a quivering soul. The painful spoken words were a memorial to a family, to a mother, father, brothers, sisters, the only testimony to their ever having existed on this blood-soaked earth. Now the responsibility rested with me, to pass on the legacy of their lives and deaths. If the tale fails, the only imprint of their existence will be a patch of blackened sky and a handful of scattered ashes.

Although I was overwhelmed with responsibility both to the memory of millions and to a new genre of Hasidic literature that we were, in fact, creating, I found the tales to be a constant source of strength and solace. Late at night, in the early hours of dawn, or whenever I wrote the tales, I felt a need to cleanse my hands, as does the scribe who is writing a sacred book.

When I began work on this book, with the help and inspiration of my Brooklyn College students, I had no idea what the final shape would be. Only after I was well advanced in my work did distinct literary themes become apparent.

The tales fall naturally into four major parts, reflecting four stages in the life of the victim and his struggle with a debased civilization, a civilization that waged a war against him first to destroy him spiritually, then to annihilate him physically. The four major organizing categories of the book are: Ancestors and Faith, Friendship, The Spirit Alone, and At the Gates of Freedom.

The first part, "Ancestors and Faith," shows the reaction of the Jew, the innocent victim, when he came face to face with the executioner and was instantly transformed from a citizen of a country into the ultimate victim destined for destruction. This was a period when one calamity swiftly followed another with accelerating speed. Yet,

despite the harsh realities, the victim was still familiar with his surroundings: his native country, language, home, family, and a tradition of thousands of years that manifested itself in the daily observance of rituals, laws, and customs. Even in the ghetto, where death
was a way of life, one still lived within a community that resembled
some aspects of the prewar existence, and generally a few members of
one's own family were still alive.

Rabbi Israel Spira, the Rabbi of Bluzhov, could look to his Hasidim for help in Russian-occupied Lvov ("The Son of the Shohet of
Medzhibozh"). The Fischelberg family cared for one another in the
ghetto of Bochnia ("The Little Slave Girl from the Toy Factory").
Bronia Koczicki was able to save her two nieces from certain death
and get spiritual help from the Boyaner Rebbe, a resident in a nearby
ghetto ("God Is Everywhere . . . But . . .").

Even when uprooted from the ghetto, shipped away from their familiar surroundings, and thrust into the Kingdom of the Night, during the first weeks and months in the concentration camp many victims managed to stay together, mostly in groups of two: two brothers, two sisters, father and son, or mother and daughter. They were
able to hold on to each other and to some shreds of a lost past. Livia
of "A Bowl of Soup" did not part from her mother for a single moment. Kalman and his son Yitzhak of "Who Will Win This War?"
lived only for each other. Others, even when left totally alone, their
last surviving relatives having disappeared forever into the maw of
the crematorium, held on to a belief in their ancestors and family,
whose strength and protective merit could transcend the reality of
imminent death. In "Hovering above the Pit," Rabbi Israel Spira
believed that he was physically carried over the open graves at the
Janowska death camp by his ancestors' merit.

During their first months in the concentration camp, people still
had faith in God and man. A multitude of starved inmates at Bergen
Belsen still had enough hope to assemble and to witness the kindling
of the Hanukkah lights by the Rabbi of Bluzhov. A young Hasid was
willing to risk his life in Skyrzysko Kamienna to make a shofar for his
beloved rebbe.

But the war continued. The condition of the victims was deteriorating. As the executioner perfected his methods he made Job's Satan look like a novice; eventually the concentration-camp reality could have put even Dante's Inferno to shame. Many inmates lost their last surviving family member and were robbed of all shreds of individuality; their very appearance was destroyed. Yet even this concentration-camp reality could not completely rob man of his capacity for faith and friendship as is shown in Part Two, "Friendship." Camp "brothers" and "sisters" were common. The woman in "A Girl Called Estherke" was willing to risk her life to save a child she had just met. Friendships were formed in the shadows of the blazing chimneys and old friendships reborn in the infernal glow of the crematorium. In "The Mosaic Artist's Apprentice," an old Polish Jew befriends a young Hungarian lad on the selection line and saves his life. In "Two Capsules of Cyanide," a lawyer from Borislav is willing to share his most precious possession—a capsule of cyanide—with the Rabbi of Bluzhov, whom he befriended in the Janowska hell.

With the continuing progress of the war, man descended deeper into the abyss as is shown in Part Three, "The Spirit Alone." The camp inmate was stripped of everything: family, friends, and even his flesh, as it was eaten away by disease and starvation. Hundreds of thousands of living human skeletons inhabited the Holocaust kingdom and moved on the endless frozen roads that linked one death factory with another. Walking skeletons, rib cages suspended from bare bones, they continued to cling to life. The Nazis could snuff out their lives but not their spirits. These "musselman," more spirit than flesh, clung to their visions, to their dreams, to the only inner reality left when humanity betrayed them. They were oblivious to their physical existence. They functioned in limbo, skeletons living in a world which was more dream than reality.

The dying girl in Bergen Belsen crawled with her last iota of strength to a distant hilltop. Delirious with typhus, she heard her dead father's voice, felt his comforting hands promising her life and health ("A Hill in Bergen Belsen"). The young lad in Mauthausen, starved, emaciated and dying, dreamed of the third Sabbath meal at his grandfather's cozy home, and his grandfather invited his grandson to eat with him. The reality of the dream overshadowed the physical existence of the camp. Ignac "ate" with his grandfather and the food sustained him ("The Third Sabbath Meal at Mauthausen"). Young Hershkowitz, dying of typhus, was sure that his dead parents were at his bedside feeding him. He recovered and a few days later was liberated ("A Father's Blessing").

Liberation (Part Four, "At the Gates of Freedom"): Through the gates of the camps, returning to familiar landscapes, lonely, emaciated survivors went back home. The roads were bombed, the earth was scorched and the skies were covered with smoke. When the survivors reached home, they generally discovered that their last hopes were false and all the other members of their family were dead. Strangers now lived in their homes, and the townspeople wished that the survivors had not returned. Some survivors, in desperation, denied their heritage, as in "Puff . . . ." Others were physically and mystically drawn to their tradition and heritage. A young boy in a Displaced-Persons Camp felt as if the letters of the Bible were pulling him back ("The Grip of the Holy Letters"). Many survivors settled in Israel and became a major force in rebuilding a new state. Others, as in "The Plague of Blood" and " 'I Envy You,' " came to America, built new lives, and became an inspiration to those who were spared the agonies of the Holocaust.

Once the internal organization of these stories emerged and my work on the book became structured, I felt that yet another element was missing: the transformation of the material from testimony to art was not yet complete without historical verification. Until that point, I had satisfied only two of my disciplines: Hasidism and Holocaust, but not history. I took the tales through yet another phase, completing a cycle from documentation to art and back to documentation. I examined each tale for its historical accuracy and plausibility: Did such an incident indeed take place on a particular date and location as told by the original storyteller? Whenever possible, I verified the events and the credibility of the tale.

In the verification process two facts were of great help: Jewish-sacred-national time and family time, the latter concept identified by Tamara K. Hareven. Paul Tillich wrote that "Judaism is more related to time and history than to space and nature." Jewish tradition, by its very nature, is time oriented. Time is classified into two major units: sacred and profane. Those two fundamental dimensions of time dominate Jewish law (Halakha) and life. Its most obvious manifestation is the Jewish lunisolar calendar with its division of the days of the year into sacred and secular days, into holidays and regular days. Many precepts (mitzvot) can be fulfilled only at very specific times of the day and night. The Sabbath and holidays begin and end at a precise minute. The holidays are governed by the clock, by the sun and the moon. The cycle of the week, the phases of the moon (the new moon coinciding with the new month and the full moon with the fifteenth of the month), the seasons and their prescribed holidays, dominate the life of the individual Jew.

Even in the skies about Auschwitz, the full moon always appeared on the fifteenth of the Jewish month. A person brought up in this tradition, where time plays such a major role, has a constant awareness of time. The many handwritten Jewish calendars compiled in camps and hiding places confirm this time-consciousness. The survivor telling his tale is scrupulously aware of Jewish-sacred-national Time. Zvi M. in " 'Jew, Go Back to the Grave!' " in Part One, when recalling the massacre of Eisysky's Jews, remembers without a shadow of a doubt that it took place on the fourth and the fifth of Tishrei 1942, dates that follow Rosh Hashana (the Jewish New Year) and the Fast of Gedalia, September 25 and 26, 1941. Bronia Koczicki is sure that the large transport of foreign nationals left Bergen Belsen on the eve of the Jewish holiday of Simhat Torah 1943, the eve of October 23 ("The Rebbetzin of Gur . . . ," Part One). In both these tales, the process of verification yielded very important information. Contrary to what I expected, the German document listing the date, place, and number of murdered Eisysky Jews is inaccurate. The Koczicki date was corroborated by an entry in the Auschwitz notebooks. There remains a discrepancy as to the number of victims on that ill-fated Bergen Belsen transport.

In addition to the major role of Jewish-sacred-national time in the life of the Holocaust victim, there is also family time, the commemoration of special days on the family calendar such as

anniversaries and birthdays. Victor Frankl remembers very vividly
the date of a particular event in Auschwitz—"For on that same day
someone [his wife] had a twenty-fourth birthday." Remembering
particular dates with accuracy is the link between the tale and historical reality in the verification process.

Checking the historical accuracy of some of the tales was a tedious
and time-consuming process. The group of tales that took place in
Janowska and deal with one of the major protagonists of the book,
the Rabbi of Bluzhov, posed a particular problem due to the erratic
administrative structure of the camp and the fact that only a handful
of people survived the Janowska hell. The three extant diaries written by Janowska inmates during the war, various Russian sources,
and documents from the Nuremburg Trials were valuable sources
corroborating particular events mentioned in the tales, as well as describing the background of the events. One example of the verification process concerning the Janowska tales should be described since
it is typical of so many others.

The huge pit in Janowska, mentioned in "Hovering above the
Pit," haunted me because it seemed so improbable. I discussed it
with a few who are familiar with both the terrain and the history of
Janowska. They tried to discourage me from searching for evidence
of such pits, since the Germans erased all traces of the mass murder
as the eastern front approached. I persisted. After a long search, I
found a photograph of the pit (which was a bomb crater from World
War I) in the photograph collection of the archives at Kibbutz
Lohamei Hagetaot in northern Israel. This particular quest ended
successfully; others still need to be resolved.

An attempt was made to confirm each historical factor: dates,
places, and events. No detail was too unimportant or too obscure.
Other issues that were carefully researched include the color of the
armband worn by members of the Hungarian Jewish Labor Battalion
("Who Will Win This War?"); the precise date of the departure of a
certain transport from Bergen Belsen to Auschwitz ("The Rebbetzin
of Gur . . ."); the date and number of victims of the Hospital Aktion
in the Bochnia ghetto ("No Time for Advice"); the location of the

hiding place on the Backenroth oil fields in Schodnica ("Rejoining the Human Race,"); and the Canadian congressional records of a bill permitting the admission of a nine-year-old Polish Jewish orphan ("The Merit of a Young Priest"). Each story, whenever possible, was researched and verified.

However, some tales in this collection, because of their very nature, cannot be authenticated: tales about dreams or the perception by an individual of a particular reality. To a young woman in a sealed cattle car somewhere on the tracks between Auschwitz and Stutthof, a white line in the sky seen through a crack in the wall becomes to her a white lifeline, a message of hope and survival, a source of strength—a miracle. Even George Bernard Shaw would agree that in some cases historical verification is superfluous:

> A miracle, my friend, is an event which creates faith. That is the purpose and nature of miracles. They may seem very wonderful to the people who witness them, and very simple to those who perform them. That does not matter: if they confirm or create faith they are true miracles.
>
> [*Saint Joan*, SCENE II.]

These unverified tales also have value as documents, for they help us to understand the inner spiritual world of the Holocaust victim. They reveal and illustrate what Victor Frankl has identified as that special human capacity to preserve a vestige of spiritual freedom under the most difficult physical condition and stress. For the person of Hasidic background, it might have been the zaddik's blessing, the zaddik's melody, the zaddik's goblet, or man's capacity for love and faith that affirmed his own faith.

Victor Frankl describes in *Man's Search for Meaning* how during moments of the bleak Auschwitz reality, when it was cold and dark, he imagined himself lecturing in a warm, well-lit room before an audience seated in upholstered, comfortable chairs. The topic of his imaginary lecture was "The Psychology of the Concentration Camp." Each person in the camps drew on the resources of his or her innermost spiritual world, which, in combination with fate, became the key to survival.

The tales in this collection, with or without historical footnoting, are documents of primary importance. They offer a glimpse into man's spiritual struggle for his survival. But it is important to remember that these are only the tales of the survivors. It is possible that thousands, tens of thousands, millions of innocent victims who did not survive had the same dreams, the same boundless faith, and the same will to live. We will never know what tales they have taken with them. All that we can do is talk to the living and salvage remnants of the spiritual activity that sustained them.

This collection of Hasidic tales is not a mystification of the Holocaust, nor is it a negation of the value of armed resistance and the physical struggle for one's life or death with honor. It is simply an attempt to bring to light yet another, unexplored aspect of the Holocaust. The tales become a link, a historical continuum between the spiritual world of the period before the Holocaust and the rebirth afterward.

The Hasidic tale of the Holocaust is rooted in the Auschwitz reality, yet it soars to heaven and higher. It can carry the faithful above pits filled with bodies. Despite Auschwitz, the tale still expresses belief that man is good and capable of improvement; it can restore order to a chaotic world and offer unlimited freedom to the creative mind attempting to come to terms with the Holocaust. Its rich Jewish heritage and European tradition make it a unique genre of modern literature. The tales in this collection completed a full cycle from documentation to art to documentation and back to art. For in the beginning there was a tale.

In listening to these Hasidic tales of the Holocaust, in writing and in reading them, one hears echoes of the words of Bertolt Brecht: "The imagination is the only truth."

*Tel Aviv–New York, 1981*

# ONE

## Ancestors
## and Faith

Every day, every child, after studying the daily lessons prescribed by our sages, should learn about the Holocaust, for it says in our holy Torah: "Then it shall come to pass, when many evils and troubles are come upon them, that this song shall testify before them as a witness" (Deuteronomy 31:21). The suffering and the testimonies, when told by Holocaust survivors, are a song, a hymn of praise, a testimony to the eternity of the Jewish people and the greatness of their spirit.

*The Rabbi of Bluzhov, Rabbi Israel Spira*

# Hovering
## above the Pit

IT WAS A DARK, COLD NIGHT IN THE JANOWSKA ROAD CAMP.[1] SUD-
denly, a stentorian shout pierced the air: "You are all to evacuate the
barracks immediately and report to the vacant lot. Anyone remaining
inside will be shot on the spot!"

Pandemonium broke out in the barracks. People pushed their way
to the doors while screaming the names of friends and relatives. In a
panic-stricken stampede, the prisoners ran in the direction of the big
open field.

Exhausted, trying to catch their breath, they reached the field. In
the middle were two huge pits.[2]

Suddenly, with their last drop of energy, the inmates realized
where they were rushing, on that cursed dark night in Janowska.

Once more, the cold, healthy voice roared in the night: "Each of
you dogs who values his miserable life and wants to cling to it must
jump over one of the pits and land on the other side. Those who miss
will get what they rightfully deserve—ra-ta-ta-ta-ta."

Imitating the sound of a machine gun, the voice trailed off into the
night followed by a wild, coarse laughter. It was clear to the inmates
that they would all end up in the pits. Even at the best of times it
would have been impossible to jump over them, all the more so on
that cold dark night in Janowska. The prisoners standing at the edge
of the pits were skeletons, feverish from disease and starvation, exhausted from slave labor and sleepless nights. Though the challenge
that had been given them was a matter of life and death, they knew
that for the S.S. and the Ukrainian guards it was merely another devilish game.

Among the thousands of Jews on that field in Janowska was the
Rabbi of Bluzhov, Rabbi Israel Spira. He was standing with a friend,

3

a freethinker from a large Polish town whom the rabbi had met in the camp. A deep friendship had developed between the two.

"Spira, all of our efforts to jump over the pits are in vain. We only entertain the Germans and their collaborators, the Askaris. Let's sit down in the pits and wait for the bullets to end our wretched existence," said the friend to the rabbi.

"My friend," said the rabbi, as they were walking in the direction of the pits, "man must obey the will of God. If it was decreed from heaven that pits be dug and we be commanded to jump, pits will be dug and jump we must. And if, God forbid, we fail and fall into the pits, we will reach the World of Truth a second later, after our attempt. So, my friend, we must jump."

The rabbi and his friend were nearing the edge of the pits; the pits were rapidly filling up with bodies.

The rabbi glanced down at his feet, the swollen feet of a fifty-three-year-old Jew ridden with starvation and disease. He looked at his young friend, a skeleton with burning eyes.

As they reached the pit, the rabbi closed his eyes and commanded in a powerful whisper, "We are jumping!" When they opened their eyes, they found themselves standing on the other side of the pit.

"Spira, we are here, we are here, we are alive!" the friend repeated over and over again, while warm tears streamed from his eyes. "Spira, for your sake, I am alive; indeed, there must be a God in heaven. Tell me, Rebbe, how did you do it?"

"I was holding on to my ancestral merit. I was holding on to the coattails of my father, and my grandfather and my great-grandfather, of blessed memory," said the rabbi and his eyes searched the black skies above. "Tell me, my friend, how did *you* reach the other side of the pit?"

"I was holding on to you," replied the rabbi's friend.

*Based on a conversation of the Grand Rabbi of Bluzhov, Rabbi Israel Spira, with Baruch Singer, January 3, 1975.*

# The Son of the
# Shohet of Medzhibozh

AT THE OUTBREAK OF WORLD WAR II, RABBI ISRAEL SPIRA MOVED from Istrik to Lvov. Lvov was then under Soviet rule.[1] According to Soviet practice, each person was supposed to be employed in a productive job; otherwise he was classified as a parasite and was liable to be exiled to Siberia.

All Hasidic rabbis had to find productive positions, and were forbidden to use the title rabbi.

The Rabbi of Bluzhov,[2] Rabbi Israel Spira, became an insurance agent. At the end of each month, he had to prove that he had earned at least one thousand rubles. In those days the rabbi still had many followers. To produce at the end of the month a receipt for one thousand rubles and a list of insured individuals was no great task. Thus, the rabbi was able to satisfy the Russian demands while continuing to serve his Hasidim.

One evening the Russian commissar called for a regional meeting of all insurance agents. Attendance was mandatory. Among the insurance agents was one other Hasidic rabbi, the Rabbi of Boyan, Abraham Jacob Friedman,[3] of sainted memory. The night of the regional meeting coincided with the first night of Hanukkah.

It was customary for many Hasidim to assemble at the rabbi's house for the festive kindling of the first Hanukkah light and for the celebration that followed. Rabbi Israel Spira searched the ways and means to excuse himself from the forthcoming meeting so that he might celebrate the first night of Hanukkah in the company of his Hasidim.

Suddenly he had an idea. He smiled to himself and left for the commissar's office. On the way there he took from his pocket his snuff box and began to sniff tobacco without stopping. By the time he reached the commissar, his nose was red and he kept sneezing. Between one sneezing attack and another, the rabbi explained to the commissar that he had a very bad cold and would be unable to attend the evening meeting.

The commissar, decorated with many medals, sat behind a huge desk covered with neatly arranged piles of paper. He listened to the rabbi with an obvious expression of disbelief. "A strange coincidence," he said to the rabbi while looking straight into his eyes. "Only a few minutes ago another insurance agent was here, an agent with a beard and sidelocks, and just like you, his nose was red as a flag and he did not stop sneezing. He too claimed that he had caught a cold and asked to be excused from tonight's meeting."

It was probably the Boyaner Rabbi, the rabbi thought to himself as he tried to conceal his smile. He composed himself and replied, "It is quite natural for two people to catch a cold at this time of the year."

The commissar did not reply. He got up from his chair and walked out of the room.

After a short while he returned with a broad smile on his face and resumed his seat beneath the huge portrait of Stalin. "Now I understand the cause of your sickness," he said. "I have just checked my Jewish calendar. Tonight is Hanukkah and the kindling of the first light. You should have known better. In Russia, when concocting a story, one should make sure it is a good one. One can never be sure who is hiding behind the uniform of a Soviet commissar. If another commissar were sitting in my chair, you and your other sneezing friend would be nursing your colds in the Siberian plains. I am the son of the shohet of Medzhibozh.[4] Go home and kindle the first light of Hanukkah."

*Based on a conversation of the Grand Rabbi of Bluzhov, Rabbi Israel Spira, with Aaron Frankel, January 1974. I heard it at the rabbi's house.*

# The Kiss

I WOULD LIKE TO TELL YOU A STORY ABOUT A KISS. "SOMETIMES A kiss can break a man more than a vicious slap or a ringing blow," said the Rabbi of Bluzhov, Rabbi Israel Spira.

"In Lemberg,[1] I had a foreign passport from a South American country.[2] It was a passport for myself, my rebbetzin, of blessed memory, and for a young child. But when I received the passport, it was too late. There was no longer a rebbetzin, and my beloved grandson, as well as my daughter and son-in-law, were all gone too. Upon receiving the passport, I realized that I had an opportunity to save two Jewish souls, a middle-aged woman and a young child. When this became known, about forty children were brought to me by their parents, little boys crying and begging to be saved. They promised to be good and not to be a burden to me. How could I choose? How could I prefer one child over another?! I told the Judenrat that I was returning to my apartment and that they should bring me a child.

"Two days later, a father came with a small son, age six. 'I am Perlberger from Auschwitz,' he introduced himself. Then he went on: 'Rebbe, I am giving you my child. God should help you, so that you should be able to save my son!' He bent down, kissed the child on his head and said, 'Shraga, from this moment on, this Jew standing here next to you is your father.'

"That kiss I can't forget. Wherever I go that kiss follows me all my life. Before he shut the door behind him, the father took one more lingering look at his son. Then I heard the echo of his painful steps as he descended the stairs. A few days later, when we were deported to Bergen Belsen, a Gestapo man took a look at my passport, at the young child, and at me. He bent down to the small boy and with a big friendly grin said, 'Tell me the truth, who is this old man next to you?' Shraga glanced at me with big, childish loving eyes, took my hand in his, turned to the Gestapo man, and said, 'My father.'

"God helped us. The boy and I managed to survive Bergen Belsen together. Despite many difficulties, I studied with him every single day in camp. With God's help we were liberated by the American Army on a death train on Rosh Hodesh Iyar [April 13, 1945].

"After liberation, together with other children who survived the war, Shraga was brought to the Land of Israel. He studied at a Talmud Torah and later at the yeshiva of Hasidei Gur. He grew up into a fine, gentle lad who did very well in his studies and was liked by all.

"Shraga's father, Mr. Perlberger, also survived the war and was privileged to see his son once more, during one precious meeting. Mr. Perlberger had been in hiding for more than two years, in the pits and damp cellars on the property of Christian friends. When he was liberated he was a very sick, crippled man. Nevertheless, he soon began his search for his young son. He made his way from Poland to Belgium, for he was told that his son and I were in Belgium. Upon reaching Belgium, he learned that I had left for America in November of 1946 and that his beloved son was in the Holy Land. Despite the British blockade around Palestine, the sick father reached the shores of the land of Israel with other illegal immigrants. When he finally reached Eretz Yisrael, he was very sick man and near death. He saw his son one single time and then passed away. He had managed to survive all that time just to see his beloved child once more and be at peace knowing that his son was indeed alive and well. People told me that he passed away with a tranquil smile on his lips.

"Through the years I kept in touch with the boy and followed his progress in his studies. When I married the present rebbetzin, her two sons, Zvi and Yitzhak, became as dear to me as my own sons. Shraga was my third son, and our close contact continued. Years later, Shraga married a very nice girl. Their house in London became known as a home of Torah and culture.

"A few years ago Shraga came to visit me with his wife and three daughters. When we parted, he said to me, 'Rebbe-Father, I wish we had a son, to carry on my father's name!' I told him, 'Shraga, you will have a son and I will come, with God's help, to be the godfather at the boy's circumcision.' A year later I received a phone call from London. I rushed to the phone. 'Don't be afraid, nothing bad happened,' I heard Shraga's reassuring voice. 'My wife just gave birth to a son.' There was a moment of silence on the other end of the line. I sensed that Shraga wanted to say something but did not dare to impose upon me.

" 'I know, Shraga,' I said. 'You probably would like to refresh my memory about my promise, to be godfather to your son. Next Sunday, with God's help, I will come to the circumcision of your son. But I want you to understand that I am not coming as the Rabbi of Bluzhov. I will not take kvitlach nor in any other way will I act as rebbe. I am simply coming as a father to rejoice, to celebrate the birth of a child to his own son.'

"On Sunday we left for London. The overwhelming welcome at the airport is difficult to describe. The welcome at Shraga's home outdid the one at the airport. It was a beautiful reception in a house with well-behaved children, a house filled with sacred books and the comforts of life. I thanked the Lord for making me His messenger to save the father of this family. We did not sleep a wink that entire night. We were telling and recalling stories and events from our common past.

"Very early in the morning Rabbi Ashkenazi came, and in the name of the community and Hasidim begged me to remain in London for a few more days. I told him that my coming to London was to realize what I had lost during the war and to appreciate what I had found. Our sages say that he who raises an orphan in his house is considered by the Scriptures as one who has actually given birth to him.[3] Why does the Gemara say it? I told Rabbi Ashkenazi: it is natural for a father to raise his own biological son, but the spiritual satisfaction in raising an orphan is especially great.

"That morning, when we walked to the circumcision wearing our shtraimlach and dressed in our Sabbath finery, I was flanked by my three sons. I experienced the height of spiritual pleasure. That moment had no equal. I asked Rabbi Ashkenazi not to beg of me anymore to remain in London, for I wanted to retain the impact of the spiritual elevation of fatherhood without diluting it with anything else.

"We left for the airport and boarded the plane. That evening I prayed Maariv, the evening prayer, here at my beit midrash on 58th Street in Brooklyn.

"The great elevation of soul that I felt during my London visit was indeed part of the realization of what I have lost and the great treasures I have found. But all that time the echo of the kiss that little Shraga received on his head resounded in my ears. I saw before my eyes a father bending and kissing his beloved son, pointing to me and saying, 'From now on this man is your father.' This last kiss of a father to his son follows me all my life. But that day in London it was even more vivid than a generation ago in Lemberg.

"I hope that the merit of that kiss, which protected me in the past, gave me the great treasure of children and grandchildren who are brought up in the Jewish tradition, will protect all of us in the future."

*Based on a conversation of the Grand Rabbi of Bluzhov, Rabbi Israel Spira, with his daughter-in-law, Dina Spira, May 12, 1976. I heard it at the rabbi's house.*

# The Halatl of Rabbi Baruch of Medzhibozh

WHEN RABBI ISRAEL SPIRA OF BLUZHOV WAS A LITTLE BOY, HE loved to travel with his illustrous father, Rabbi Joshua of Ribatisch. He especially enjoyed their Passover visits to his maternal grandfather, Rabbi Jacob of Delatin. His most memorable trip to the small Rumanian border town of Delatin was during his Bar Mitzvah year.

On that occasion, Grandfather Jacob gave Israel one of the family's most precious possessions, a halatl, a silk robe that had belonged to the Baal Shem Tov's grandson, Rabbi Baruch of Medzhibozh [1757–1811].[1] Rabbi Jacob gave the beautiful snow-white halatl to his beloved grandson and said: "May its merit protect you now and save you in difficult times to come."

Israel was especially pleased with the unique gift, not only because of the accompanying blessing, not only because it had belonged to the grandson of the founder of Hasidism, but because his own grandfather, Rabbi Jacob of Delatin, used to wear it to synagogue on Passover when reciting the Prayer for Dew.

Israel had often helped his grandfather put on the beautiful snow-white halatl. Then he would stand close to his grandfather in front of the open holy ark as he prayed in his melodious voice:

We pray for dew . . .
For thou art the Lord our God who causeth the wind to blow and the dew to descend.
May it be a blessing and not a curse! May it be for life and not for death. May it bring plenty and not scarcity.

The halatl became Israel's most cherished possession. He wore it on all important occasions in his own life and in the life of the community. Israel Spira grew up to be one of the prominent Hasidic personalities in Poland. Each time he wore the snow-white halatl, his grandfather's melodious voice would ring in his ears and fields blessed with dew and peace would stand before his eyes.

World War II broke out. The rabbi decided to put on the halatl under his regular clothing and not to part with it. After much suffering in ghettos and death camps, the rabbi was transported to the infamous Janowska Road Camp. Under his concentration-camp clothing, he was still wearing what had once been his snow-white halatl.

One day, Rabbi Israel Spira was driven with a group of Janowska inmates to the bath house on Shpitalna Street in Lvov. Each of these trips to the showers ended in a bloodbath. The strange procession of tired, filthy inmates was accompanied by the S.S. Untersturmführer Rokita, the most bloodthirsty Askaris, and empty carriages for bringing back the dead. Each inmate knew that in entering the portals of the Shpitalna bath house, he was standing at the threshold between life and death.[2]

On that particular day, the Rabbi of Bluzhov was among the victims selected at random to die. Outside the bath house, those in the unfortunately selected group were ordered to strip naked. One by one, they were bludgeoned to death while Rokita showered insults upon them and a group of Askaris played sentimental Ukrainian tunes on their harmonicas.

The rabbi's turn came. He refused to remove the halatl of Rabbi Baruch of Medzhibozh. The Askaris began to inflict blows with their truncheons. Rokita, in a state of rage, kicked the rabbi with his blood-stained boots. But all Rabbi Israel Spira could hear was his grandfather's melodious voice praying for dew, life, and peace. They tried to undress him forcefully, but the rabbi crossed his hands so they would not be able to remove his halatl. One Ukrainian pulled on one sleeve, a second on another. They pulled the halatl up to the rabbi's neck and began to choke him. His face turned pale. Blood covered the once pure-white halatl wrapped around his neck. "The dog is dead," pronounced one of the Askaris. They kicked him once more. His body did not respond to their boots. He was thrown onto the wagon with the other dead bodies.

One of the rabbi's Hasidim, the cousin of Menachem Freifeld, and a few other Jews were ordered to bury the dead. As they lifted the bodies, Menachem's cousin felt a reflex in one of the rabbi's toes. He touched the body and it was still warm. With the help of a few inmates, he carried the body back to the barracks. There he located a Jewish doctor by the name of Solomon, who was known for his dedication to saving human lives even in the Kingdom of Death. Dr. Solomon rushed to the barracks with stolen medicine and gave the rabbi two injections. Slowly Rabbi Israel Spira opened his eyes and rejoined the living. The famous halatl of Baruch of Medzhibozh, which his grandfather Jacob gave him before his Bar Mitzvah, was still wrapped around his bloody neck.

*I heard it at the house of the Grand Rabbi of Bluzhov, Rabbi Israel Spira, April 26, 1979.*

# The First Hanukkah Light in Bergen Belsen

IN BERGEN BELSEN, ON THE EVE OF HANUKKAH, A SELECTION TOOK place. Early in the morning, three German commandants, meticulously dressed in their festive black uniforms and in visibly high spirits, entered the men's barracks. They ordered the men to stand at the foot of their three-tiered bunk beds.

The selection began. No passports were required, no papers were checked, there was no roll call and no head count. One of the three commandants just lifted the index finger in his snow-white glove and pointed in the direction of a pale face, while his mouth pronounced the death sentence with one single word: "Come!"

Like a barrage of machine-gun fire came the German commands: *"Komme, komme, komme, komme, komme."* The men selected were marched outside. S.S. men with rubber truncheons and iron prods awaited them. They kicked, beat, and tortured the innocent victims. When the tortured body no longer responded, the revolver was used . . . .

The random selection went on inside the barracks and the brutal massacre continued outside of the barracks until sundown. When the Nazi black angels of death departed, they left behind heaps of hundreds of tortured and twisted bodies.

Then Hanukkah came to Bergen Belsen. It was time to kindle the

Hanukkah lights. A jug of oil was not to be found, no candle was in sight, and a hanukkiah belonged to the distant past. Instead, a wooden clog, the shoe of one of the inmates, became a hanukkiah; strings pulled from a concentration-camp uniform, a wick; and the black camp shoe polish, pure oil.

Not far from the heaps of the bodies, the living skeletons assembled to participate in the kindling of Hanukkah lights.

The Rabbi of Bluzhov lit the first light and chanted the first two blessings in his pleasant voice, and the festive melody was filled with sorrow and pain. When he was about to recite the third blessing, he stopped, turned his head, and looked around as if he were searching for something.

But immediately, he turned his face back to the quivering small lights and in a strong, reassuring, comforting voice, chanted the third blessing: "Blessed art Thou, O Lord our God, King of the Universe, who has kept us alive, and hast preserved us, and enabled us to reach this season."

Among the people present at the kindling of the lights was a Mr. Zamietchkowski, one of the leaders of the Warsaw Bund.[1] He was a clever, sincere person with a passion for discussing matters of religion, faith, and truth. Even here in camp at Bergen Belsen, his passion for discussion did not abate. He never missed an opportunity to engage in such a conversation.

As soon as the Rabbi of Bluzhov had finished the ceremony of kindling the lights, Zamietchkowski elbowed his way to the rabbi and said, "Spira, you are a clever and honest person. I can understand your need to light Hanukkah candles in these wretched times. I can even understand the historical note of the second blessing, 'Who wroughtest miracles for our fathers in days of old, at this season.' But the fact that you recited the third blessing is beyond me. How could you thank God and say 'Blessed art Thou, O Lord our God, King of the Universe, who has kept us alive, and hast preserved us, and enabled us to reach this season'? How could you say it when hundreds of dead Jewish bodies are literally lying within the shadows of the Hanukkah lights, when thousands of living Jewish skeletons are walking around in camp, and millions more are being massacred? For this you are thankful to God? For this you praise the Lord? This you call 'keeping us alive'?''

"Zamietchkowski, you are a hundred percent right," answered the rabbi. "When I reached the third blessing, I also hesitated and asked myself, what should I do with this blessing? I turned my head in order to ask the Rabbi of Zaner and other distinguished rabbis who were standing near me, if indeed I might recite the blessing. But just as I was turning my head, I noticed that behind me a throng was standing, a large crowd of living Jews, their faces expressing faith, devotion, and concentration as they were listening to the rite of the kindling of the Hanukkah lights. I said to myself, if God, blessed be He, has such a nation that at times like these, when during the lighting of the Hanukkah lights they see in front of them the heaps of bodies of their beloved fathers, brothers, and sons, and death is looking from every corner, if despite all that, they stand in throngs and with devotion listening to the Hanukkah blessing 'Who wroughtest miracles for our fathers in days of old, at this season'; if, indeed, I was blessed to see such a people with so much faith and fervor, then I am under a special obligation to recite the third blessing.' "[2]

Some years after liberation, the Rabbi of Bluzhov, now residing in Brooklyn, New York, received regards from Mr. Zamietchkowski. Zamietchkowski asked the son of the Skabiner Rabbi to tell Israel Spira, the Rabbi of Bluzhov, that the answer he gave him that dark Hanukkah night in Bergen Belsen had stayed with him ever since, and was a constant source of inspiration during hard and troubled times.

*Based on a conversation of the Grand Rabbi of Bluzhov, Rabbi Israel Singer, with Aaron Frankel and Baruch Singer, June 22, 1975. I heard it at the rabbi's house.*

# Seder Night in Bergen Belsen: "Tonight We Have Only Matzah"

A FEW WEEKS BEFORE PASSOVER, ABOUT SEVENTY JEWS IN THE SEC-
tion for foreign nationals in Bergen Belsen organized into a group.
Most of them were Hasidic Jews who had arrived at the camp from
the Bochnia ghetto. The majority of the people from the Bochnia
transport were holders of South American passports; a few held British papers from Eretz Yisrael.[1] They organized the group in order to
request flour for baking matzot in honor of the approaching Passover
holiday. They addressed their written request to the camp commandant, suggesting that instead of their daily ration of bread they be
given flour from which they would bake matzot. In this way they
would not strain the camp food supplies. Each of the seventy people
signed the petition, and the Rabbi of Bluzhov, Rabbi Israel Spira, an
old-timer in Bergen Belsen, was selected as the group's spokesman.

Adolf Haas, the camp commandant, read the petition carefully,
then looked at the rabbi with open contempt and ridicule. "I will forward the request to Berlin," he said, after a long silence, while non-
chalantly toying with his revolver, "and we will act according to their
instructions."[2]

Days passed and there was no reply from Berlin. With each passing day, the signers of the petition became more depressed. Some
were convinced that they had made a grave mistake by signing the
petition, for in doing so, they separated themselves from the rest of
the inmates and probably signed their own death sentence, thus
making their own "selection." Knowing from their past experience that the Germans set apart the Jewish holidays as days of terror, torture, and death, the seventy petition signers feared that they
would probably be the Passover sacrifice, the Paschal lambs of
Bergen Belsen.

Passover was only a few days away and the reply from Berlin had not yet arrived. At the height of their despair, when all hope appeared lost and a bitter fate seemed to be inevitable, two tall S.S. men with two huge dogs briskly entered the section for foreign nationals. They summoned the Rabbi of Bluzhov to the camp commandant. In those dark days a summons by an S.S. officer clearly spelled one thing for a Jew: death. The rabbi parted from his friends and began to recite the Vidduy, the prayer one recites before death, as he walked in the direction of the commandant's office.

Camp cap in hand, the rabbi stood before the commandant and listened to what he had to say: "As always, Berlin is generous with the Jews. You can bake your religious bread." The rabbi remained standing, waiting for the horrible decree to follow the commandant's statement, but to the rabbi's great amazement, none did.

Instead, the commandant called in a few inmates from another section in camp who were already waiting at the office entrance, and ordered them to help the rabbi build a small oven for baking matzot in the section for foreign nationals. The rabbi thanked the commandant and rushed back to the barracks in disbelief that they had indeed been granted permission to bake matzot.

The building of the oven began with feverish haste, the Hasidim fearing that the camp commandant would change his mind at any minute and stop them. In the few days before Passover, matzot were baked from the meager rationed flour, matzot that only in name resembled the pre–World War II matzot baked at home. But the people were thrilled with the shapeless black matzot, especially for the children's sake, so they might see and learn that a holiday is observed even in the Valley of Death.

Passover arrived. A Seder was arranged in one of the barracks. Three-tiered wooden bunk beds served as tables and as traditional seats for reclining. Three precious unbroken matzot were placed on the table. An old, dented, broken pot was used as the ceremonial Seder plate. On it there were no roasted shank bone, no egg, no haroset, no traditional greens, only a boiled potato given by a kind old German who worked at the showers.

But there was no shortage of bitter herbs; bitterness was in abundance. The suffering of the Jews was reflected in their eyes.

The Rabbi of Bluzhov sat at the head of the table. He was surrounded by a group of young children and a few adults. The rabbi began to recite the Haggadah from memory.

He uncovered the matzot, lifted the ceremonial plate, and began to tell the story of the Exodus.

This is the bread of affliction that our fathers ate in the land of Egypt. All who are hungered—let them come and eat, all who are needy—let them come and celebrate Passover. Now we are here; next year may we be in the land of Israel! Now we are slaves; next year may we be free men!

The youngest of the children asked the Four Questions, his sweet childish voice chanting the traditional melody: "Why is this night different from all other nights? For on all other nights we eat either bread or matzah, but tonight only matzah."

It was dark in the barracks. The moon's silvery, pale glow was reflected on the pale faces. It was as if the tears that silently streamed down their cheeks were flowing toward the legendary angel with the huge jug of tears, which when filled to its brim would signal the end of human suffering.

As is customary, the rabbi began to explain the meaning of Passover in response to the Four Questions. But on that Seder night in Bergen Belsen, the ancient questions of the Haggadah assumed a unique meaning.

"Night," said the rabbi, "means exile, darkness, suffering. Morning means light, hope, redemption. Why is this night different from all other nights? Why is this suffering, the Holocaust, different from all the previous sufferings of the Jewish people?" No one attempted to respond to the rabbi's questions. Rabbi Israel Spira continued.

"For on all other nights we eat either bread or matzah, but tonight only matzah. Bread is leavened; it has height. Matzah is unleavened and is totally flat. During all our previous sufferings, during all our previous nights in exile, we Jews had bread and matzah. We had moments of bread, of creativity, and light, and moments of matzah, of suffering and despair. But tonight, the night of the Holocaust, we experience our greatest suffering. We have reached the depths of the abyss, the nadir of humiliation. Tonight we have only matzah, we have no moments of relief, not a moment of respite for our humiliated spirits. . . . But do not despair, my young friends."

The rabbi continued in a forceful voice filled with faith. "For this is also the beginning of our redemption. We are slaves who served Pharaoh in Egypt. Slaves in Hebrew are *avadim;* the Hebrew letters of the word *avadim* form an acronym for the Hebrew phrase: David, the son of Jesse, your servant, your Messiah.[3] Thus, even in our state of slavery we find intimations of our eventual freedom through the coming of the Messiah.

"We who are witnessing the darkest night in history, the lowest moment of civilization, will also witness the great light of redemption, for before the great light there will be a long night, as was promised by our Prophets. 'But it shall come to pass, that at evening time there shall be light,' and 'The people that walked in darkness have seen a great light; they that dwelt in the land of the shadow of death, upon them hath the light shined.'[3] It was to us, my dear children, that our prophets have spoken, to us who dwell in the shadow of death, to us who will live to witness the great light of redemption."

The Seder concluded. Somewhere above, the silvery glow of the moon was dimmed by dark clouds. The Rabbi of Bluzhov kissed each child on the forehead and reassured them that the darkest night of mankind would be followed by the brightest of all days.

As the children returned to their barracks, slaves of a modern Pharaoh amidst a desert of mankind, they were sure that the sounds of the Messiah's footsteps were echoing in the sounds of their own steps on the blood-soaked earth of Bergen Belsen.

*I heard it at the house of the Grand Rabbi of Bluzhov, Rabbi Israel Spira, June 22, 1975.*

# The Berlin–Bucharest Express

IN SLOTWINA BRZESKO, BRONIA LIVED NEAR THE TRAIN STATION and the Wehrmacht headquarters. It was an advantageous location. Every night at exactly 1:20 A.M. the express train stopped for one and a half minutes, long enough for Bronia to step on or get off the train. Bronia served as a courier, delivering Aryan papers and foreign passports to Jews in various parts of Poland. She had two wonderful connections, Benjamin Sander Landau in Bochnia, who had in his possession seals from all the desirable consulates in the free world, and the ticket seller at the train station, a kind Gentile who arranged for Bronia the correct tickets needed for each occasion.

One day Bronia was traveling to Lvov to bring Aryan papers and make travel arrangements for Reb Hirsch Landau and his wife, formerly from Litvatz and now living in Lvov. It is difficult to describe the despondent condition of Reb Hirsch and his wife. When Bronia entered the cold, dark little room, their faces lit up with such gratitude as she never had seen before. They were overjoyed that they were not forgotten and that their distant relative had come to their rescue. Reb Hirsch was praising the Lord that He had not forgotten His humble servant, and Mrs. Landau kept telling Bronia that if an angel had come down from heaven it would have been less of a miracle than Bronia's coming in this difficult time to rescue them. Bronia placed them on a truck and two days later they safely arrived in Tarnow.

Bronia boarded the Bucharest–Berlin Express. It was December 1941. A gentle snow was falling. The train was packed with soldiers from the eastern front going home for Christmas. Next to Bronia sat a woman, a German secretary who worked at a German company in the occupied territories. Now she too was traveling home for Christmas.

20

At Gorodenko the train came to a sudden halt for passport control. The woman next to Bronia became very frightened. She turned to Bronia and said, "We are all dark in my family. In the past it was considered an asset. We used to be referred to as the Spanish beauties, but now my dark complexion is a curse. Each time I travel they suspect me, you know, that I am one of them. My family is one of the oldest German families. We never even intermarried with the Austrians!"

"Passports please!" Bronia was searching for her passport. "No need, comrade," the officer who checked passports said to blond, blue-eyed Bronia. "Follow me!" he ordered the German secretary. She left the compartment, never to return. Bronia finally found her passport. It was issued in Berlin, where she had lived since childhood, in her real name, Bronia Koczicki née Melchior, born in Sosnowiec. It even stated her correct date of birth. Slowly, Bronia placed the passport back into her pocketbook.

A German officer took the secretary's place and sat next to Bronia. He looked as if he were in his mid-thirties, with a very handsome face that expressed much suffering and pain. The train proceeded once more on its way. Snow was still falling and the compartment was lit by a dim light from the narrow corridor. Tears began to stream from the officer's closed eyes. He seemed to be having a nightmare. His face twitched and his lips mumbled soundless words. He opened his eyes and turned to Bronia. The tears were still falling on his hollow cheeks. He told Bronia that he was on his way home because he could not take it any longer. "In Zhitomir¹ it was especially horrible." He was responsible for it, too; he was in command and he gave the orders to shoot. "They assembled them all, men, women, and children. We murdered them all, all of them," he said as he wept. He showed Bronia pictures and documents to support his horrible tale. Bronia looked at them in the dim light. She felt her head spinning; she was afraid she was about to faint. How was this possible? How was it possible to murder innocent people, unsuspecting Jews dressed in their Sabbath finery? Bronia's blood was screaming, Why, why, why? She controlled her emotions, but the officer sensed her great pain, which he interpreted as sympathy for his troubled state of mind. Bronia asked for a picture for evidence. But he told her that as much as he would like to give it to her, he could not do so.

The officer asked Bronia to continue traveling with him. Her understanding and sensitivity would be of great assistance to him, he said, to ease the terrible burden he could not carry alone. Bronia replied that she would like to accompany him, but her duty did not allow her this great pleasure. At Tarnow she quickly parted from the officer and stepped down off the train into the cold, sorrowful December night.

Bronia brought back the news of Zhitomir to the town's leaders. They listened to her gruesome tale and then said, "Here it will not happen. They kill Jews only in the formerly held Russian territories because they can not distinguish between Communists and Jews. But here they know we are not Communists. We were never under Russian rule."

Bronia saw before her eyes a picture of the dead children. She questioned the spokesman of the group: "How does one mistake infants, small children, babies at their mothers' breasts for Communists?" she demanded.

"Here it will not happen," she was told over and over. "Just don't scare the people with unnecessary tales of horror."

Every night when Bronia was at home, when the Berlin–Bucharest Express rolled by, she would hear in the clickety-clack of its wheels new tales of terror, new names of other Jewish communities. Long after the train had disappeared into the frosty winter night, Bronia would clearly hear the voice of a German officer telling the gruesome tale of Zhitomir.

*Based on a conversation of Rebbetzin Bronia Spira with her daughter-in-law, Dina Spira, May 10, 1976.*

# The Vision
# of the Red Stars

IN THE TURMOIL OF THE SUMMER OF 1941, BRONIA, HER TWO SMALL
sons, her husband, and other members of the Koczicki family were
among the huge stream of refugees who were on the run in search of a
haven. Somehow, in the confusion, the family became separated.
Bronia and her two young sons went to Dembitz while her husband
managed to reach Warsaw, which had been under German occupation since September 1939.

One day Bronia received a letter from her husband asking her and
the children to join him in Warsaw. He had discussed the matter with
his rebbe, the Grand Rabbi of Radomsk.[1] They both felt that Bronia
and the children should return to Warsaw as soon as possible.

Bronia feared Warsaw. She felt that in time of war, small towns
were safer than large cities. In Dembitz, at the comfortable house of
her husband's relations, she thought they would all have a better
chance of survival. Even so, after receiving her husband's letter,
Bronia immediately started packing. Who was she, she thought to
herself, to question a grand rabbi's advice?

Her husband's uncle, Joseph Koczicki, a resident of Palestine who
had been stranded by the war in Dembitz, comforted Bronia. He
sensed her troubled heart and felt that the best way he could ease her
burden would be to help her pack and to play with the children. For
the decision had already been made in Warsaw and there was nothing
one could say in Dembitz.

When the packing was finished, Bronia, exhausted, fell asleep on
the couch, surrounded by the scattered bundles of their possessions.
She dreamed that she, the children, and a large Jewish multitude
were herded together into a gigantic open space. It is very cold there.
Everything is covered with ice and snow and the wind is whistling.
The people try to get warm, to seek shelter, but guards are posted in

all directions. The uniformed guards beat the rag-clad prisoners with truncheons and long whips. The Jews try to run between the blows but the huge space is sealed off without any exits. They are all trapped.

Suddenly, they are all in Warsaw. Groups of Jews are being led to their death. Slowly Warsaw is emptied of its living Jews and is filled with corpses. A strange silence descends upon Warsaw. All is quiet; not a single sound is heard. Then, suddenly, the night flares up. Warsaw is burning—the houses, the courtyards, the streets— everything is one huge flame. The fires die. Warsaw is reduced to charred, sooty ruins, amidst which grows a tree trunk with five leaves.

Only five people remain alive among the ruins, Bronia, her children, and two adult strangers whose faces Bronia does not recognize. Together they search for other living people, but in vain. There are none. As they walk, the earth under their feet begins to rumble. The sewers open and, underground, huge gray pipes rise up and fill the streets. Red stars begin to flow in a powerful stream from the pipes, rivers of red stars. But Bronia and her children and the two strangers remain standing on solid ground. The stars turn into the rows and columns of a marching army, the Red Army. . . .

Frightened by her own dream, Bronia fell off the couch. Sitting there on the floor among the scattered bundles, she decided not to travel to Warsaw, but to remain in Dembitz. Then feverishly she began to unpack, while mumbling to herself, "At times one must follow one's own dreams."

*Based on a conversation of Rebbetzin Bronia Spira with Dina Spira, May 2, 1976, and my own conversation with the rebbetzin, June 22, 1975.*

# Honor Thy Mother

THE DAYS BEFORE ROSH HASHANA, 1942, WERE PARTICULARLY difficult for the Koczicki family in the ghetto of Slotwina Brzesko. It was clear that they too would soon be taken on their last journey.[1]

Bronia, Rabbi Israel Abraham Koczicki's wife, had false papers, but her husband and mother-in-law did not. After much deliberation, a painful decision was made. The family would split up again: Bronia would leave the ghetto and try to obtain Aryan papers for her husband and mother-in-law.

The parting was a painful one. Bronia took little Yitzhak with her while the older son, Zvi, age six, remained with his father and grandmother.

Bronia and her son boarded a passenger train filled with German officers. Her blond hair, blue eyes, and Berlin-accented German were a perfect cover, but she was fearful on account of little Yitzhak. Because the family had lived in Berlin until the Zbaszyn Affair[2] they all spoke the German language, but Yitzhak's German was intermingled with Yiddish words because he had been born and raised in occupied Poland. Bronia held the child in her lap, displaying his beautiful shock of blond curls. Yitzhak was asleep, and Bronia prayed that he would stay asleep until Bochnia, their destination.

The German officers seated next to Bronia struck up a conversation with her. Before long, they were discussing the Germans' favorite topic—the Jews. Their remarks were brutal and vulgar, although they apologized to Bronia for using such vile language in the presence of a lady. Soon one officer was recalling how, on a similar journey, he had discovered a Jew who was traveling on Aryan papers: "I sniffed him out, I have a special talent for it. Right here in the middle of the compartment I made him pull down his trousers. I was right. The poor devil never made it to the next station." He told his story gleefully, trying to amuse beautiful Bronia.

Little Yitzhak turned his head in his sleep. To think about the fact that he was circumcised made Bronia's heart pound louder than the locomotive's puffings, and her blood raced through her veins like the train in the dark night. But she managed to smile her calm, charming smile. She pointed to the sleeping child and said: "Gentlemen, you don't want to wake up a future soldier." The conversation continued in hushed voices. One officer remarked that Bronia was the embodiment of German motherhood. She reminded him of a beautiful madonna and child in his native Bavarian village of Saint Ottilier.

When the train stopped in Bochnia,[3] Bronia, without giving any sign that it was her stop, remained in her seat. Just as the train was about to pull out of the station, she swiftly stepped down to the platform. The train pulled out of the station and Bronia waved to the German officers from below. They responded warmly as the train sped on its way. Bronia breathed a sigh of relief. The cool, crisp air was refreshing. She hugged and kissed her little son, thanking him for being such a good boy. Moments later, she was already planning the next step, the rescue of the other members of her family.

After a few days, Bronia was able to obtain Aryan papers for her husband and mother-in-law. With a very reliable messenger and for a substantial sum of money, Bronia sent the papers to her husband in Slotwina Brzesko. Daily, Bronia went to the train station, hoping that her husband, older son, and mother-in-law would be among the passengers. But days passed and they did not arrive. Bronia began to worry. Maybe the documents never reached her husband and were intercepted by the Germans; maybe her husband and mother-in-law were recognized and betrayed on the train by an old Polish acquaintance; maybe the papers arrived too late. Desperate, Bronia decided to return to Slotwina Brzesko.

On the very day she had planned to leave, Bronia received a letter from her husband. The Aryan papers had arrived safely, the rabbi wrote, and he was very grateful. But his mother was afraid to use them. She claimed that her looks and accent would betray her and, consequently, all of them. Since the command to "Honor thy mother" is a cardinal command in the holy Torah, he could not leave his mother alone. He hoped that Bronia would agree, and would understand and forgive him.

A few days later, Bronia received a second letter from Rabbi Israel Abraham. He wrote that their fears had begun to materialize. They had all been taken in a transport to Tarnow. There the men were separated from the women and he was separated from his mother. He feared the worst; however, Zvi was well and was with him. He continued his letter, reminding her that Yitzhak would be three years old on Rosh Hashana, and she should not forget to cut his hair and make sure that he wore a tallit katan so that he would always remember that he was a Jew. Israel Abraham begged her forgiveness if he had ever offended her during their married years and especially during the difficult years of the war. He forgave her for everything and thanked her for the wonderful years God had given them together to build a family. A substantial sum of money was enclosed in the letter. After reading it, Bronia rushed to a man in the Bochnia ghetto who was known as an expert smuggler, one who was able to transport people from ghetto to ghetto.

"To Tarnow I do not travel," the man declared, shaking his head in the negative. "It is entering the lion's den without any possible exit." Bronia offered to pay double. Still he refused. She reminded him that only a few days earlier, when he had run into serious difficulties in Kolomea, she herself had endangered her own life and saved him. "I remember and I am grateful, but 'man is responsible first for himself,' " he said, "and this mission is just too dangerous."

A few days later, Rabbi Israel Abraham was sent to the gas chamber. On his last journey from Tarnow to Belzec, he was able to break one of the iron bars at the cattle car's only window. He managed to squeeze his six-year-old son through the resulting space and he tossed Zvi to freedom from the speeding train. He was sure that somehow, Bronia would find him.

*Based on a conversation of Rebbetzin Bronia Spira with Dina Spira (Yitzhak's wife), May 2, 1976.*

# A Mother's Heart

THE DEATH TRAIN FROM TARNOW TO BELZEC SPED THROUGH THE crisp autumn night. Rabbi Israel Abraham Koczicki was holding in his arms his six-year-old son Zvi. He was whispering to his sleepy child to be strong and courageous, for out there in the open spaces was a big God, father of the universe, who watches over all his children. A clink from an iron bar as it was being removed from the cattle-car window, a hurried kiss from his father's feverish lips, and Zvi flew from his father's warm arms into the dark, cold Polish countryside. He landed in the bushes near a huge pine tree. Bruised, bleeding, in a state of shock, he called out to his father in a faint voice until he was silenced by cold and fatigue. It was dark. He no longer heard the clatter of the train.

Somehow Bronia, in the Bochnia ghetto, sensed that her son would be found along the Tarnow–Belzec tracks. She hired a Polish peasant for a handsome sum of money and posted him day and night along the death road. The peasant pretended that he was gathering mushrooms in his huge basket in the nearby forest along the tracks leading from Tarnow to the death camp of Belzec.

The tracks were strewn with pictures of Jewish families, smiling faces of young and old. On the backs were scribbled frantic messages in shaky handwriting, asking for help.

One day, at the edge of the tracks and the forest, the peasant noticed a pair of small shoes on top of a bush. The shoes were on the feet of a little boy who was more dead than alive. The child matched the picture and information Bronia had given the peasant. He picked up the boy and rushed to Bochnia.

In the Bochnia hospital, Zvi began slowly to respond to what was happening around him. He opened his eyes and his lips whispered something. Bronia was sure that she heard him call for his father. But the road to recovery was still a long one.

Some time later, while Bronia was working in one of the ghetto

28

workshops, she dropped everything and ran to the hospital. She had a strange premonition that something terrible was going to happen to her son. Despite the nurses' protests, she hastily dressed Zvi, bundled him up in a blanket, and with the child in her arms ran out of the hospital. Only when the hospital building was out of sight did she slow down to catch her breath.

That night, November 11, 1942, all the people in the hospital, medical personnel as well as patients, forty-four Jews in all, were shot to death.[1] Zvi was safe in his mother's arms in a tiny corner of their ghetto apartment.

*Based on a conversation of Rebbetzin Bronia Spira with Dina Spira, May 2, 1976.*

# God Is
# Everywhere . . . But . . .

BRONIA KOCZICKI HAD MIRACULOUSLY MANAGED TO SAVE HER two small sons, Zvi and Yitzhak, ages six and three. Now she attempted to save two more children, her twin nieces Leah and Brasha. The girls' parents and five younger siblings had perished in a nearby ghetto; the twins were the last two relatives to survive from Bronia's once large family. To save the girls became Bronia's obsession.

Despite all her connections in the Bochnia ghetto, Bronia was unable to obtain working papers for Leah and Brasha. Without these papers the girls automatically became illegal residents in the ghetto, an offense punishable by death, both for the stateless residents and for those who gave them shelter.[1]

For a few days, Bronia was able to hide the twins in a tiny corner of a room she was sharing with other refugee families who had come to Bochnia in search of life. During that time, Bronia did not cease in her efforts to obtain the necessary papers. But her efforts were in vain, and the girls remained stateless refugees in the ghetto. When the Aktions became more frequent and death was stalking the streets of Bochnia day after day, Bronia's neighbors in the apartment feared for their lives and demanded that Bronia send Leah and Brasha away. Bronia was desperate. She tried once more to obtain working papers for the girls, but all her efforts seemed to lead nowhere. Then Bronia decided upon a dangerous plan. It was her last resort and she decided to act immediately. Bronia did not share her plan with anyone for fear that someone might betray her. Alone, she began feverishly to translate ideas into action.

That night, after a long day in the ghetto workshop, Bronia sat down to write an official letter in German. After she completed the letter she rewrote it several times. Finally it became apparent, from the gratified expression on her face, that she was pleased with the letter, both its content and form.

The following morning Bronia set her blond wavy hair, dressed in her best clothes, and started toward the Gestapo headquarters. She walked with an elegant, confident stride while praying to God that her true emotions of fear and desperation would not betray her. She entered the Gestapo building with a cheerful smile and warmly greeted everyone. She walked directly into the chief of police's office. There Bronia was welcomed like an old friend who was much missed. She sat on the edge of the police chief's desk. Soon a friendly conversation developed among Bronia, the head of the Gestapo, Schomburg, and the Gestapo man, Kunda, who were known in the ghetto for their unlimited lust for bribes. Bronia's voice, with its special Berlin ring, resounded in the Gestapo headquarters to the delight of all.

During the course of the conversation, Bronia slipped ten gold coins into the hands of each of the German officials, with a promise that more would follow. She soon learned that the ghetto would be liquidated in the near future and only people with foreign passports and papers would be spared. They would be transported to a special transit camp for prisoners called Bergen Belsen, and would be exchanged by the German government for Germans held prisoner in

Allied territory. "All others will be *kaput* (finished)," said Schomburg and burst into wild, vulgar laughter.

About noontime, Bronia parted from the two officials and thanked them for their hospitality. As they were escorting Bronia to the door they complimented her once more on her Aryan good looks and told her how much they had enjoyed her visit, especially her sophisticated Berlin wit. As they were about to reach the main entrance, Bronia stopped. "Oh, gentlemen, I enjoyed the conversation so much that this letter nearly slipped my mind. I am sure that gentlemen in your position will have no difficulties in forwarding the letter to Tarnow through the proper channels and getting a favorable reply."

They all then returned to Schomburg's office, where the men read the letter carefully and complimented Bronia on her perfect German and beautiful penmanship. They stamped the letter with a few official German seals, giving it the appearance of a picture with a few eagles nesting on swastikas, placed it in the pile of outgoing mail, and assured Bronia that all would be well.

On her way home, Bronia trembled with fear. She had just made her first dangerous move, a move that if successful would promise the gift of life for her twin nieces. But if it failed, it spelled disaster to all five of them: the twins, her two sons, and herself. In the letter she had just mailed to Tarnow, Bronia had assumed the identity of her dead sister-in-law Miriam, the mother of the twins, and requested her documents. Miriam was a native of Berlin and had held a British passport because she and her family had lived in Palestine for some years under the British Mandate.

A few days later, Miriam's papers arrived, all intact, from Gestapo headquarters in Tarnow. Schomburg and Kunda each received ten additional gold coins, and promised further cooperation. Only with the arrival of Miriam's British papers did Bronia's real dilemma begin. Which papers should she use, her own passport from a South American country, which included only two children, or that of her sister-in-law, which included seven?

Miriam was five years Bronia's senior, thus placing Bronia in the category of older women, a very undesirable group in the Third

Reich. To make matters worse, Miriam's passport photograph did not bear the slightest resemblance to Bronia, and Bronia's sons were slightly younger than the children nearest to them in age on Miriam's passport. But if she took the chance of using the newly arrived papers she might be able to save the twins, for they were listed on their mother's passport. By using her own papers, she had a much better chance to save her sons and herself but would abandon the girls to a certain death. Bronia was at a loss. She asked for advice but she was told that the decision must be her own since it was a matter of life and death.

Bronia then decided to seek the advice of the world-famous Boyaner Rabbi, Rabbi Moshe Friedman.[2] Reb Moshenu, as he was known by his Hasidim, had found temporary shelter in the Tarnow ghetto. Unable to reach Tarnow, Bronia sent a letter to the rebbe in which she stated her dilemma in detail. A trustworthy messenger carried the letter from ghetto to ghetto for a handsome sum of money. Reb Moshenu read the letter carefully and with great concentration. He remained sitting motionless for a long time. Only his big wise eyes looked far beyond the room. He stood up from his chair and lifted his hands to heaven in a sweeping motion, as if trying to fill up the entire space of the small room and the world beyond it. Then, in a clear and resolute tone he said to the messenger, ''God is everywhere, in Bochnia, in Paraguay, and in Eretz Yisrael. But in this particular case papers from Eretz Yisrael are preferable. Use them and may the merit of the holy forefathers and grandfathers protect her and the four children and guide their steps to safety and life. For saving a soul is among the most noble acts a person can do. As stated by our sages, 'Whosoever preserves a single soul of Israel, Scripture ascribes to him as though he had preserved a complete world.' ''[3]

The messenger returned safely to Bochnia and gave Bronia the rabbi's message. Bronia felt as if a weight had been lifted from her shoulders. The decision had been made by Reb Moshenu. She was going to assume Miriam's identity and use the Palestinian passport. Bronia rushed home to her children to tell them of the rabbi's decision and blessing.

In the summer of 1943, Bronia was deported from Bochnia with the other holders of foreign national papers to Bergen Belsen. Not long after their arrival in the camp's foreign nationals sector, the Bochnia ghetto was liquidated, in September 1943.

As the British liberating forces approached the gates of Bergen Belsen, Bronia, her sons, and the twins, together with a few thousand Jews, all holders of foreign passports, were placed aboard a train and deported to be killed. As they were taken from the train to a nearby forest to be shot, they were liberated by the American Army near Magdeburg, Germany.[4]

*Based on a conversation of Rebbetzin Bronia Spira with Dina Spira, May 2, 1976, and my subsequent conversations with the rebbetzin.*

# The Amulet of the Belzer Rabbi

IT WAS A COLD, DARK NIGHT IN THE TARNOW GHETTO. SOMEONE was impatiently knocking on Dr. Isaiah Hendler's window. "It's a Jew, a friend; open the door, doctor." Dr. Hendler rushed to the door. In the doorway stood Mr. Goldfarb, a Belzer Hasid. His distress was obvious; he spoke in great haste. "Doctor Hendler, I need your help. Money is no object; we will pay as much as you ask. The Grand Rabbi of Belz has been injured. He is in a small village near Tarnow and needs immediate medical attention." Dr. Hendler knew well the risk of leaving the ghetto without a permit: the punishment was death. But in a matter of minutes he was dressed, and with his doctor's satchel in hand he followed Goldfarb. They climbed over fences and crawled in the mud until they were finally outside the ghetto limits. There, a Polish farmer with a horse and buggy was waiting for them. Once they were in the carriage and on their way, Goldfarb briefly sketched in a few details about the plight of the

Grand Rabbi, Aaron Rokeach, since his escape from Belz. He had
suffered the death of his family and his beloved son, and now had had
a serious accident. The Belzer Rabbi, his brother, Rabbi Mordechai
of Bielgory, and two of their ardent followers had hired a taxi with a
Polish driver for an astronomical sum of money to drive them to
Bochnia. The car missed the road, turned over into a ditch, and the
frail old rebbe was badly hurt.

After a drive of close to an hour in the pitch-black Polish countryside, the doctor and his escort reached the village where the rabbi and
his party were waiting. The Polish farmer, their coachman, led them
to a barn. There, seated on a bundle of straw in the pale light of a
hanging kerosene lamp, was the world-renowned Belzer zaddik. The
rabbi's face was bandaged with a red kerchief, as if he suffered from
toothache. His beard and sidelocks were shaven and his hands and
clothes were covered with blood. Dr. Hendler attended to the rabbi
and then the other, more fortunate passengers, who had escaped the
accident with only mild injuries. When the doctor was finished, the
rabbi asked what his fee would be. "Not even a broken penny,"
replied Dr. Hendler. He told the rabbi that he had simply done his
human and professional duty; there was no limit to his joy that he
was privileged to help the rabbi, his brother, and their companions in
such a moment of distress.

The Grand Rabbi of Belz was very moved by the doctor's reply.
Before they parted, he blessed Dr. Hendler and said that he and the
close members of his family would survive the war. He gave the doctor a twenty-zloty coin, not as a payment, but rather as an amulet.
The rabbi told the doctor to watch over the amulet, for its merit
would always protect him.

On the way back to the ghetto, Mr. Goldfarb asked Dr. Hendler to
sell him the amulet. "Doctor, why do you need the amulet? You are
a Jew who does not observe tradition and law. As such, an amulet
from a Hasidic rebbe is meaningless to you." He offered the doctor
2,000 zloty for the twenty-zloty coin. Hendler did not respond.
Goldfarb raised his bid to 20,000 zloty. The doctor still remained silent. Goldfarb continued to bargain for the amulet. "I will pay any

amount you wish," he pleaded. Finally the doctor responded: "Dear Mr. Goldfarb, no matter what price you are going to offer, I am not going to part with the twenty-zloty coin given to me by the Grand Rabbi of Belz. It has no price, for it is worth my very life!" The subject was dropped, and the two men returned to the ghetto before dawn.

When the Tarnow ghetto was liquidated in September 1943, Dr. Hendler, together with other able-bodied young people, was deported to Plaszow. He took with him his most precious possessions, the amulet and a medical manuscript he had been writing in the ghetto. When the doctor faced deportation again, this time from Plaszow to a concentration camp in Germany, he buried the amulet and his manuscript near his barracks in Plaszow.

Just as was promised by the Belzer Rabbi on that dark night in a remote Polish village, Dr. Hendler survived the war. After liberation, he returned to Plaszow and began to search for his amulet and manuscript. His barracks was no longer in existence and the search was a tiresome one. But eventually he did locate the site and retrieved both the amulet and the manuscript.

Although Isaiah Hendler lost his parents in the Tarnow ghetto, and his brothers, doctors like himself, were also consumed by the Holocaust, he firmly believes that he and his sister survived because of the protective merits of the amulet and the blessing given to him by the Grand Rabbi of Belz, Rabbi Aaron Rokeach. To this very day, Dr. Hendler proudly displays, in his Tel Aviv apartment, the twenty-zloty coin, the amulet that saved his life.

*Based on Dr. Isaiah Hendler's own account in* Tarnow-Sefer Zikaron, *(Israel, 1968), vol. II, pp. 272–76, and my own interview with a Belzer Hasid, March 18, 1980.*

# Fine Generations

WHEN THE RABBI OF BELZ, RABBI AARON ROKEACH (1880–1957), stayed in the Bochnia ghetto before his dramatic escape to Hungary, many of the ghetto inhabitants came to him to ask for a blessing and to seek his advice. The frail rabbi, who slept no more than two hours a night, and survived on a few sips of coffee and a glass of milk smuggled into the ghetto by his ardent follower Mr. Kempler, did not turn away a single soul. He offered comfort and solace to all who came to him, never mentioning his own great tragedy, the loss of his entire family.

Among the many people who came to the crowded apartment in Ghetto Bochnia were Bronia and her two little sons, Zvi, age six, and Yitzhak, age three.

After the rebbe blessed her and her two children with a general blessing—"that God will help"—Bronia did not leave the rebbe's presence, but asked him to bless her sons with "fine generations in the future."

"Poor woman," someone whispered, "she probably lost her mind in these troubled times. Every day children's Aktions take place. Hundreds of children are constantly being murdered and this woman is asking for a future with fine generations, a future of living Jews!"

The Belzer Rebbe motioned to the young boys to come close to him. He placed his hands on their heads and blessed them with generations upon generations of fine Jews. "We will live through this war, we will live through this war!" Bronia kept telling her bewildered children as she walked back to her apartment, filled with hope and faith.

Today, as Bronia (who is now married to the Rabbi of Bluzhov) tells her story, she is surrounded by grandchildren and daughters-in-law. From the floor below, the beit midrash of the Bluzhover Rebbe, one can hear the melodious voices of her sons and her older grandchildren studying the Talmud with great devotion. "At times one

36

has to be aggressive when it comes to blessings," she adds as if in an afterthought, in a manner of good-natured advice. "In time of war one has to organize everything, even a blessing."

*Based on a conversation of Rebbetzin Bronia Spira with Dina Spira, May 2, 1976.*

# The Little Slave Girl from the Toy Factory

MIRIAM FISCHELBERG WAS NEARLY TEN YEARS OLD WHEN HER family arrived in the ghetto of Bochnia. The ghetto was overcrowded. The young, the old, and the weak were dying from starvation, typhus, and dysentery. All legal residents of the ghetto and children twelve years and older were given working papers for employment in the German workshops established with the initiative of Salo Greiber.

The Fischelbergs, after great effort and much bribery, were able to obtain working papers for their tiny daughter. She was very small for her age and had a leg injury which she suffered when a German driver ran her over deliberately. Despite her miniature size and the pains in her leg, after Miriam received her papers she worked like an adult, a full day from dawn to dusk. She worked in the toy factory,[1] where in order to look as tall as the other workers and to reach the table, Miriam stood on a box covered by her long full skirt. During selections, she would stand on her tiptoes and pinch her hollow cheeks so that she would look healthy. Her tiny hands would continue to assemble the little parts of the colorful toys with great diligence, proving to the overseers that she was a very valuable worker in the Third Reich's war machinery. Never did it enter Miriam's mind that she, the little Jewish slave child, was assembling toys for children her own age, free German children who would play with toys on a soft rug in front of a fireplace. "If only I could be tall and healthy," Miriam would pray silently after each selection. But with each passing day, the pains increased and the selections became more and more frequent.

At night, back at the apartment that the Fischelbergs shared with eight other refugee families, Miriam would eat her meager, rationed meal. Exhausted from a long day's work, she would curl up in her tiny corner and fall asleep. At night Miriam would dream. In her dreams she was in Palestine where it was spring. She was in a huge orange grove with many other young people, all healthy-looking and suntanned. They were picking oranges. All her friends were standing on top of boxes and ladders. Only she was tall enough to reach the oranges while standing firmly on the ground.

Her mother's touch on her shoulder at dawn would pluck Miriam out of her orange grove and thrust her back into the dark, cold, overcrowded Bochnia ghetto apartment.

One evening, when Miriam returned home from the toy factory, she found a new tenant in the overcrowded apartment, a frail old man. Despite the lack of space, a small cubicle had been partitioned off for him. Dark paper was pasted over the windows. Two men were constantly at his side. Candles were a scarce commodity in the ghetto, yet the old frail man studied by the light of burning candles, day and night.

From the moment of his arrival, the occupants of the apartment changed dramatically. People who constantly argued with one another over the position of a mattress, a turn at the kitchen stove, a cup of water, or the situation at the eastern front, suddenly spoke in hushed voices and willingly gave up a few inches of space in the crowded apartment. Everyone became polite and even greeted each other with a faint smile, as if a ray of hope had appeared in that dark corner of the Bochnia ghetto.

Miriam soon learned that the frail old man was the world-famed Belzer Rebbe, Rabbi Aaron Rokeach (1880–1957), who, like her own family, after much suffering, had come to Bochnia. Day and night people streamed into the small cubicle to ask for a blessing. As they left, Miriam watched their hopeful faces and became convinced that she too could be saved by the rebbe who could bless her with life and health.

Two days short of her tenth birthday, Miriam and her father, mother, and brother stood before the rebbe. Miriam was overcome with awe. His deep-set eyes looked at her and past her as if he were tearing away a mask from the hidden face of the future. Then he spoke: "You will live; you will survive and be blessed with a beautiful generation of good Jews."

Miriam was sure that each word uttered by that frail man held a power which gave her a lease on life and to this day she feels that it was her faith in the rebbe that sustained her during the terrible years in Bergen Belsen.

Miriam and her family were liberated on a death train near Magdeburg, Germany, by the American Army in April 1945.[2]

*Based on interview by Bella Linshitz with Miriam Fischelberg Lesser, May 1975, and on my own conversation with Miriam Lesser.*

# The Generals

THE RABBI OF BELZ, RABBI AARON ROKEACH, AND HIS BROTHER Mordechai, the Rabbi of Bielgory, were smuggled out of the Bochnia ghetto in May 1943. In charge of the rescue operation was a brave Hungarian officer who was handsomely rewarded for his bold plan.

According to his plan, the high-ranking Hungarian officer would be traveling in the service of the Hungarian Army. His "mission" would be to bring back to Hungary from Poland for interrogation two prominent generals captured on the eastern front. The two captured generals would be none other than the Grand Rabbi of Belz and his brother.

The Hungarian officer made all the necessary arrangements at the various border checkpoints both in Poland and Hungary. All the forged documents were in perfect order, as were the various license plates he prepared for his car. The only possible problem was the fact that he had forgotten to bring along two sets of Russian uniforms. When he realized his error, it was too late to go back. However, the Hungarian officer had confidence in his plan and did not foresee any major difficulties.

After long months of preparation, the journey to freedom began. First came the dramatic escape from the Bochnia ghetto. Among many bold and heroic deeds was that of the Hasid who played the rabbi's double for a few days so that the ghetto administration would not become aware that the rabbi was missing.

With the two "generals" in his back seat, both clean-shaven and dressed in civilian clothing, the brave Hungarian officer successfully passed the first checkpoint. As he passed each additional checkpoint, his confidence grew and he merrily sang Hungarian songs. At one point in the journey, he even left his two illustrious passengers alone in the parked car while he entered a bar to have a few drinks.

When he returned he could not find the car. He began to search frantically for the vanished car only to discover that the car was parked in precisely the same spot where he had left it. But it was shrouded in a heavy mist as if to conceal it from eyes that were not supposed to see it. He crossed himself, for now he was sure that all he had been told about his two passengers was indeed true.

Finally they reached the Hungarian border, the last leg of their dangerous journey. The Hungarian officer was in especially high spirits, for at last he was on his native soil. He changed the license plates on the car and discarded the old ones in a nearby potato field where he buried them deep in the ground.

At the first major checkpoint in Hungary, the officer did not foresee any mishaps. As they stopped at the barrier, he presented all the necessary papers to the young border guard. The guard looked at the pictures in the documents, carefully compared them to the two passengers in the back seat, then checked their names against a list in his possession. "Sorry, I can't let you pass. I have no order from my superiors to expect the arrival of two captive generals," the young soldier said. "Check with your superior," the Hungarian officer suggested in a commanding voice. The superior appeared moments later. He apologized for the inconvenience, but he confirmed the young soldier's statement. He had no instructions to allow the passage of two captured Russian generals. "Where are your uniforms?" he asked the gentlemen in the back seat. They remained silent. "They are under strict orders to speak to no one except at headquarters. How long do you expect us to wait at this godforsaken place?" The Hungarian officer continued speaking in a confident tone while he tried to figure out what had gone wrong and to work out an alternative plan.

Just then, out of the mist appeared three Hungarian generals mounted on beautiful horses. They ordered the border guards, both the junior officer and his superior, to let the captive generals through. As the car crossed the border, the three mounted Hungarian generals saluted the two "generals" in the car. Once more the car was on its way to freedom with its two prominent passengers.

The Hungarian officer was bewildered. "I know all the high officers in the Hungarian Army, but I must frankly admit to you I did not recognize the three high-ranking military men who came to our rescue at the border."

"We did," responded the Rabbi of Bielgory. "They were our father, Rabbi Issacher Dov Baer (1859–1927), our grandfather, Rabbi Joshua (1825–1894), and our great-grandfather, Rabbi Shalom the Seraph (1779–1855), all top-ranking generals in God Almighty's Army!"

*I heard it from a Belzer Hasid who in turn heard it from the Rabbi of Bielgory himself, February 24, 1980.*

# A Shofar
# in a Coffee Cauldron

WOLF FISCHELBERG AND HIS TWELVE-YEAR-OLD SON WERE WALK-
ing among the barracks of the sector for privileged people
(Bevorzugenlager) in Bergen Belsen, trying to barter some cigarettes
for bread. As they were turning into another row of barracks, a stone
was thrown across the barbed wire separating one sector from another. The stone flew over their heads and landed at their feet. It was
clear that it was aimed at father and son.

"What does it mean?" Wolf turned to his son Leo.

"Nothing! Just an angry Jew hurling stones," replied the son with
a defiant note in his tone.

"Angry Jews do not cast stones; it is not part of our tradition,"
replied the father.

"Maybe it is time that it should become part of our tradition," the
son snapped with restrained anger.

Wolf Fischelberg looked around to see if all was clear. Only then
did he bend down to pick up the stone. A small gray note was
wrapped around it. Wolf slipped the note into his pocket. They
walked into a safe barracks where other Polish Jews lived. In a corner, at a distance from the others, Wolf read the note. It was written
in Hebrew by a Dutch Jew named Hayyim Borack who had
Argentinian papers. After establishing his credentials, Hayyim wrote
that he was fortunate to have obtained a shofar and it was in his possession. If the Hasidic Jews from the Polish transports wished to use
the shofar for Rosh Hashanah services, Borack could smuggle the
shofar in one of the coffee cauldrons of the morning distribution. In
doing so they would lose a cauldron of coffee, for the Shofar would be
covered with a minimal amount of coffee, just enough to conceal it.

A vote was taken among the Polish Jews. Those in favor of the plan
to smuggle in the shofar held a clear majority. They all agreed to give
up their morning coffee ration on the first day of Rosh Hashanah.

At the time and place specified in the note, a stone once more made its way over the electrified barbed wire, this time from the Polish Jews to the Dutch. "You see, my son, Jews never throw stones in vain," said Wolf to his son as his eyes followed the stone making its way from one sector to another.

The smuggling of the shofar was a success. Nobody was caught and the shofar was not damaged. But now a new problem arose. In order to fulfill the mitzvah, the obligation of shofar blowing, all present must clearly hear the voice of the shofar. The risk was great. If the sounds of the shofar reached German ears, all present would pay with their lives.

A heated debate developed among the scholars and rabbis in the barracks as to whether one could properly fulfill the commandment of sounding the shofar if it could not be heard distinctly. In the absence of books, all discussants relied on their memory and quoted precedents from various Jewish sources. Based on Halakha (Jewish law), a decision was reached to blow the shofar quietly. God would surely accept the muffled sounds of the shofar and the prayers of His sons and daughters just as he had accepted the prayers of Isaac atop the altar of Mount Moriah, thought Wolf Fischelberg as he was about to blow the shofar.

As little Miriam, Wolf's daughter, listened to the shofar, she hoped that it would bring down the barbed-wire fences of Bergen Belsen just as the blasts of the shofar had in earlier times made the walls of Jericho come tumbling down. Then the service was over. Nothing had changed. The barbed wires remained fixed in their places. Only in the heart did something stir—knowledge and hope: knowledge that the muffled voice of a shofar had made a dent in the Nazi wall of humiliation and slavery, and hope that someday freedom would bring down the barbed-wire fences of Bergen Belsen and of humanity.

*Based on interview by Dina Spira with Wolf Fischelberg, December 20, 1976.*

# "Avremele,
# You Are Going
# to Siberia!"

ABRAM GRINBERG WAS A YOUNG TAILOR IN JEZIERZYCE, POLAND.
He joined the Red Army and managed to escape with the retreating
Russians when the Germans occupied his town.

Some time later, his unit was split into two groups. One group of
volunteers was to be sent to Siberia and the other to join the regular
fighting forces. After long deliberation, Abram Grinberg decided to
join the combat unit. He promptly informed his commander of his
decision.

That night, his mother appeared to him in a dream and told him,
"Avremele, you are going to Siberia!" She repeated the sentence
several times. The following morning, Abram asked his commander
to be transferred back to the volunteer unit leaving for Siberia. He
was transferred.

After the war, Abram Grinberg learned that the entire combat unit
had been killed at Stalingrad.

*Based on interview by Zelda Grinberg (daughter) with Abram Grinberg,
May 4, 1977.*

# The Zanzer Kiddush
# Goblet

RABBI MENDEL HALBERSTAM, THE LAST RABBI OF CHRZANOW, was herded into the ghetto with the entire Jewish population of Chrzanow. Life in the ghetto became more difficult with each passing day. Despite the many hardships, the rabbi's household was hopeful. The family was together and they still had their most precious possession, the miraculous Kiddush goblet of their illustrious great-grandfather, Rabbi Hayyim Halberstam, founder of the Zanz dynasty (1793–1876).[1]

The Kiddush goblet had been given to the rabbi by a childless Hasid who requested that the rabbi and his descendants forever after use the goblet for Kiddush every Sabbath and holiday for the restoration of the Hasid's soul. The rabbi agreed.

Some time after the death of the Hasid, the rabbi pawned the goblet. He gave the money to a poor widow as a dowry for her daughter's forthcoming marriage. Several weeks later, the deceased Hasid came in a dream to the gabbai (personal secretary) of the rabbi and angrily demanded an explanation of why the rabbi was no longer making Kiddush over his goblet. The next morning, the gabbai dressed in great haste and ran to the rabbi's house. As he opened the door, the rabbi was awaiting him. "I know," he said, in his quiet voice. "You came about the goblet. We will redeem it as soon as possible." The goblet was redeemed.

When the rabbi died, he did not bequeath the golden Kiddush goblet to any of his eight sons. After a long family dispute and recourse to a Din Torah (rabbinic court) to determine the lawful ownership of the goblet, it was awarded to Rabbi David Halberstam (1821–1894), the Rabbi of Chrzanow, since it was he who had redeemed the pawned goblet. It was agreed that the cup would never leave the possession of the Zanzer Rabbi's descendants. Upon his death, his son Naftali inherited the goblet. Like his grandfather, Reb Naftali did not bequeath the cup to anybody. His two sons, Rabbi Mendel and Rabbi David, drew lots for it. Rabbi Mendel, the last Rabbi of Chrzanow, became the owner.

Rabbi Mendel of Chrzanow guarded the golden Kiddush goblet. It became the family's most precious belonging, and Rabbi Mendel would not let the goblet out of the sight of his watchful eyes. When the goblet developed a leak, Rabbi Mendel himself made a trip to Cracow since he trusted no one with the goblet. He waited for long hours at the goldsmith's while the cup was soldered and repaired under his supervising gaze.

Every Sabbath and holiday, Rabbi Mendel Halberstam would recite the Kiddush while holding the beautiful golden goblet. The glow of the Sabbath candles would be mirrored in the polished, delicate flower etchings of the golden goblet. The faces of the rabbi's six daughters and only young son, Naftali, would glow with the pride of owning the Zanzer cup.

World War II came. The Germans entered Poland and darkness took over Europe. The lights of the Sabbath table were extinguished. The Zanzer goblet was wrapped and hidden in a dark corner in the rabbi's home. But the belief that the Zanzer golden Kiddush cup would protect them from the Nazi beast glowed in the hearts of the rabbi's family.

The ghetto grew smaller and smaller and the deportations to Auschwitz larger and larger. One evening, after a large transport had left, the rabbi called in his children. He took out the golden goblet and handed it to Rivka, the second of his six daughters. "My child, I am entrusting the Zanzer Kiddush cup to you. May the merit of my great-grandfather, the Divrei Hayyim, protect you and your sisters."

Rivka understood the awesome meaning of that transaction in the small room in the ghetto of Chrzanow. Death was about to cross the threshold of the rabbi's house, and she was being blessed with life. With trembling hands, Rivka took the Zanzer Kiddush goblet.

That night no one slept in the rabbi's house. Rivka made a hole in one of the walls of their house in the ghetto, placed the cup inside, and carefully plastered up the wall. The family watched her in silence as their shadows flickered for the entire night against the precious wall.

In 1943, Rabbi Mendel, his wife, his oldest daughter, her husband, child, and the rabbi's only son, Naftali, were taken to Auschwitz on their last journey. Rivka and her sisters Chana, Rachel, Miriam, and Zipporah were deported to Parnitz in Sudeten.

Rivka and her four younger sisters survived somehow. When the war was over they returned to Chrzanow. The entire city was still intact. All the Jewish homes had been taken over by local Poles, except one house which had been damaged by a bomb that had exploded nearby and blown off its roof. It was the rabbi's house in the ghetto. Rivka entered the bombed-out shell, the place that had been her home. The wall was intact. She retrieved the precious goblet.

In May 1945, Rivka, her four sisters, and the Zanzer goblet left Chrzanow, the town that had been their ancestral home for generations, and left for the D.P. camp in Wolfratshausen in Germany. To assure the safety of the goblet, Rivka smeared it with blackberry jam so that its luster would not attract attention. In December 1948, the five sisters and the golden Zanzer Kiddush goblet arrived in the United States and settled in Brooklyn, New York.

Once more the warm glow of the Zanzer cup sparkles in the eyes of the rabbi's descendants. It is the Zanzer cup that welcomes newborn babies into the Halberstam family and touches their lips on the day of circumcision. Its luster reflects the blushing faces of young brides under the marriage canopy; its magic touch reassures feverish hands in illness. Its golden tradition spans the abyss of anguish with a gleaming bridge of ancestral faith.

*Based on interview with Rivka Halberstam Schachner by her daughter Rachel Schachner on May 15, 1975. Rivka Halberstam Schachner is the present owner of the Zanzer Kiddush cup.*

# No Time for Advice

MOISHE DOVID WAS THE YOUNGEST SON AND SIXTH CHILD OF Simcha and Menucha Faluch. Rabbi Simcha was a Gerer Hasid and a director of the Talmud Torah at 116 Kilinskiego Street in Lodz. His family lived next door at Number 120. Rabbi Simcha was known as a scholar and wise man. People came to seek his advice, especially in time of trouble.

When World War II broke out, people flocked to Rabbi Faluch for advice and comfort. "We Jews must understand that this war is not just a usual war with one country fighting another. This will be a war against the Jews and Judaism, and we must act accordingly." To his own family his advice was more specific. "When our Patriarch Jacob was 'greatly afraid and . . . distressed . . . he divided the people that was with him . . . into two camps. And he said: If Esau came to the one camp, and smite it, then the camp which is left shall escape.' "[1] We must follow our Patriarch's example and do likewise. We must part and scatter to the four corners of the land. Perhaps this way a few of us will survive this war."

The children listened to their father's advice. Each of the Faluchs' married sons and daughters ran with their families in different directions. Moishe Dovid was then twenty-two years old and single. His older sister Bluma was newly engaged. The two of them, at their father's urging, decided to go to Warsaw. Rabbi Simcha reasoned that since Warsaw was the capital, its defenses and fortification would be superior to anything found in the rest of the country; its large Jewish community also encouraged him to think of Warsaw as a likely refuge.

With heavy hearts, Moishe Dovid and Bluma parted from their parents. The roads to Warsaw were clogged with people. It seemed as if the number of people who were trying to get there equaled the number of refugees trying to flee. German planes were flying overhead, alternately bombing and strafing. In one such attack, as every-

48

one was running for cover, Moishe Dovid lost his sister, never to find her again.

Despondent and alone, he attached himself to a Hasidic group on the run like himself. It was a party of the Grand Rabbi of Pabianic, Mendel Alter, the son of the famed Sefat Emet.[2] At Brzezyn the bombing was especially heavy. It was a Thursday night. A small crescent moon shone, but the fires lit up the night like high noon. The house where the Hasidic party sought shelter was not spared. Half of the house was blown away. Dovid was frightened. He began to doubt that leaving Lodz had indeed been a sound decision and he feared that he would never make it alive to Warsaw. He decided to seek advice and ask the Grand Rabbi of Pabianic for guidance. But Moishe Dovid was shocked by the answer he received. The Grand Rabbi Mendel Alter, a man who had always found the right word for each situation, told him: "Don't ask me any questions! This is no time for advice."

Moishe Dovid had to act according to his own intuition, and that very same day he turned back toward home. It was Friday morning. He ran most of the way home, not stopping even when his hat blew away.

When Dovid reached Lodz, the Germans had already conquered the city. At the gate of their home his father was standing crying, tormented by the advice that he had given his two youngest children to leave home. When he saw his son running toward him, he was grateful that for at least one of his children his prayers had been answered.

Moishe Dovid was still troubled by the fact that the grand rabbi had not been able to offer any advice when Dovid had so desperately needed it. He turned to his father for an explanation. His father responded with a Talmudic proverb: "When the shepherd is angry at his flock, he inflicts with blindness [its leader] the ram of the herd."[3]

His father continued: "It is a time when the biblical curse has materialized: 'The Lord shall smite thee with madness, and with blindness, and with astonishment of heart. And thou shalt grope at noonday, as the blind gropeth in darkness . . . and thou shalt be only oppressed and robbed alway, and there shall be none to save thee."[4]

"It is a time such as we have never experienced before. Each of us must make his own decisions, for each of us will ultimately be called to be a member of the Sanhedrin and sit in judgment in matters of life and death, to judge his own life. My son, the Grand Rabbi of Pabianic was right. I was wrong and my dear beautiful daughter, Bluma, the flower of my life, has paid dearly, with her life, for my decisions and advice."

Moishe Dovid listened closely to his father. Each word became engraved on his memory and in his soul. For the next six years, under German occupation, in the Lodz ghetto, in death and labor camps, he made his own decisions about how to survive German tyranny. In Lodz, he was one of the organizers of the Gerer Hasidic underground. In Auschwitz, he managed to survive a selection; in Trydland, a labor camp on the Czech border, he was a spokesman for his fellow inmates. He was liberated by the Russians on May 8, 1945, and was fortunate to find his wife, whom he had married in the Lodz ghetto. After many more struggles, he arrived in Israel in 1949.

*Based on interview by Zeev Falk with Reb Moishe Dovid Faluch in 1970 in Israel. I am grateful to Zahava Ben-Zeev for giving me the transcript of the interview.*

# "The Messiah Is Already Here!"

ON THE EVE OF ROSH HASHANA, 1941, MORE THAN 4,000 JEWS FROM Eisysky and its vicinity were herded together by the Lithuanians into the shtetl's synagogues. Men were wrapped in their prayer shawls; women and children carried pillows, blankets, and pots filled with the food and delicacies that had been prepared in honor of the Jewish New Year of 5702. More people kept arriving at the already congested main synagogue and the overcrowding became unbearable.

About sixty Jewish lunatics from the nearby insane asylum at Selo were put in charge of the crowd in the packed synagogue by the drunken Lithuanian armed guards. The lunatics' wild laughter, gestures, drooling, and gibberish created a strange scene, as if from another planet.

Huddled together like other families in the main synagogue, in an attempt to protect each other from the unknown, sat three brothers with their wives and children. They were all shoemakers, known in Eisysky as Yankel the shoemaker, Eli Dovid the shoemaker, and Chaim Yitzhak the shoemaker. While the two latter brothers made a decent living, owned cobbler chairs, and were respected members of the shoemaker's shtibel, Yankel the shoemaker was poor and begged for alms. With a big empty potato sack thrown over his shoulder, he would make the rounds in the neighboring shtetlach begging for food and money. On Friday he would return to his native Eisysky and make his rounds there. His brothers were mortally embarrassed and they avoided being seen in public with him. But now they were all sitting together. Yentel, Eli Dovid's wife, was holding on to a pot of golden chicken soup filled with carrots and stewed chicken. Yankel was clutching his empty, coarse potato sack.

Near the holy ark at the Mizrach (Eastern) wall, not far from the three brothers, stood Rabbi Scholem, Eisysky's mystic. His beautiful black beard was neatly combed, its few gray hairs looking like silvery threads. Dressed in white kittel and prayer shawl, with a tall white satin yarmulke on his head, he was an impressive, solemn figure. How many nights had Reb Scholem spent in solitude with the holy scrolls? Night after night, burning candle after candle until daylight filtered in from the arched windows, he had stayed there alone.

Many rumors had circulated in Eisysky about Reb Scholem, for Eisysky was a town of Mitnaggedim, opponents of Hasidism and mysticism. But even they loved him, for in his prophecies he had singled out their beloved shtetl as the place where the Messiah was going to come. Some said that Reb Scholem came to Eisysky from Russia from a prominent Hasidic dynasty, and in his youth had been an ardent revolutionary. According to the stories, disappointed by the Revolution and its false Red Messiah that failed, he returned to the fold and came to Eisysky to bring the true Messiah. For years every night, alone in Eisysky's main synagogue, surrounded by the Zohar, the Book of Splendor, and other mystical writings, Reb Scholem had tried to calculate the date of the coming of the Messiah and induce him to hasten his arrival.

Now Reb Scholem was sure that the Messiah would come. Everybody was here in the synagogue, men in their prayer shawls, women, children, babes in arms, the sick, the lame, the insane, just as it says in the Scriptures.[1] Reb Scholem stood with his eyes closed, his hands stretched out to the open holy ark. In the two-tiered shelves of the ark, the holy scrolls stood next to each other like the rest of Eisysky's community. Some of the scrolls in this holy ark were as old as Eisysky's most ancient families. Bedecked in pure-white velvet mantles, ornamented with gold and silver embroidery as befitting the High Holiday season, they too awaited the verdict.

Reb Scholem lifted his hands to heaven and in a powerful voice commanded the Messiah to come! Silence fell in the synagogue. Even the lunatics from Selo froze in their bizarre positions. Just then, Yankel the shoemaker lost his balance and tripped over his sister-in-law Yentel's chicken soup pot. The soup spilled and quarters of stewed chicken scattered all over the floor. Yankel picked up the largest *polke* (drumstick) and began to chew on it. With the *polke* in one hand and his beggar's bag in the other, he walked over to Reb Scholem in front of the Holy Ark. His eyes were gleaming with exhilaration. He began to talk, at first in a quavering voice that became more powerful with each word he uttered: "Prominent households of Eisysky, brothers and sisters! Do you see with your own eyes that I, Yankel the shoemaker, the beggar, am holding a chicken *polke* in my hand and standing at the Mizrach wall reserved only for the privileged? If I am standing here next to the great scholar, Reb Scholem, my friends, the order of the universe must indeed have changed! Your troubles are at end, for the Messiah has just arrived here in our own shtetl of Eisysky. The Messiah is already here!"

During the following days, on September 25 and 26, 1941, all of

Eisysky's Jews were murdered at the old Jewish cemetery. Among them were Reb Scholem the mystic and Yankel the shoemaker.

*Based on my interview with Zvi Michalowsky on September 14, 1980.*

# "Jew, Go Back to the Grave!"

ON ROSH HASHANA, 1941, WHEN ALL THE JEWS OF EISYSKY AND nearby towns awaited their fate in the shtetls' synagogues, watched over by lunatics whom their Lithuanian captors had appointed as their supervisors, it was clear to the Rabbi of Eisysky, Rabbi Shimon Rozowsky, that his beloved shtetl was doomed. A few days earlier he had called the town's notables together and told them, "Jews, our end is near. God does not wish our redemption; our fate is sealed and we must accept it. But let us die with honor, let us not walk as sheep to the slaughter. Let us purchase ammunition and fight until our last breath. Let us die like judges in Israel: 'Let me die with the Philistines.' "[1]

Some had supported him, but the opposition, led by Yossel Wildenburg, prevailed.[2] Now it was too late. From the synagogues, they were led to the horse market. At the head of the strange procession, more than 4,000 Jews, walked Rabbi Shimon Rozowsky, dressed in his Sabbath finery and his tall silk yarmulke. Next to him walked the handsome hazan of Eisysky, Mr. Tabolsky. The hazan, wrapped in his talit, was holding the holy Torah scrolls. The rabbi and the hazan together were leading the congregation in reciting the Vidduy, the confession of the dying.

In groups of 250, first the men and then the women, the people were taken to the old Jewish cemetery in front of the open ditches. They were ordered to undress and stand at the edge of the open graves. They were shot in the back of the head by Lithuanian guards with the encouragement and help of the local people. The chief executioner was the Lithuanian Ostrovakas. Dressed in a uniform, a white apron, and gloves, he personally supervised the killing. He reserved for himself the privilege of shooting the town's notables, among them Rabbi Shimon Rozowsky, and he practiced sharpshooting at the children, aiming as they were thrown into the graves.[3]

Among the Jews that September 25, 1941, in the old Jewish cemetery of Eisysky was one of the shtetl's melamdim (teachers), Reb Michalowsky, and his youngest son, Zvi, age sixteen. Father and son were holding hands as they stood naked at the edge of the open pit, trying to comfort each other during their last moments. Young Zvi was counting the bullets and the intervals between one volley of fire and the next. As Ostrovakas and his people were aiming their guns, Zvi fell into the grave a split second before the volley of fire hit him.

He felt the bodies piling up on top of him and covering him. He felt the streams of blood around him and the trembling pile of dying bodies moving beneath him.

It became cold and dark. The shooting died down above him. Zvi made his way from under the bodies, out of the mass grave into the cold, dead night. In the distance, Zvi could hear Ostrovakas and his people singing and drinking, celebrating their great accomplishment. After 800 years, on September 26, 1941, Eisysky was Judenfrei.[4]

At the far end of the cemetery, in the direction of the huge church, were a few Christian homes. Zvi knew them all. Naked, covered with blood, he knocked on the first door. The door opened. A peasant was holding a lamp which he had looted earlier in the day from a Jewish home. "Please let me in," Zvi pleaded. The peasant lifted the lamp and examined the boy closely. "Jew, go back to the grave where you belong!" he shouted at Zvi and slammed the door in his face. Zvi knocked on other doors, but the response was the same.

Near the forest lived a widow whom Zvi knew too. He decided to knock on her door. The old widow opened the door. She was holding in her hand a small, burning piece of wood. "Let me in!" begged Zvi. "Jew, go back to the grave at the old cemetery!" She chased Zvi away with the burning piece of wood as if exorcising an evil spirit, a dybbuk.

"I am your Lord, Jesus Christ. I came down from the cross. Look at me—the blood, the pain, the suffering of the innocent. Let me in," said Zvi Michalowsky. The widow crossed herself and fell at his blood-stained feet. "*Boże moj, Boże moj* (my God, my God)," she kept crossing herself and praying. The door was opened.

Zvi walked in. He promised her that he would bless her children, her farm, and her, but only if she would keep his visit a secret for three days and three nights and not reveal it to a living soul, not even the priest. She gave Zvi food and clothing and warm water to wash himself. Before leaving the house, he once more reminded her that the Lord's visit must remain a secret, because of His special mission on earth.

Dressed in a farmer's clothing, with a supply of food for a few days, Zvi made his way to the nearby forest. Thus, the Jewish partisan movement was born in the vicinity of Eisysky.

*Based on my several interviews with Zvi Michalowski and my interviews with several other people from Eisysky.*

# God's Messenger, the Grandson of the Pnei Yehoshua

YITZHAK STEINBLAT LIVED WITH HIS FATHER AND MOTHER IN Stoczeklukowski, Poland, where he worked in the family flax business. It was difficult work, especially during the "season," when Yitzhak and his father stayed in the countryside for six days and did not return home until late Friday afternoon for the Sabbath.

One Friday evening, at the height of the flax season, the Steinblat family had just completed the festive Sabbath meal. Yitzhak, a

Raziner Hasid, was also a member of Mizrachi. As was his custom every Friday night, he was about to leave for a Mizrachi gathering. It was raining heavily and his mother pleaded with him not to go. "You are so exhausted; you can barely hold your head straight, you will do a bigger mitzvah if you go to bed instead of going to the organization. It is pouring outside. I am sure no one will show up except you. Not even a dog would venture outdoors in this type of weather." "Listen to your mother," his father agreed. "I know you hardly slept a wink during the entire week." But Yitzhak persisted. He was lonely and longed very much to be with his friends.

The streets were deserted. There was not a living soul outdoors, only the sound of raindrops on the cobblestones. Then, suddenly, he heard a voice, a choked voice attempting to shout: *"Gevalt! Gevalt!"* ("Help! Help!") "Who is it?" Yitzhak asked in Polish. But no one answered. The voice calling for help grew fainter and fainter. Yitzhak began to run in the direction of the voice. He felt as if the faint voice were calling to him. There, in the middle of the street in a huge puddle, lay a Jew. Three Polish teenagers were beating him. Yitzhak gave the tallest of the three a healthy slap, directly on his face. The boy fell to the ground and the other two ran away. The tall fellow soon picked himself up and joined the others in the flight, while nursing his bloody nose.

On the ground was an old Jew with a long white beard. Yitzhak helped him to his feet, cleansed him of blood and mud, and asked him, "Who are you, Reb Yid?" "I am the grandson of the Pnei Yehoshua."[1] "And where are you going, my dear Jew, in this heavy rain?" continued Yitzhak. "I am coming from the house of Mottel Becker. I ate the Friday evening meal with them and was on my way to the guest house[2] when the three Polish *shkotzim* attacked me. You know, you just saved my life. In doing so, you have earned this world and the entire world to come. Please, take me to the guest house. But I have a problem. The guest house is not part of an *eruv hazerot*[3] (an amalgamation of courtyards), and I have some articles in my pockets that I may not carry around on the Sabbath. I would like to put them away somewhere."

Yitzhak suggested that they stop at the Raziner shtibl, leave the articles there, and on Saturday night, after Havdalah, retrieve them. They reached the Raziner shtibl, and only then, in the dim light of the shtibl, did Yitzhak notice the beautiful, glowing eyes of the man whose life he had just saved. Yitzhak took down the tractate Shabbat[4] from the bookshelf and suggested to the grandson of the Pnei Yehoshua that he put his articles inside the book. The old man took out of his pocket a tallit clasp, a tiny ivory snuff box, his eyeglass case, his handkerchief, and some other items, all beautifully and delicately made. Yitzhak placed the Gemara back on the shelf, leaving it sticking out a bit farther than the rest of the books as a marker.

Yitzhak then took the grandson of the Pnei Yeshoshua to the guest house. He looked for a good spot and a clean mattress for his very special guest. He wished him a *Gut Shabbes* and was about to leave. "You hear, all of you in the guest house, this young man saved my life tonight and thus earned this world and the entire world to come!" the grandson of the Pnei Yehoshua declared. Yitzhak parted again from the old man and told him that what he had done was not so outstanding, that any other young man would have done the same. The old man did not pay attention to Yitzhak's humility and once more repeated his blessing.

On the way home, Yitzhak stopped at the Mizrachi but no one was there. They all had left some time ago. When Yitzhak returned home, his father and mother were still up, waiting for him. He was soaking wet. "*Nu* ("Well"), was anybody at the organization?" his mother asked him.

"If only you knew what happened to me tonight!" Excitedly, Yitzhak told his parents the entire story, from the minute he heard the old man's faint call for help until their parting in the guest house. He repeated the awe-inspiring old man's blessing word for word. His parents' faces lit up with joy and pride as they listened to their son's account of how he saved a human life.

"In all my life I did not have the privilege of performing such a deed, such a mitzvah, to save another Jewish life, my son. You have great merit," his father said to him.

"What's the matter with you? Are you jealous of your own son? May God do His share so that the promise will be fulfilled," Yitzhak's mother said.

The following day, very early on Shabbat morning, Yitzhak rushed to the Raziner shtibl. The tractate Shabbat was pushed back against the wall in line with the rest of the Talmud. He pulled it out, but there was nothing inside the Gemara except distinct imprints of the articles placed there the night before by the old man. It looked as if they had been removed only seconds ago. Yitzhak inquired about the old man but was told that he had left at dawn.

A year passed, but Yitzhak never forgot that Friday night, his fateful meeting with the grandson of the Pnei Yehoshua and his blessing. Circumstances changed. World War II broke out. The Germans occupied the town, the Mizrachi club and the Raziner shtibl were closed, the flax business was taken away from the Steinblat family and given over to local Poles, and Jewish blood began to flow like water.

Again it was a Friday night. It had been quiet in town for the last few days and Yitzhak, despite his mother's warning and pleading, ventured out of the house. He walked for a few blocks unharassed. Then, from nowhere, a German soldier suddenly appeared in front of him. "Are you a Jew?" "Yes, I am a Jew," replied Yitzhak. No sooner had he uttered the word *Jew* than a barrage of blows descended upon him. When the German's hands began to hurt, he switched to another weapon, and thrashed Yitzhak's back with the butt of his gun. Then he shoved Yitzhak against the wall, aimed the gun at him, and gleefully announced, "I am going to kill you, dirty Jew!"

At that moment, before Yitzhak's eyes, appeared the image of the old man, the grandson of the Pnei Yehoshua. "Where is your promise?" Yitzhak managed to utter between his broken teeth, with a mouthful of blood. At that very second, a door across the street opened in great haste. A Christian woman, the wife of the local school principal, came running. She flung herself at the German's feet and started to plead with him to pity the poor young man, for he was an honest person. The German lowered the gun and turned to the woman. "What do you want, dirty Polish pig?" "I beg of you, spare the life of this young man." Something in the woman's tearful plea touched the German soldier. He placed the gun back on his shoulder and said, "Fast, *schnell!* Go home, dirty Jew and Polish pig!" The Christian woman took Yitzhak by the hand as if he were her own son and led him back home.

"God has mysterious ways and mysterious messengers," concluded Yitzhak Steinblat, "and I was privileged to have met one of them, the grandson of the Pnei Yehoshua."

*Based on interview by Goldie Merenstein with Yitzhak Steinblat, 1974.*

# "If You Will Grow Hair on the Palm of Your Hand"

HE WAS THE BAKER AT MY CHILDREN'S SUMMER CAMP, CAMP Massad in the Pocono Mountains. He did not speak much prior to the accident. I loved to watch him on birthdays when he carried his beautifully decorated cakes into the dining room. One could sense his great respect and joy for the celebration of life. I especially remember his eyes as he carried in the cake, shaped like a book and decorated in blue and white, in honor of my son Yotav's Bar Mitzvah. Mr. Slucki looked like a high priest entering the Holy of Holies.

After our automobile accident, he came to visit me wearing his baker's hat and white apron, with his sleeves rolled up. He carried with one hand, like a skillful waiter, an aluminum tray, and on it one of his artistically decorated cakes. In fine calligraphy, it wished my daughter Smadar and me a full and speedy recovery. He said that he was very happy to see me practically unharmed and with only minor injuries. After seeing the car when it was towed away, he had expected to find me in a much worse state.

I told him that it was one of these strange cases when not being strapped in by seat belts had been advantageous. As the car rolled down the hill in the Poconos after its brakes failed, I had thrown myself over my daughter to protect her from the caving-in roof and the seat's springs that rolled out from below.

"Don't attribute it to the seat belts. It is rather the miracle of living in order to save someone very dear to you. Even if you had been strapped in with your seat belts, you would have torn them loose like Samson," he said to me. Then, without stopping for my comment, he began to tell me his story.

"You see, I had a little sister who was the most beautiful person on earth both in body and soul. There wasn't a thing in the world that was too difficult for me to do for my sister. When the Germans occupied our town, we hid her for we knew that they would take her away with the rest of the young women. In the ghetto we worked very hard to provide food for an additional mouth. But we looked upon it as a special privilege. We all lived for her safety and well-being. The knowledge that she was safe and with us gave us the strength to go on living in the most difficult times. Even in the ghetto under the most horrible conditions, having her there made our little room seem like a palace. It was as if the Sabbath Queen was always dwelling among us.

"One day as we were returning home, a strange silence hung on the streets . . . the silence that follows death and Aktions. The closer we got to our building, the more we could sense that something was wrong. When we got there, we discovered that the door to our room had been broken in, everything was looted, and my sister was gone! While avoiding our eyes, neighbors told us that she had been taken by the Gestapo. Without thinking, I began to run to the Gestapo. My mother begged me to return; she did not want to lose two children in one day. But I just continued to run.

"I entered the Gestapo building as if it was the most natural thing for a Jew to do. I was greeted by a young soldier at the desk. 'What's your wish, Jew, to be shot now? If you are in great haste, I can accommodate you.'

" 'You took my sister,' I said.

" 'Who's your sister?'

" 'The beautiful girl you just brought in.'

" 'That's fascinating. Tell me, how do all ugly Jews have beautiful sisters?'

The soldier at the desk called in another Gestapo man from the next room. He briefed him.

" 'So she's your sister?' he said to me while his eyes examined me from head to toe.

" 'Yes,' I said.

" 'What do you want?'

" 'Give me back my sister.'

The German burst into wild laughter. ''What strange ideas Jews have these days,' he choked. Suddenly he stopped laughing. 'You know, Jew, I will let your beautiful sister go on one condition. If right now you will grow hair on the palm of your hand.'

"I opened the palm of my hand—it was covered with black hair. The Gestapo man's face twisted into a horrible grimace. He began to shout hysterically, 'You Jewish satan, devil, take your sister and run before I machine-gun the two of you!' Then he went to get her from another room and pushed her toward me, all the while continuing to scream. I grabbed my sister's hand and with all our strength we began to run, never looking back. We stopped for only a moment at our home to tell our parents that we were alive, and then we fled to the forest. Never in my life did I run faster than on that day. I am sure that I would have been a world champion at all the Olympic running tournaments.''

When he finished this story, he opened his clenched fist. His palm was covered with a thick growth of black hair. I was so surprised that I could not utter a single word. I had known him for several years and never noticed it before.

"You see," he went on, "when I was a very young man, a boy, I worked in a factory. My hand was caught in a machine. It was a terrible accident. How they managed to save my shattered hand I still marvel till this day. As you can see, there is not a task I can't perform with my hand, from the most difficult, strenuous movement to the most delicate. Apparently, the skin that was grafted onto my palm was from a hairy part of my body. In my late teens, hair began to grow on the palm of my hand. Doctors tell me today that this is impossible, but the palm of my hand did not go to medical school.

"But let me tell you something. Even if I had not had hair on the palm of my hand, if this had been the only way to save my sister's life, I would have grown hair on the palm of my hand right there before the German's eyes! Don't attribute your daughter's surviving the accident to seat belts; attribute it to love, to a mother's love for her child."

*I heard the story from the baker, Mr. Slucki, August 12, 1970.*

# The Miracle of a Doorless Back Wall

LEIB FISHMAN WAS BORN IN RADAWIEC, WEST OF LUBLIN. IT WAS A small town with shtiblach of many Hasidic rabbis, among them the Trisker, Radziner, and Kotsker. But no one in town was more famous than Reb Pesach Radowiczer, a Kotsker Hasid and the maternal grandfather of Leib Fishman. People from all over came to seek his blessing and advice, and even Gentiles respected him greatly. When people came to him in times of stress to seek his blessing, Reb Pesach used to say, "Please, good people, leave me alone. Go to the rebbes for a blessing. I am just a simple Jew who sits in the beit hamidrash and learns." And indeed, that was where Reb Pesach spent his life when he was not helping the needy and the sick. His wife ran the family store. The only time Reb Pesach crossed the store's threshold was on market days. He would storm into the store to check the weights so that his wife would not, God forbid, inadvertently cheat either her Jewish or her Gentile customers.

Little Leib loved to listen to his grandmother tell stories about her husband, Reb Pesach. Bread-baking time was usually story time, and naturally Leib was at her side. Grandmother often told how many years ago it was a very cold night and, just as now, she was baking bread. Grandfather had still not returned home, but Grandmother did not find any cause for alarm. She was sure that "my Pesach" was still sitting and studying in the beit hamidrash. Just as she was about to remove the bread from the oven, the door opened with a great bang, and cold winds blew in and almost extinguished the fire. Two Gentiles, all bundled up against the cold, walked in. One was carrying Reb Pesach's clothes, the other Reb Pesach himself, naked and wrapped in sheepskins.

"Pania Pessachowa, you are lucky that you are not a widow this very moment," the Gentiles told Grandmother. "On our way home, we noticed Rabbin Pesach making a hole in the ice and just about to jump into the river beneath it, so we picked him up and, despite his protests, brought him back to you." Later, Reb Pesach explained to his wife that since the town's mikveh was broken, he had gone to the icy river to immerse himself in the water.

"Tell me"—Grandmother would at such a point in the story turn to the children and ask—"do you think that this is a proper way for a human being to behave?" And then, with a twinkle in her eye, she would continue to tell more stories about her Reb Pesach.

But Grandmother's favorite story was about the doorless back wall. Little did Leib know then that this particular wall would one day save his life.

Like all East European shtetlach, Radawiec had had a big fire in its history. The entire town was burnt to the ground. Among the houses that went up in smoke was the house of Reb Pesach. But Radawiec showed a remarkable sense of vitality, and in a very short time the town was rebuilt except for Grandmother's house. This lot remained empty, for Reb Pesach refused to build a new house. "Man does not need property," he insisted to Grandmother. "It causes only hardships and worries. Our sages said so. What's wrong with living in rented rooms at Mate Soreh's place, as we do now?" But he failed to convince her; she wanted a house. So Grandmother decided to take matters into her own hands.

She gave the lot to a builder. In return, he was to build two houses in it: a big one for himself and a smaller house for Grandmother. Reb Pesach had no knowledge of this transaction.

One morning when Grandmother woke up she could not believe her eyes. Her wooden house was up! The builder had apparently worked the entire night. But it was a strange house, the likes of which Grandmother had never seen before. The back wall was doorless and there was no side entrance. Whoever heard of such a strange house? Every other house in Radawiec had a back door. How could one live in a house without one? Grandmother argued with the builder, but to no avail. He just smiled as he put the hinges on his own back door. Grandmother was at a loss, and like every Jew in trouble in Radawiec, she ran to Reb Pesach for help.

Reb Pesach was sitting in his usual place in the beit hamidrash and studying. She told him that he must call the builder to a Din Torah, a Rabbinic court. Grandfather said to Grandmother, "Quiet, woman, quiet. If the builder did build two houses, his big house with a back door and your small house without a back door, it was probably not his own idea. It must have been decreed in heaven that Pesach Radowiczer and his wife and their children should live in a house without a back door."

Grandmother continued to argue with Grandfather, pleading for his help. She kept explaining to him how difficult life would be, how she was probably the only woman in the world doomed to raise children in a house without a back door. Nothing helped. Grandfather was sure that it was God's will. He never called the builder to a Din Torah.

Years passed. Reb Pesach was fortunate enough to die a natural death. But for his family and the entire House of Israel, matters were quite different. War came and Radawiec was occupied by the Germans. When the ghetto was liquidated, Reb Pesach's family were deported to their deaths. But two of his grandchildren, Leib and his brother, escaped the deportation and took refuge in the house without the back door. They made a hiding place under the floor and covered up its entrance with a huge crate.

After the deportation of the Jews, the Germans posted guards in front of the Jewish homes to safeguard the property left behind so that all valuables could be shipped to Germany. However, the local Polish population outmaneuvered the German guards and looted the houses by breaking in through the back doors. While looking for Jewish treasures, they would often come upon Jews in hiding. To appease the Germans for their thievery, they would hand over the Jews they found. Thus the Poles were allowed to hold on to the looted goods, and the eradication of the Jews was made virtually complete.

Leib and his brother were sitting in their hiding place and listening to the macabre events outside their home. They could hear Poles breaking into the builder's home through the back door. They heard the pleading voices of members of the builder's family, begging not to be turned over to the Gestapo, and the sound of their being dragged away. Moments later, shots were heard from the direction of the marketplace.

The looters returned and tried to force their way into Reb Pesach's house, but without success. There was no back door! Leib Fishman and his brother held their breath. Between them and death stood only a few inches of a doorless wall. The peasants consulted among themselves and decided to move on to the next house, which had an accessible back door. Leib squeezed his brother's hand in joy and drew a deep breath, filling his lungs with the damp, musty air of the small cubicle under the floor.

Late at night when all was quiet outside, Leib and his brother crept out of their hiding place and made their way into the adjacent backyard. From there they reached the outskirts of the town and the surrounding fields. They found temporary refuge in a forest and obtained food from a friendly shepherd. A few days later they reached a neighboring town which still had a ghetto. It served as a labor camp for young able-bodied men and women who worked in a German factory. There they learned that during the Aktion in Radawiec all the people had been shot, including all who were found in hiding. Leib was sure that what saved him and his brother from the horrible fate of the rest of Radawiec's Jews was Grandfather's doorless back wall. For if a door had been built as Grandmother had wished, he and his brother would now be sharing the mass grave with so many of Radawiec's Jews.

Weeks later Leib and his brother, with other young able-bodied men, were deported to Majdanek and from there to Auschwitz. During his long ordeal and his constant struggle with death, Leib was always sure that his escape from death because of Grandfather Pesach's doorless back wall was a good omen, a promise that Grandfather's merit would always shield him and his brother like an impenetrable wall through which death could not enter. Leib and his brother indeed survived Majdanek and Auschwitz, escaped from a death march, and lived to witness the day of liberation.

*Based on interview by Barry Fishman (son) with Leib Fishman, May 12, 1975.*

# Mothers

WHEN A SMALL POLISH GHETTO WAS LIQUIDATED, A HANDFUL OF Jews managed to escape and hide in a pit on the property of Polish acquaintances. Among the group of people hiding in the pit were the young widow Esther and her six-year-old daughter Ann. The pit was dark, crowded, and lined with damp straw. Food, air, and light were scarce commodities and the abundance of fear and lice made life very difficult. For Esther the ordeal was unbearable. Her husband, parents, and all the other members of her own family had been shot in the ghetto before her eyes, immediately after the German occupation. She and her young child were the only survivors of a large family. The people in the pit knew of her vulnerable position and took advantage of it.

Esther's entire existence centered around her little girl. Saving the child, the sole remnant of her family, became the guiding force of her life. She tried to protect little Ann from the ugly realities of the world "up there," and from the roughness of some of the people in the pit. She gave most of her rationed food to the child and survived on mere crumbs and morsels.

One day, an abscess developed in one of Esther's teeth. She ignored the pain and discomfort, hoping that the abscess would disappear as suddenly as it appeared. But as the swelling increased, her fever rose and Esther could hardly see, hear, or move. The people around her were of no help. There was no medication, no doctor or dentist. Esther kept caressing her little girl, reassuring her with a loving touch. But the child understood her mother's critical condition and cried silently.

Suddenly, Esther distinctly heard her dead mother's voice. "Estherke, why do you and the rest of the people in the pit sit and do nothing? Do what I am telling you and you will recover." She gave Esther detailed instructions on how to treat her abscess. Esther instructed the people around her to act according to the instructions of her dead mother.

In a matter of a few days the swelling went down and Esther's life was saved. "You see, my child, Grandma would not allow anything bad to happen to Mama or to you. She will always come to care for us," she told Ann. Little Ann wanted to ask why Grandma did not save herself, Papa, and Grandpa from the German guns, but she knew that grownups were very annoyed each time she asked a question. So she kept quiet and huddled against her mother, the safest place in the pit and in the whole wide world.

*Based on interview by Florette Kardysz (daughter) with Ann Kardysz, November 22, 1977.*

# Number 145053

SAMUEL ROTHKOPF WAS BORN IN LUBRANIEC, POLAND, A TOWN with a huge flour-milling industry where his father was a successful grain dealer and a devout Sochaczewer Hasid. His mother, a pious woman, was busy raising her nine children, spending much of her time with her eighth child, Samuel, a sickly boy who suffered from an incurable coughing illness. The local doctors, unable to help the child, warned the parents of their son's grave condition and his probable death. But the parents did not despair and traveled with the child from doctor to doctor.

One day when little Samuel had a severe coughing attack, his father decided to take the child to the famed Sochaczewer Rebbe, Rabbi Samuel (1856-1926). Early the following morning, the Hasid himself polished the carriage and harnessed the horses as befitted such an important journey. Little Samuel, all bundled up, was brought out to the carriage by his mother while eight siblings stood around and watched in awe.

After a long, tiring ride, they arrived at the Sochaczewer Rebbe's house. The rebbe welcomed them with a big *"Shalom aleichem,"* a welcome befitting a devout Hasid and a relation of the famed Rabbi Israel Joshua Trunk (1820-1893).

While stroking his full beard, the Sochaczewer Rebbe looked at the child with gentle, reassuring eyes. He went to a huge bookcase, took a small package of herbs out of a drawer, put a teaspoon of the herbs into a glass, filled it with hot, steaming water from the samovar, mixed it well, and gave it to young Samuel to drink. "Drink, my child, and you will recover," the rabbi told him in a voice in which mingled strength and gentleness. It was a drink that tasted like very bitter tea, but the rebbe commanded Samuel to drink it nevertheless.

Reluctantly, little Samuel finished the bitter tea to the very last drop, while the rabbi watched in silence. "Your son will recover," he said to the father. "He will live and survive grave and difficult times." When they were about to depart and Samuel was already seated in the carriage, the rabbi stood framed in the doorway, and stroking his long, white flowing beard, once more repeated his blessing, "Your son will recover and survive dark and difficult times."

The year was 1920. A few days later the cough mysteriously stopped, and the pale six-year-old Samuel started to blossom into a healthy, vigorous child.

Years passed. Samuel, the delight of his parents, attended the yeshiva of Rabbi Kowalski (1862–1925), the Mizrachi leader and a member of the Polish Senate. Later, Samuel was drafted into the Polish Army and distinguished himself as a marksman. It was quite an achievement for a Jewish boy.

During World War II, Samuel was taken prisoner with other soldiers, but managed to jump from a moving train, and afterwards joined the Polish underground. During one of their attacks on a German unit, Samuel was captured and taken to Posen. There, in camp, he was reunited with one of his brothers and a nephew, only to watch them hang a few days later for smuggling a piece of bread inside.

On September 1, 1943, just a few days before Rosh Hashana, Samuel found himself on a train with a death convoy from Lodz to Auschwitz. More fortunate than others, he passed his first selection by the notorious Dr. Joseph Mengele,[1] who declared him a "healthy-looking Jew." Later that afternoon, when the tatoo was burned into his flesh, he glanced at his arm and instantly knew that he would survive. His number was 145053. The sum was eighteen, the numerical value of the letter *chai*, spelling the promised message of life, the fulfillment of the Sochaczewer Rabbi's blessing.[2]

*Based on interview by Baruch H. Hilsenrath with Samuel Rothkopf, May 1978.*

# Save This One Grandchild

GINA WAS ONLY ELEVEN YEARS OLD WHEN SHE WAS DEPORTED with her parents and grandparents to the labor camp of Pionki[1] near Radom, Poland. The only way to save Gina's life was to have her classified as an adult capable of a long day of work.

From early in the morning until late at night, Gina worked together with her mother. In the hot, humid summer months or blustery winter days, Gina dug trenches, mixed cement, or loaded ammunition crates. Not a single sign or word of complaint escaped her parched lips. Her little hands continued to slave for the German war effort as if this was the only thing they were ever meant to do. For she well understood that only the useful and the strong would be spared.

The supervisor of Gina's work detail was a German prisoner arrested because of his Communist ideas when Hitler came to power. He was a kind man who tried to alleviate the suffering of others. He especially took pity on little Gina. Whenever possible, he would assign her to an indoor job where she would be sheltered from the heat, rain, and snow and where he could share with her his sandwich.

With the help of this kind German foreman, Gina was able to survive an entire year in Pionki. In July 1944, Gina, her parents, and grandparents were deported to Auschwitz. After the initial selection on the infamous Auschwitz platform, Gina and her mother were placed in Camp B in Birkenau next to the gypsy camp.[2] Mother and daughter tried to conceal their tears when they looked at each other. Heads shaven, dressed in oversized, grotesque camp uniforms, they looked like strange creatures from another planet. Yet a moment later they were in each other's arms, grateful that they were still together. In Auschwitz, as in Pionki, they posed as sisters, for mothers and daughters staying alive together were not considered an acceptable phenomenon in the Nazi slave labor kingdom.

One day in camp they met a cousin who had been like a sister to Gina's mother before the war. Now she had risen to a prominent position in the camp and, as such, had more food and clothes. Gina's mother asked her cousin if she could give them a few crumbs of bread or whatever she could spare so that she might save the life of her daughter. The cousin looked with disgust at Gina and said, "If my daughter could die, let your daughter die too." After that, Gina's mother did not ask anyone else for help.

The winter of 1944–1945 was an especially harsh one. Gina came down with measles. She became very sick and was running a high fever. Her mother was desperate. She was afraid to put Gina in the infirmary block for she feared that she would never see her daughter again. Despite her mother's pleas, Gina stopped eating and drinking. Yet the mother did not give up hope, and saved Gina's and her own meager rations for the moment when Gina would recover and be able to eat again. Every morning and evening she carried the feverish girl outside into the freezing roll-call square and stood her up on the snow between herself and another inmate. The two women supported the girl, for Gina could not stand up alone. Gina's fever kept rising. The girl became delirious and was wasting away before her mother's eyes. One evening she even feared to carry her out to roll call. She left Gina on the top of a bunk bed, covering her in such a way that she resembled a pile of rags, so that she would not attract the attention of the vicious blokhova, who was rumored to be the daughter of a Polish rabbi. That evening, by a stroke of luck, they dispensed with the eternal roll call and Gina's absence was not noticed.

The mother knew that her daughter's life was hanging in the balance, but without medication, proper food, or even a warm drink, she was helpless to do anything for her dying child. She had only her own body with which to keep Gina warm. That night, Gina's mother dreamed that her father, dressed in the camp's striped uniform, came to her and said, "My child, I stood before the Almighty God and beseeched Him to save this one grandchild of mine, your daughter."

The following morning Gina woke up and asked her mother for a piece of bread.

On Jaunary 27, 1945, silhouettes with gun butts appeared on the gray snow of Auschwitz—Russian soldiers. Gina and her mother, with hundreds of other living, crawling skeletons, kissed the liberators' boots in gratitude.

For Gina's grandfather, liberation came too late. The chimneys were his road to heaven.

*Based on interview by Rebecca Zweibon with Gina Gotfryd, March 29, 1979.*

# A Pail of Potato Peels and Two Halberstams

"BEING A COOK IN A CONCENTRATION CAMP WAS LIKE BEING A KING of a country," recalls Mendel Halberstam. [Another man by the same name, a rabbi, perished in Auschwitz. He is mentioned in an earlier tale, "The Zanzer Kiddush Goblet."] But he missed his chance, and all because of a decision made in the Sosnowiec ghetto. One day his father called him aside and said, "My dear son Mendel, for fifteen generations in an unbroken chain from father to son, the Halberstam family gave Jewry in general, and Polish Jewry in particular, scholars, rabbis, and Hasidic zaddikim. But times have changed. The light of the Torah is not wanted anymore in this dark, debased world. Learn a trade, my son; become an electrician. For this spark is the only one understood by technology-oriented diabolical murderers. Sparks of metal and steel, fires of machine guns and bombs, sparks that grow into flames of destruction—these are the guiding lights of today's world. May the merit of your holy grandfathers protect you so that one day you might ignite once more the sparks of holiness."

And so Mendel Halberstam became an electrician, the first to learn a trade in fifteen generations of the Halberstam family. It was his trade as an electrician that saved his life in the ghetto of Sosnowiec and in six camps. But, he thought, if his father had advised him to become a cook, he would now be inside that warm kitchen and eating to his stomach's content. Instead, on that miserable cold and rainy day in Buchenwald, he was a hungry electrician outside of the magic kingdom—the concentration-camp kitchen.

How well he knew the schedule of that kitchen—when they sliced the bread, cooked the soup, peeled the potatoes, distributed the food, and sent out the two boys with the potato peels.

One day when Mendel could no longer stand the hunger pains, he had an idea. For days afterward he meticulously worked out his plan in detail, and when the time came, Mendel felt confident of his scheme.

At dusk, he hid behind a bush alongside the path where two lads carrying the potato peels would pass. When the kitchen door slammed, Mendel moved to the position of attack. His pulse quickened as he waited for the two boys with their precious cargo to turn down the path flanked by two bushes, where he was out of sight momentarily.

When zero hour approached, Mendel leaped out from behind his bush. Just at that very second, from the bush across the path, another figure in striped uniform also jumped for the potato peels, something Mendel had not allowed for in his elaborate plan. "We will split," the two voices simultaneously said in the dark. The other voice had a familiar ring. It was Mendel's cousin, another Halberstam!

The two cousins, scions of one of the most prominent Hasidic families, met in the concentration camp of Buchenwald, while raiding a pail of potato peels reserved for camp commandant's hogs!

Weeks later the cousins were separated once more. Mendel Halberstam was again saved because of his skills as an electrician and was transferred to Flossenberg. While listening to the constant rumbles of his hungry stomach, Mendel began to notice additional sounds, the rumbles of American artillery. They grew stronger and louder on April 23, 1945, and the liberating Third Army entered Flossenberg.[1]

Mendel was among the first to welcome the liberating American soldiers. The first American soldier that he met with he spoke to in Yiddish, while his tears gushed uncontrolled, his first tears in six years. "Do you know my grandfather, Rabbi Hayyim Halberstam, he lives in New York?"

"Sure," said Private William Wineless in Yiddish. "I am a member of his congregation. My family are very close friends of Rabbi Halberstam."

Weeks later, when the boat that brought Mendel Halberstam to America passed near the Statue of Liberty with her shining beacon, Mendel wondered about his father's blessing in the Sosnowiec ghetto. What would the future generations of the Halberstam family be like? What sparks would they kindle on American soil?

*Based on interview by Samuel Goodman with Mendel Halberstam, May 21, 1978.*

# A Brother's Tefillin (I)

SHE WAS IN HER TEENS. HER BROTHER WAS A FEW YEARS younger. Their entire family had been deported with thousands of other Rzeszow Jews to the Belzec death camp.[1] She, her brother, and a young cousin were the sole survivors of a very large family. In November 1942, when the many transports to the death camps reduced the Rzeszow ghetto population, the ghetto was transformed into a forced-labor camp and divided into two smaller, isolated parts: "A" for slave laborers and "B" for the members of their families. The three young people found themselves in camp A. When they arrived in the camp, her brother realized that in the great haste of deportation from the larger ghetto, he had left behind his tefillin, which he had received for his Bar Mitzvah at the outbreak of the war. He believed that if he prayed while wearing his tefillin, he, his beloved sister, and his cousin would survive the war, for the tefillin had belonged to his great-grandfather, a prominent Hasid, and been handed down from father to son.

Before his sister had a chance to stop him, he ran back to the large ghetto to retrieve his tefillin. Upon entering the ghetto he was caught by the Germans and sentenced to be executed for the crime of looting. When the sister heard of her brother's fate, she immediately ran to the Gestapo headquarters and pleaded with the commander to free her only surviving brother. The Gestapo commander looked at her in bewilderment and amusement and said, "You are a very pretty, brave young girl to come to the Gestapo headquarters and plead for your brother's life. For Jews, this place is the gateway to eternity. Give me one good reason why I should listen to you."

"For a very good reason," replied the sister without any hesitation. "My brother returned to the large ghetto to rescue a religious object with special protective powers. If you release my brother, nothing will ever happen to you on the battlefield and you will return in good health to Germany and will be reunited with your family at the end of the war."

There was a silence in the room that to the sister lasted an eternity. The Gestapo commander looked through the window as if searching for a distant place. Without turning his face to her, he commanded, "Let the young man join his sister."

*Based on interview by Debbie Kaiserer with Mrs. Glatt on April 25, 1976.*

# The Rain (II)

SECTIONS OF THE LABOR CAMP IN RZESZOW, POLAND, WERE LIQUI-
dated in November 1943. The sister, her brother, and their cousin,
all who were left of a large family, were deported to Auschwitz. With
the advance of the Red Army, they were evacuated from Auschwitz
in great haste.

During the bitter-cold European winter months of 1945, tens of
thousands of innocent human beings —starving, frozen, and scantily
dressed—were driven across Europe on foot and in open cattle cars to
various concentration and labor camps deeper into Germany. The
sister was separated from the boys and found herself in one camp
while the brother and cousin reached Gardelegen in Germany.

It was a sunny, bright spring day, April 14, 1945, in a camp near
the town of Gardelegen. Liberation was close. The Red Army was
racing from the east toward the Elbe river and armored divisions of
the American Army were advancing toward the river from the west.
The Nazis and their collaborators were running out of time and
searched for a quick way of killing the slave laborers. Under the direction of a Wehrmacht soldier, young German boys in S.S. uniforms rounded up 1,100 inmates of various nationalities, including
one American, herded them into a huge brick hay barn lined with
gasoline-soaked straw, and set it afire. Among the 1,100 human
beings in the burning inferno were the two young cousins.

The screams and prayers in the barn are difficult to describe. As
the smoke grew more intense and the leaping flames grew higher, the
screams subsided and were drowned by the sounds of coughing. But
the prayers did not stop. All the individual prayers, all the glimmers
of hope, united in one phrase—the cry of men, in a babel of languages: "Oh God, save us!" "Shema Yisrael!" "Hear O Israel, the
Lord our God, the Lord is One!" With each wave of engulfing
flames, the screams of the burning men became more distant and

faint. Suddenly the skies turned black. Thunder shook heaven and earth. The rains came down in streams like a flood.

The flames went out. A handful of young people made their way out of the barn and threw themselves on the flooded ground. The young cousins had won another round with death. On the barn floor were the charred bodies of 1,016 young men.

On the following day, American soldiers liberated Gardelegen. As their report stated: "The 2nd Battalion, 405th Infantry, discovered near Gardelegen an atrocity so awful that it might well have been committed in another era, or indeed on another planet."[1]

*Based on interview by Debbie Kaiserer with Mrs. Glatt on April 25, 1976.*

# A Passover Melody (III)

RAINS HAD EXTINGUISHED THE FLAMES OF THE BARN IN Gardelegen, Germany, where the 1,016 slave laborers perished. When the rains stopped, the survivors from the burning barn, other inmates and POW's, were loaded on trucks guarded by Germans and gendarmes, and driven to the woods to be shot. The woods were a few kilometers from camp. The air smelled fresh and clean. The young brother and his cousin were on one of the trucks.

"I am bored," said one of the guards. "Hey, you Jew boy, sing for me one of your church songs and hymns!" The cousin, a young Hasid, had a very beautiful voice.

It was April 15, 1945, only five days after the holiday of Passover. The young lad started to sing a song from the Passover Haggadah, *"Ve hi she amdah la-avoteinu."* The melody was a beautiful one. Soon the other slave laborers of various nationalities and the guards joined in the singing. The gentle spring wind carried the song to the other trucks in the death convoy and they, too, hummed the melody.

As they approached the forest, the German guard stopped the

singing. "Tell me the meaning of your song; translate it for me."
The Hasidic lad translated:

> And this it is which has succored our ancestors and us. For it was
> not one alone who rose against us to annihilate us, but in every
> generation there are those who rise against us to annihilate us. But
> the Holy One, blessed be He, ever saves us from their hand.

When the boy concluded the translation, the German burst into a
wild, mocking laughter. "Let's see how your God will save you from
my hands."

"I am still alive, but I am not afraid to die," replied the lad.

They reached a clearing in the forest. In groups of six, they were
taken to a ravine in the forest and shot. The two cousins were among
the last group. On the face of the German guard was an expression of
triumph as the young lads were led to their death.

Suddenly, a motorcycle arrived with two high-ranking German officials. They ordered all remaining prisoners to be taken back to
camp. Gardelegen had just surrendered to the American Army.

"Call it fate, call it a miracle, call it anything you want," said Mrs.
Glatt as she concluded the story about her brother and cousin. "But
one thing is clear. We, the Jewish people, with our abundance of
faith, will somehow manage to survive forever."

After a brief silence she added: "I am the great-granddaughter of
Rabbi Raphael Zimtboim, the personal secretary (gabbai) of the
Zanzer Rabbi, Rabbi Hayyim Halberstam (1793–1876). The rabbi
was lame, and many times my great-grandfather, Reb Raphael,
carried him around. Maybe it was his merit, my brother's innocent
faith, and the merit of his tefillin that protected all of us. The tefillin
belonged to Reb Raphael."

"And your brother, where is he now?"

"Shortly after liberation, he died. His lungs were very damaged by
the Gardelegen fires. But he died a free man!"

*Based on interview by Debbie Kaiserer with Mrs. Glatt on April 25,
1976.*

# A Natural Victory:
# Churchill and the
# Rabbi of Gur

AFTER THE SPECTACULAR RESCUE OF THE RABBI OF GUR,[1] RABBI
Abraham Mordechai Alter (1866–1948), from the Warsaw ghetto,
the following story circulated.

The British wartime prime minister, Winston Churchill, invited
the Hasidic Rabbi of Gur to come to see him and advise him how to
bring about Germany's downfall. The rabbi gave the following reply:
"There are two possible ways, one involving natural means, the
other supernatural. The natural means would be if a million angels
with flaming swords were to descend on Germany and destroy it. The
supernatural would be if a million Englishmen parachuted down on
Germany and destroyed it."

Since Churchill was a rationalist, he chose the strategy based on
natural means, angels with flaming swords. . . .[2]

*I heard it on May 31, 1976.*

# The Rebbetzin of Gur:
# Two Passports

IN THE SUMMER OF 1943, SOME OF POLAND'S MOST PROMINENT
Jews arrived in Bergen Belsen's foreign nationals sector. Most of
them were scions of ultra-Orthodox and Hasidic families. One such
transport originated in the ghetto of Bochnia. They had traveled a
tortuous route that included Cracow, a stopover at the Montelupich
prison and Berlin, before finally arriving in Bergen Belsen on July
11, 1943. A second transport arrived in August 1943. They came di-

rectly from the infamous Pawiak prison in Warsaw where they had been tortured and humiliated. Among this artistocratic group of Warsaw Jewry were a famous rebbetzin and her son, the wife and son of Rabbi Israel Alter.[1]

The news of the arrival of the rebbetzin and her son spread quickly through Bergen Belsen. Their arrival raised new hopes that the day of deliverance was indeed just around the corner. Even in Bergen Belsen it was known that the saintly Rabbi of Gur, Rabbi Abraham Mordechai Alter, and his son, Rabbi Israel, had been miraculously saved from the European hell and were residing in the Holy Land. People in the camp were convinced that the Grand Rabbi of Gur, with the help of Almighty God and the British Empire, would surely save his daughter-in-law and grandson from the Nazi beast.

In addition, people in Bergen Belsen were convinced that because of the merit of this great family, all the people in the sectors for foreign nationals and, ultimately, perhaps even the entire camp would be saved. These hopes were fanned higher when the camp commandant, Rudolf Haas, made his famous speech to the holders of foreign passports, visas, and citizenships.[2] He informed them that the exchange of foreign nationals incarcerated in Bergen Belsen for Germans stranded in Allied territory would finally take place. However, Haas warned his eager listeners, the German administration had concluded that all the obstacles and snags to date had been due to Allied reluctance to accept the inmates of Bergen Belsen. Despite this pessimistic note, hopes were high. News began to circulate in the camp that the long-awaited exchange would take place in the very near future, and possible locations for the pending exchange were even being mentioned.

On Hoshana Rabbah, the seventh day of Sukkot, October 21, 1943, it was announced that all those holding South American and Palestinian passports, visas, papers, and citizenship should report to the camp square with all their belongings. Joy overwhelmed the people in the barracks. They hastily packed all their meager belongings and rushed to the square so as not to delay, even by one minute, the hour of freedom. Close to 3,000 people of all ages assembled in the square, awaiting further instructions—but there were none. It was getting cold and dark. Tired, hungry children began to beg for food. Among the frightened adults, rumors circulated that, as Haas had warned might happen, the British had refused to accept the Bergen Belsen inmates and the Germans were now making desperate, last-minute attempts to convince them that the exchange was vital to their interests and should take place.

The chilly October night brought no news, just a biting, early frost. Children cried, mothers fed them their last morsels of food, while some men prayed, for it was the beginning of the holiday of Shemini Atzeret. Slowly children fell asleep. As their cries grew faint, 3,000 souls tried to sleep while awaiting the unknown under the cold stars of the Bergen Belsen sky.

Morning came. A loaf of bread was distributed to each person, food for the long-awaited journey. Again spirits soared; the food was the most reassuring sign that the miracle of freedom was only a few hundred kilometers away. At noon, S.S. officers appeared. The checking of papers began. Two lists were compiled, one consisting of holders of South American papers, the other, holders of Palestinian papers. Accordingly, the people were divided into two groups. The South American group far outnumbered the Palestinian one, which contained only about three dozen people.

The Rebbetzin of Gur faced a dilemma. She had two sets of papers, South American and Palestinian, but on that fateful day in Bergen Belsen only one set could be used. She asked for advice, but even friends were reluctant to express their opinion. Her choice could be between citizenship in the land of the living or in the habitations of death. The rebbetzin was desperate. "The group of South American citizens is getting bigger by the minute; surely they can't kill such a large group of people, holders of foreign passports," someone remarked. The rebbetzin was despondent. Her turn was getting nearer, the decision could not be postponed any longer. She looked at the handful of people in the Palestinian group, at the huge crowd with South American papers, at her young son Leibl. Frantically, she tore up her Palestinian visa and swallowed the tiny white flakes of paper. Her turn came. With trembling hands she presented two South American passports, her son's and her own.

In the afternoon, more than twenty-four hours after the initial assemblage in the square, all names were once more checked against the two freshly compiled lists. Close to 3,000 people were in the South American group and only thirty-six people were holders of papers from Eretz Yisrael.

As the evening approached, it was becoming clear that the holders of South American passports would leave Bergen Belsen and the Palestinian group would stay behind. Among the people in the South American group was a Christian Pole. When the woman he loved, a beautiful, tall, slender Jewish girl named Estherke, was taken to the camp, he decided that freedom without her was meaningless. He had joined her and had been deported with her. Now they were standing, holding hands, hoping that somewhere outside the barbed wires, freedom and a common future awaited the two of them. Wolf Fischelberg, from the Palestinian group, walked over to the Pole, with whom he was friendly, and asked him to mail him a postcard when he reached freedom.

The Pole put his arm around Fischelberg's shoulders and said, "My friend, I will send you a postcard in any event, even if we never cross the borders of occupied Europe. You may believe the Germans, or have faith in the protective merits of the rabbi's wife and her son. I don't have faith in either. I have seen too much. I come from a town where the Jews also had a great rabbin. On Jewish holidays the town was black with Hasidim. His merit did not save the town from its terrible end. Most of the Jews were buried in one huge pit at the edge of the old Jewish cemetery. The few who survived that fateful day are now dying in concentration camps. If the train that we board takes us back to Poland instead of to Switzerland or Turkey, Estherke and I are going to jump off the train. In this little bundle of clothing I have concealed some carpenter's tools. These tools will be our passport to safety. I will break through a door, a wall, whatever it takes. Estherke and I will run! My friend, no matter what, you will receive a postcard from us."

The friends embraced each other once more and parted in the dark. Others among the Palestinian group also made arrangements with the departing South American group. It was agreed that when they reached the train that was to take them to their destination, they would signal those left behind in the camp. If the train was a passenger train and not cattle cars, they would wave white handkerchiefs to show that all was well. If it was a cattle train, God forbid, there would be no need for signals. . . .

Orlian, a Hasidic Jew, suddenly shouted at the top of his voice: "Jews, do you realize Simhat Torah has just begun? On our most joyful holiday of the year, it is time to sing, dance, and rejoice in the holy Torah!" Circles of men formed around Leibl, the young grandson of the Gerer Rebbe, around Orlian and other prominent Jews. People began to sing and dance, and the words of the famous Simhat Torah chant echoed from the huge Bergen Belsen square:

> O Lord, save, we beseech thee,
> O Strong Redeemer, answer us
> On the day that we call.

"*Achtung! Achtung! Achtung!* All people holding South American papers form a column, five abreast, facing the main gate!" a voice announced in German over the loudspeakers.

The circles slowly dissolved into a huge column while faint echoes of singing still clung to the disappearing shadows of the column—"O Lord, save, we beseech thee . . . answer us on the day that we call."

In the chilly, dark night of Bergen Belsen, white handkerchiefs began to flutter in the dark, like wings of doves, like memorial candles, like departing souls returning to their makers. Night swallowed the column. A deadly silence descended upon Bergen Belsen. The thirty-six holders of Palestinian papers returned to the empty barracks. Among them were Wolf Fischelberg, his wife, son, and tiny daughter Miriam, Bronia Koczicki, her two small sons, her twin nieces, and a handful of other Jews.[8]

A few weeks later, Wolf Fischelberg received a postcard from his

Polish friend. It carried the postmark of a small Polish town in Silesia. The coded message read:

The train with all its passengers arrived at its final destination in Auschwitz. May heaven bless their souls.

Except for the Polish Christian and his beautiful Estherke, no one from the South American group was ever heard of again, including the Rebbetzin of Gur and her beloved young son.[3]

*Based on a conversation of Rebbetzin Bronia Spira with Dina Spira, May 2, 1976, my own several conversations with the rebbetzin, June 1976–June 1981, and an interview by Dina with Wolf Fischelberg, December 20, 1976.*

# The Shofar of the Rabbi of Radorzytz

MOSHE WAS BORN IN PIETROKOV IN 1914. HE WAS A STUDENT AT A Pietrokov yeshiva and later at the Yeshiva of Keter Torah at Czestochowa. Back home, Moshele, as he was called, had become very close to the Grand Rabbi of Radorzytz, Rabbi Yitzhak Finkler.[1] Moshele especially loved to spend the High Holidays with the rabbi. His pleasant, melodious voice and his great devotion and concentration during prayer made a deep impression upon Moshe and were a constant source of inspiration to him.

When the Germans occupied Pietrokov, after much humiliation and suffering, Moshe found himself in the Skarzysko Kamienna camp at barracks 14 together with his beloved rabbi, Yitzhak Finkler of Radorzytz. It was 1943, and even by the standards of the concentration-camp universe, Skarzysko was hell on earth. The barracks of Grand Rabbi Finkler became a center for prayer and study, as much as the camp's horrendous conditions permitted. The rabbi's behavior and faith were a source of strength and comfort. As the High Holidays of 1943 (the Jewish year 5704) were approaching, the Rabbi of Radorzytz bought a ram's horn from a Gentile for a very high price. Now it had to be shaped into a shofar. With tears in his eyes the Rabbi of Radorzytz walked over to Moshe and said, "Moshele, I've known you since you were a child and I knew your father very well. I am entrusting you with this great mitzvah of making a shofar. The holy merit of making this shofar will protect you, and you will survive this war."

Moshe was greatly moved by his beloved rabbi's devotion to the observance of God's commandments even in the valley of death, and by the rabbi's blessing, but he was also very frightened. As it happened, on the previous day a young Jewish man had been shot on the spot for having in his possession an unauthorized piece of leather. In Moshe's case the danger was even greater. First he had to smuggle the ram's horn into the workshop, and work on it instead of going to his regular job. Then he had to smuggle the shofar back to camp. For each of these violations the penalty was death. But how can a Hasid refuse his rabbi?

Moshe undertook the task. Needless to say, he had never in his life made a shofar.

Moshe successfully smuggled the ram's horn into the workshop. He soon realized that without help, the task of making the shofar would end in failure. Help came from a most unexpected source. The supervisor of the carpentry shop was a devout Polish Catholic, and understood the importance of the shofar for the Grand Rabbi of Radorzytz. He gave Moshe permission to work on it and was helpful in getting all the necessary tools. Moshe finished the shofar on time. One hour before the holiday of Rosh Hashana began, the shofar was in the rabbi's hands.

The following morning at dawn, before they left for work, the mitzvah of blowing the shofar was observed in barracks 14 at

Skarzysko. The rabbi's joy knew no limit. "You see, Jews are willing to endanger their lives to worship their God as commanded," he said, pointing to Moshele and to all those present.

But the tale does not end on Rosh Hashana, 5704. Rabbi Yitzhak Finkler was murdered by the Nazis, as were the other members of his dynasty. Moshe was transferred to Hasag at Czestochowa and was able to take the shofar along. At Hasag he was taken while at work and deported to Buchenwald. The shofar was left behind.

Moshe survived the war, as he was promised by his beloved rebbe. When the war was over, he made his way to Israel and settled there. However, with each passing day Moshe felt that his return to his homeland was incomplete. He felt an obligation to locate the shofar and bring it to Israel, so that at least one thing that had been dear to Rabbi Yitzhak Finkler's heart should be in Israel, as a memorial to him. The search for the shofar began. Moshe tracked down survivors who had remained in Czestochowa after his deportation from the camp. The search led to Europe, Israel, South America, and North America, but to no avail. No one knew the shofar's whereabouts.

Then, from an unexpected source, the link between the shofar and Moshe was established. Author Vladka Meed, a former Warsaw ghetto fighter and now a resident of New York, learned that the shofar was in New York. After liberation someone had taken the shofar, brought it to Czestochowa, and given it to the representatives of the newly reestablished Jewish community. In 1945, the Yiddish author Jacob Fet visited Czestochowa and was given the shofar as a gift. He took it with him back to the United States. Vladka Meed located the shofar in the possession of Jacob Fet's widow, and brought it to Israel. According to Moshe's wish, it was presented to Yad Vashem as a lasting tribute to the memory of Moshe's beloved Rabbi of Radorzytz.[2]

*I heard it from Vladka Meed, May 1979.*

# The Keepers
# of the Holy Temple

IN APRIL 1944 THE GERMANS ENTERED SATMAR, ESTABLISHED A ghetto, and began the deportation of the Jews to Auschwitz. One of the most wanted Jews was the Satmar Rabbi, Joel Teitelbaum (1887–1979). His followers and friends were well aware of the grave danger to the grand rabbi's life. A bunker was built for the rabbi with an entrance through a garden adjacent to his home.

One day the Germans stormed into the rabbi's house. There, sitting on a chair surrounded by books, was a man with a full, white, flowing beard. The S.S. man aimed his revolver and at point-blank range shot at the sitting man. He missed. The bullet zoomed by, a millimeter away from the man's head, and embedded itself in a book behind him. "Your name!" demanded the S.S. man, still pointing his pistol. "Ashkenazi," responded the old man.[1]

"Where is the Rabbiner Teitelbaum?" inquired the S.S. officer.

"He left this house some time ago," responded Rabbi Ashkenazi.

After the officer left, the pale, shaking Rabbi Ashkenazi took out the Bible that was hit by the bullet. The bullet had stuck at the verse: "So they and their children had the oversight of the gates of the house of the Lord. . . ."[2] For Rabbi Ashkenazi and the rest of the rabbi's close Hasidim, the message was clear. No harm would come to those who took care of the Satmar Rabbi and watched over him, for he was the holy Temple and they were the priests who served him.

The holy book that saved Rabbi Feifush Ashkenazi's life was also miraculously saved, and made its way to the Rabbi of Satmar's study in Brooklyn. Frequently the rabbi would take out the book and look at it with tears in his eyes.

*I heard it from a Hasid of Satmar, June 26, 1979. This story appears in a*

*slightly different version in* Shlomo Rozman, Sefer Rashei Golat Ariel
*(Brooklyn, N.Y., 1975), vol. I, pp. 46–47.*

# The Kasztner Transport
# and a Zionist Leader's
# Dream

WHEN THE LIST FOR THE FAMED KASZTNER TRANSPORT OF HUN-
garian Jews was drawn up in the spring of 1944, the name of Rabbi
Joel Teitelbaum, the Rabbi of Satmar, was not among the prominent
Jews chosen to be rescued.[1] But the rabbi did not despair. He hoped
that the Almighty would come to his aid just as he had done in the
past. Indeed, salvation was soon to come, and from a most unexpected source, the Zionist camp itself, the very group to which the
Rabbi of Satmar was vehemently opposed and which he blamed for
the many ills that had befallen Judaism, including the Holocaust. It
happened that Dr. Jozsef Fischer, who was Kasztner's father-in-law,
had a dream. In his dream, his mother of sainted memory told him
that if the Rabbi of Satmar were not included in the special transport,
the entire test convoy would be doomed.

Dr. Fischer then demanded the inclusion of Rabbi Teitelbaum on
the list, but he was opposed by the Zionist leader majority in the
Klausenburg ghetto. Only after he revealed to them his dream and
his mother's warning did they yield to his pressure. The Rabbi of
Satmar and his wife, as well as Rabbi Joseph Ashkenazi and other
close members of the rabbi's entourage, were added to the list which
carried with it the promise of life.[2]

Eventually, when 388 of the 18,000 Jews in the ghetto of
Klausenburg arrived in Budapest via a special train on Saturday,
June 10, 1944, the Rabbi of Satmar was among them. When they dis-
embarked to make their way to the ghetto, the rabbi and other orthodox Jews left their belongings on the train so as not to carry anything

on the Sabbath, even though they were sure that their belongings would all be looted. But to their amazement, some time later a Gentile came to their new headquarters at the Wechselmann Institute for the Deaf on Columbus Street and gave the Rabbi of Satmar his prayer shawl and tefillin. All saw in this incident a good omen for their eventual journey to freedom.

With the initial leg of the journey completed, the controversy over the list of those who would in the end travel on the test convoy train continued in Budapest. The original list was constantly being altered. As a result, many of the Jews who were finally selected did not meet any of the criteria originally agreed upon with Adolf Eichmann, the S.S. officer in charge of Jewish emigration, and Wisliceny. Many wealthy Jews fought bitterly over a few seats that had been put up for sale by the Vaada,[3] the rescue committee, in order to finance the transport and bribe the ever-greedy German officials.

At last the test convoy, or Noah's ark, as Kasztner referred to it in his report, numbered 1,684 Jews.[4] When they left Hungary the train carried aboard it the Orthodox Jews on the Philip V. Freudiger list; Neolog Jews on the Samuel Stern list; Polish, Slovak, and Yugoslav refugees; Palestine certificate leaders; young Zionist leaders; a handful of orphans from Poland; prominent Jews and paying Jews; and the Klausenburg group, which included many family members of Rudolf Kasztner, the principal organizer, and the Rabbi of Satmar and his close associates.[5]

When the transport was finally ready for departure, the Vaada suggested that it go to Palestine via Rumania and Turkey. Adolf Eichmann objected, claiming Germany's obligation to its allies among the Arabs. Late on the night of June 30, 1944, the train finally pulled out of the Budapest station and left for the Austro-Hungarian border. The passengers were told that the train would stop at Strasshof, near Vienna, and continue to Lisbon, Portugal. But it did not stop at Strasshof. Instead, the train was to switch tracks at the Auspitz junction. Passengers on the train overheard the guards' conversation and mistook "Auspitz" for "Auschwitz." Panic broke out; their worst fears seemed to have materialized. Two passengers jumped from the train. One made his way back to Budapest to Rudolf Kasztner. Kasztner immediately called upon Eichmann, who reassured him that all was well with the transport.

After making several stops, the train passed through the Auspitz junction and reached Linz, Austria. The passengers were told to go into the showers for disinfection. Once more fears were intensified that this was indeed the last leg of their journey. But the fears proved false; hot water came pouring down from the showers!

The train, however, never reached Lisbon. On July 8, 1944, the test convoy arrived at the Bergen Belsen concentration camp.

The Rabbi of Satmar and other passengers of the rescue convoy suffered much in Bergen Belsen, even in the "privileged" sector. In December 1944, six months after their arrival at the camp, the group was suddenly informed that they would be allowed to proceed to Switzerland. Their release was due to Kasztner's efforts. He had worked relentlessly arranging a deal with Heinrich Himmler whereby 20 million Swiss francs would be paid by the Jews and ear- marked for the purchase of Swiss products for the Germans. Five million francs were to be paid in advance and the balance of 15 mil- lion would be paid later. Two German officials named Krell and Kettlitz were already waiting for the transport at the Swiss border.[6]

Not all of the passengers who were on the first leg of the rescue convoy's journey were permitted to board the Kasztner transport. Eihcmann himself reviewed the list. Out of anger at Joel Brand of the Vaada, and what he considered Brand's defection, Eichmann kept Brand's mother and three sisters at Bergen Belsen.[7] Other people who had left Budapest as part of the original convoy were also de- tained in Bergen Belsen for having broken some rule of camp disci- pline. Among them were parents who had learned that their children were inmates in different sectors of Bergen Belsen and had contacted them despite regulations forbidding them to do so. For that "crime" they were to pay with their lives.[8]

As the train approached the Swiss border, a cable arrived from Himmler demanding the complete payment of 20 million Swiss francs on account for further deliveries of Jews, and above all for keeping alive the Jews still in Budapest and in the camps. Although Himmler ordered that the dispatch of the convoy into Switzerland would depend on the payment of the francs, his orders were not obeyed. On December 8, 1944, Kasztner cabled Andre Biss in Budapest that the train had crossed the border.

According to Satmar tradition, Himmler's instructions arrived in Switzerland just as the train was to cross the Swiss border. A Swiss station master, a Gentile, one of the Righteous among the Nations, admitted the train and marked the cable "received" one minute after the train had already crossed the border.[9]

At nine o'clock, a train was waiting at the Swiss station of Lustan to meet up with the special convoy. One hour after midnight, the train crossed the bridge on the river Rhine and arrived at St. Gallen. In their first moments of freedom, the passengers were met by the cold, biting winds at the St. Gallen train station. Rabbi Joseph Ashkenazi tried to shield the Satmar Rabbi with his own body. Their eyes filled with tears of gratitude, the passengers of the Kasztner transport were escorted to a nearby public school. Despite the late hour, crowds of people, many of them Hasidic Jews, lined the streets to welcome the long-awaited test convoy.

Suddenly a Hasidic Jew broke away from the crowd, ran through the lines, and stopped in front of the Rabbi of Satmar. From a white handkerchief, he unwrapped his precious gift for the rabbi, a big, beautiful, shining apple—a welcoming gesture to freedom.

That day, the twenty-first day of the month of Kislev, December 7, 1944, was established by the Rabbi of Satmar and his Hasidim as a day of thanksgiving. Every year, it is celebrated with great joy. Until the last year of his life, the rabbi told of the many miracles that happened to him on that journey and how God delivered him from the hands of the Nazi beast.[10]

*Based on my interviews with Satmar Hasidim and passengers on the Kasztner transport, and an interview by Eydie Schwartz with Rabbi Jacob Jungreis, December 1, 1977.*

# A Holy Book

THE BERKOWITZ FAMILY WERE CONSIDERED AMONG THE MOST fortunate of Hungarian Jews, for they were included among the 6,841 Jews deported from Debrecen to Strasshof, Austria, in 1944.[1] Their deportation to Strasshof was due to a stroke of good luck. During the negotiations of the "blood for trucks" deal between Adolf Eichmann and Rudolf Kasztner, a new element was introduced. Thirty thousand Hungarian Jews were to be "put on ice" in Austria instead of being shipped directly to the Auschwitz gas chambers.[2] This was to demonstrate Eichmann's goodwill and sincerity in the negotiations. One of the immediate conditions was the payment of 5 million Swiss francs by Kasztner to Eichmann. The Austrians, including Mayor Blascke of Vienna, were also pleased with the arrangement, for it provided them with a desperately needed fresh source of slave labor.

In Strasshof, families were permitted to stay together. The Berkowitz family arrived there at the end of June 1944. They did not mind the harsh camp realities, the disease and starvation, as long as the members of the family were permitted to stay together. Grandfather Berkowitz, an ardent Hasid, was even able to take along a holy book that had belonged to his family for generations. He was sure that the merit of the holy book would protect and save his family from all evil.

During the entire week, the adult members of the Berkowitz family saved part of their meager food rations for the holy Sabbath. In the cold, long evenings of fall and winter they huddled together, sitting in the dark and listening to Grandfather's Hasidic tales, many of them about the family's holy book. Grandmother did not permit them to use their few, tiny rationed candles. She saved them for Friday night. She would melt the bits of paraffin and make pencil-thin candles so that she, her daughters, and daughters-in-law could kindle the Sabbath candles and welcome the Sabbath with the number of candles they were accustomed to light in the pre-Hitler days.

As the Russian front approached, the camp officials at Strasshof became restless. Food and candle rationing stopped while they waited for orders from Berlin about what to do with their Jews. The orders came quickly: they were to load all the Jews on freight cars and ship them to an extermination camp. Amid constant Allied bombardments, the Jews were loaded on the trains. To Grandfather Berkowitz the destination was clear, but he did not despair. While the women were holding on to the children, the food, and their few belongings, Grandfather was clutching his most precious possession, the holy book.

On the train in the sealed freight car, Grandfather Berkowitz found a corner for his family. He sat in the middle surrounded by his family so that they would all be able to hold on to the holy book during the journey, for he was convinced that its merit would protect them all. Mr. Berkowitz was very worried; he noticed that wagons with munitions were attached to their train. With the constant air attacks by Allied and Russian air forces, he fully understood the perils of the journey. Yet he kept reassuring his family that all would be well and with God's help the holy book would protect them.

The train never left the station. Allied bombers appeared in the sky and bombarded the train just as it was about to pull out. The explosions were powerful. Shrapnel and bullets flew in all directions. Those who survived the bombs were killed by the exploding ammunition. Through the entire air raid, Grandfather Berkowitz was in full control of his family. They all lay on the floor attempting to touch the holy book. "Keep your heads down and your hand on the book," Grandfather commanded between explosions.

Hours later, when all was quiet in the charred train station, Grandfather Berkowitz permitted his family to get up from the floor of the bombed train. Miraculously, the entire Berkowitz family survived the bombing raid, and with them, the family's precious possession, the holy book. In the spring of 1945, when Strasshof was liberated by the Russians, "The return of whole families seemed like a miracle."[3]

*Based on interview by Layah Tomor with Vera Landau, née Berkowitz, November 27, 1977.*

# The Yellow Bird

LIVIA ADORED HER FATHER. SINCE THE DAY HE WAS TAKEN AWAY to the Hungarian labor battalions, Livia had hoped that each new day would bring her father back home. But the days kept passing and Livia's father did not return.[1]

One night Livia dreamed that she was standing with her father in the small, dark storage room in back of their store. The door was ajar. Through the partially open door, beams of light were streaming into the dark room. Livia's father was wearing his gray overall coat, which he always wore while in the store. His face was very pale. A bird flew in as if it were gliding on a ray of light. It was a yellow bird, the most brilliant shades of yellow. The bird seemed flattened in the stream of light. Its dazzling yellow colors were set aflame by the sunbeam, and Livia was overcome by the bird's strange, hypnotic beauty. But not her father, who grabbed her arm in terror and repeatedly said, "Look at it, look at it, look at that bird!" She looked at the bird again, and only then did she realize that the splendid yellow bird was indeed terrifying, a peculiar firebird whose glow set everything ablaze.

All that time her father held on to her and repeated the same sentence: "Look at it, look at it, look at that bird!" His face was even paler than before and his terror-stricken eyes followed the bird in its strange, acrobatic, silent flight.

Livia woke up covered in a cold sweat, trembling with fear, and with a strange premonition that her father would not return home and she would never see him again.[2]

A few months later, Livia, her mother, brother, and aunt, with the rest of the Jews of Nagymagyar, were deported to Auschwitz.

*Based on interview by Emily Bitton (daughter) with Livia Bitton Jackson, May 1979.*

# A Bowl of Soup

ON A BEAUTIFUL SPRING DAY IN 1944, LIVIA AND HER MOTHER, brother, and aunt were deported from their ancestral home in Czechoslovakia. At the age of thirteen, Livia found herself on the threshold of death—the Auschwitz platform.[1]

Dr. Joseph Mengele himself was conducting that selection. The tall, slender, graceful girl was holding on to her mother. While the line of women was nearing Mengele, Livia's mother was braiding her daughter's long blond hair which had become tangled during the horrible three-day train ride from Czechoslovakia to Auschwitz.

With her deep-blue, smiling eyes and child's curiosity, Livia tried to comprehend what was happening around her. Livia's main concern was her aunt, a sickly woman who was clinging to her mother. Somehow Livia sensed that this strange place would not tolerate the sick, the old, or the very young.

The three women stood before Dr. Mengele. Just as Livia feared, the aunt was sent to the left, with the other group of older, sickly-looking women and young mothers with small children. Livia's mother instinctively took a step in her sister's direction. Mengele motioned her to stop. "What beautiful long golden hair you have, my child," Mengele said as he picked up one of Livia's heavy braids with white-gloved hands. He looked into her deep-blue eyes and asked in an almost fatherly voice, "Are you Jewish?" "Yes, I am." "Are you sure that you are Jewish?" "Yes, I am," replied Livia in her melodious voice and perfect German. "How old are you, my child?" "Thirteen." "From now on you will say that you are six-

teen." He looked at Livia's mother. "Is this your mother?" Livia
nodded her head in the affirmative. "A mother should always be
with her daughter," Mengele said and motioned both mother and
daughter to the right. He looked handsome and even kind as his eyes
followed the mother and daughter joining the column of young
women on the right side.[2]

In camp, mother and daughter lived for each other. They did not
part for a second; they shared their food and their clothes. They constantly kept encouraging one another that one day it would all be over
and they would be free again and reunited with their loved ones,
Livia's father and brother.

After a few weeks in Auschwitz, they were shipped to the Nazi
forced-labor camp of Plaszow on the outskirts of Cracow. But even in
Plaszow, neither the cruelty of the camp commander, Amon Goeth,
nor the subhuman conditions in the factories could dampen the spirits of the mother and her daughter, or diminish their devotion to each
other.[3] Together they withstood hunger, disease, and the harsh
winds of the Polish fall.

One morning, at the beginning of a bitter cold day, Livia, her
mother, and thousands of other Plaszow inmates were driven to the
train station and loaded in packed cattle cars. After an excruciating
journey, Livia and her mother found themselves once more on the
Auschwitz platform.[4]

One night one of the three-tiered, flimsily constructed bunk beds
in an Auschwitz barracks gave way under its human cargo and twelve
girls came crushing down on Livia's mother and the other women
who slept on the lowest tier. Livia's mother suffered severe back and
neck injuries and became partially paralyzed. Livia's despair was beyond words, yet she decided that she would not succumb and would
nurse her mother back to health. After four weeks in the camp infirmary and with the constant attention of Livia, who somehow managed to be with her constantly, Livia's mother regained her ability to
walk. That day, Livia arranged for her mother to be discharged from
the infirmary, for she had heard rumors of an impending selection.
Despite the fact that the mother's paralysis was gone and only three

fingers on her left hand remained numb, her back and neck pains persisted in their full intensity. She was unable to bend down, to dress herself, or to stand upright, unsupported. Livia did not leave her mother's side. She supported her at Zeilappell (call-up), helped her to dress, and did for her whatever was humanly possible.

Then came another fateful selection. Able-bodied women were selected for slave labor in Germany and the sick and elderly doomed to remain eternally at Auschwitz. As they neared the selection point, Livia's fears that her mother would not pass this selection were too much to bear. Then the selection baton in front of Livia's eyes moved. Her mother was sent to the right, to slave labor; she to the left, to the gas chambers. Livia's mind went blank. All she could see was the growing distance between herself and her mother. Her eyes never lost sight of her mother as she staggered to catch up with the others. *"Schnell, schnell!"* Livia heard the S.S. woman shouting as she beat her leather truncheon on her mother's back.[5] Madness overtook Livia. She broke away from her column and in a frenzy ran to her mother's rescue. She attacked the S.S. woman. The blows were now directed at Livia's body and head. But somehow the S.S. woman stopped and did not club Livia to death. Instead, she shoved her with her mother to the waiting trucks. From there they were transported to the train station where open cattle cars awaited them. In each other's arms, comforting and shielding each other from the biting frost, they arrived in a labor camp in Germany. Conditions in this camp were far better than in Auschwitz. They each received a blanket and Livia's mother could even sit down while slaving in the munitions factory.

One day in the midst of a blizzard a multinational girls' work detachment was ordered to clear the snow. The girls pleaded with the overseer, explaining that shoveling the snow in those conditions was useless since they would die in the blizzard. "This is what you are here for," snapped back the German overseer. But the girls refused to shovel the snow and disobeyed orders. They were punished. For twenty-four hours they worked in the factory without food or even water. Livia was among them. When she returned to her barracks, her mother was waiting for her with a bowl of soup that she had saved for her, her own soup portion. She had held it under the blanket to keep it warm. Knowing how sickly her mother was, Livia refused to eat the soup.

"I kept it especially for you."

"Mother, I will not touch it. It is your soup and you need it more than I do."

"My child, I would rather spill it on the floor than let it touch my lips after you have fasted for twenty-four hours."

"I will not touch it," Livia insisted.

The mother spilled the soup. Mother looked at daughter, daughter at mother, while between them lay the empty, miserable camp soup bowl. They fell into each other's arms and started to cry. They cried the entire night. Despite the many hardships they endured together, the grief that overcame them that night was the most painful of their concentration-camp experiences.

A few days later, Livia, her mother, and other camp inmates were hastily put on an evacuation train, since the American armies were nearing the camp. The train began its journey toward death. Without food or water it made its hopeless rounds from station to station, trying to avoid Allied bombing and strafing. At one station they found a bombed train filled with male inmates from other camps. Many were dead, others wounded, and some were still alive. A pair of familiar blue eyes was staring at Livia from one of the cars. She and her mother walked over. They pulled out the body that belonged to the eyes. It was Livia's only brother, Armin, from whom they had parted on the Auschwitz platform. He was wounded in the head by American strafing. They dragged him to their train, tore off a piece of dress, bandaged his head, and covered it with a kerchief so that he might pass for a female inmate.

Some hours later they were liberated by the American Army near the town of Dachau. The American commander forced the local townspeople to come and see what the glorious Third Reich had done to humanity. An elderly woman, meticulously dressed in a black dress, wearing a broad-brimmed black hat with a feather and white,

short crocheted gloves, and clutching a black pocketbook, stared at
Livia with great compassion. Finally she said to her, "It must have
been very difficult for people your age to endure all this suffering."

"How old do you think I am?" Livia asked her.

"Maybe sixty, maybe sixty-two," replied the German woman.

"Fourteen," replied Livia.

The German woman crossed herself in horror and fled.[6]

In a convalesence home set up by the American Army, Livia's
mother learned that her back and neck had suffered multiple frac-
tures. Armin was recovering from his head wound. Livia saw herself
in a mirror for the first time in a year. The face that stared back at her
from the mirror bore no resemblance to the girl with long, golden
braids and smiling blue eyes. It was only one year since she was ban-
ished forever from her home and childhood.

One day they met a man who had been with their father and husband in the Hungarian labor battalion, concentration camps, and
later on the death march to Bergen Belsen. He told them everything,
including the fact that Livia's father was shot near the gates of
Bergen Belsen when his feet refused to carry him any longer. "Do
you remember the exact date of his death?" "Yes," replied the man.
It was on the same evening when the incident over the bowl of soup
took place, that same night when Livia and her mother were overcome with grief, the night when there were no words of comfort, only
tears.

*Based on the interview by Emily Bitton (daughter) with Livia Bitton
Jackson, May 1979.*

# The "Blessing"
# of the Munkacser Rebbe

IN THE TOWN OF MUNKACS LIVED A BELZER HASID, MOSHE SILBER,
scion of the prominent Hasidic Zanz dynasty. Peace did not dwell between the Munkacser Rabbi, Hayyim Eleazar Shapira (1872–1937),
the author of *Minhat Elazar*, and the Belzer Hasid, Reb Moshe
Silber. The latter was an opponent of the rabbi through his involve-
ment in the continuing dispute between Belz and Munkacs, a dispute
that had raged ever since the Belzer zaddik, Issachar Dov Rokeach,
lived in Hungary from 1912 to 1921, seeking refuge from World
War I.

One day, during a lively argument, the Munkacser Rabbi turned
around and in a moment of anger said to the Belzer Hasid, "You will
die with your tallit katan on!" The Belzer Hasid kept the rabbi's
words in his heart.

Years passed. World War II engulfed Europe. In April 1944 a brutal deportation Aktion was initiated in Munkacs, and by May 30 the
city was pronounced Judenrein. The ghetto had been liquidated and
all its Jews deported to Auschwitz. Among the deportees was the
Belzer Hasid, Reb Moshe Silber.

Despite the hunger, disease, slave labor, and the constant threat of
selections, the Belzer Hasid was sure that he was going to survive the
war, for in Auschwitz it was impossible and punishable by death to
wear a tallit katan. Since words spoken by a zaddik (saint) must be
fulfilled, the Belzer Hasid was sure that death had no power over him
so long as he was not wearing his ritual garment.

Indeed, the Belzer Hasid survived the Auschwitz inferno. Today,
wearing a tallit katan, he resides in Monsey, New York, and though
not a Munkacser Hasid, frequently tells about the miraculous powers
of his former adversary, the Munkacser Rebbe.

After telling his tale, Reb Moshe Silber added, as if in an afterthought, "A Hasidic rebbe is like a master diamond cutter. He takes a man and cuts away all the roughness, all the waste. He does it with a tale, a niggun (a Hasidic tune), and lots of wisdom. What you get is a polished precious stone—a Hasid. Only great masters can do it. The Munkacser was such a rebbe."

*Based on interview by Hilari Patasnick with Moshe Silber, May 1977.*

# Who Will Win This War?

WHEN KALMAN AND HIS SIXTEEN-YEAR-OLD SON YITZHAK WERE caught in a *razia* (Aktion) on a Budapest street in the summer of 1944 and placed in a labor batallion, they knew what to expect.[1] Kalman had been a prisoner in a labor battalion for two years, and Yitzhak, though only sixteen, was also a veteran of forced labor. Both father and son had managed to escape and return to Budapest.

In Budapest, with the help of the Zionist organizations, Yitzhak was able to infiltrate the Green Shirt fascist youth movement of the Arrow Cross party.[2] He lived in a youth camp where he was able to gather information about impending Aktions against Jews and then relay the news back to Zionist leaders in Budapest.

One day, as Yitzhak was on a line with other youths to receive his dinner, the Hungarian official who was dishing out the food bent down into the huge cauldron and said to Yitzhak, "Don't you like the thick soup from the bottom of the pot . . . ?" Then he whispered in Yiddish: "They suspect you, run!"

Yitzhak was simultaneously dismayed, astonished, and amused. This jolly fellow, who was full of patriotic fascist jokes, slogans, and songs, and looked like a Hungarian peasant, was a Jew like himself! That very day Yitzhak left camp.

A few days later, Yitzhak and his father were picked up during a dreadful *razia*. Only a few days before Yitzhak had been safe and could even forewarn others of such an action. Now he and his father

were again in a labor battalion, just as they had been before. Their
earlier escape seemed futile.

"You are now under the direct command of the Todt Organization, and as such, you are soldiers of the Third Reich.[3] You are fortunate people, who will benefit from the generosity of the German Fa-
therland." The men listened intently to the German officer's speech
and a glimmer of hope appeared on their taut faces. Kalman Mann
tried to conceal his bitter smile. He had heard that speech before.
The clean-shaven, well-fed, meticulously dressed German officer
could no longer fool him. Kalman knew well, from firsthand experience, what it meant for a Jew in wartime to be a so-called soldier in
the Jewish labor battalions. It meant digging antitank ditches, building roads, and burying murdered Jews. He could still see the faces
of the dead scattered like fallen sheaves in the open fields of the
Ukraine, murdered Jews dressed in their Sabbath finery.

Being a "German soldier" also meant being a living mine
detector.[4] Kalman remembered the day when, as they approached a
Russian minefield, 250 Jews of the labor battalion were selected.
They were given a pep talk about how honored they should feel that
they were selected to help Germany in its great war against Commu-
nism and Judaism. After the talk, they were ordered to march into
the minefield. Only fifty Jews returned. Kalman Mann had been
among the fifty lucky ones. Now as he listened to the German officer's speech about their privileged position as part of the German
Army, the experiences of the past two years kept flashing before his
eyes. But around him he saw faces clinging to hope as the German officer continued his "induction" statement. "And now you will be
given your uniforms," the officer finally concluded. The "uniforms" were distributed, yellow armbands for the Jews and white
armbands for the group of Jewish converts to Christianity.[5] Kalman
could not take his eyes off the German officer: he was a strange cross-
breed between a peacock, a wooden soldier, and a mechanical toy;
both fascinating and frightening.

Life in the labor battalion was even more difficult than Kalman
had anticipated. The Germans were now retreating in haste. Food ra-

tioning was more meager than ever, injuries from work were on the increase, and because of minimal medical attention, oozing open wounds were everywhere in sight.

On the eve of Rosh Hashanah, 1944, the Russians launched a big offensive and the German retreat hastened. The labor battalion was given orders to demolish all communications, transportation, and dwellings. Telegraph and electricity poles were sawn into small cubes of lumber, railroad tracks were uprooted, bridges blown up, main highways destroyed, and houses set to the torch. Only the scorched earth remained behind the retreating German Army. The labor battalion was constantly on the move, never sleeping in the same location. They were given only a few hours to sleep under the open sky before being moved to the next demolition assignment. On the eve of Yom Kippur they reached the Polish mountain of Bornemissza, between Osmoloda and Tacev, on the Slovakian border.

The German commander stepped out from his covered wagon and gave one of the long speeches they had learned to accept as part of their daily suffering. "I know that tomorrow is one of your most important holidays, Yom Kippur. It is an important fast day in your religion. I want to remind you that you are soldiers, soldiers at a time of war on the battlefield, and as such, it is strictly forbidden for you to fast. All those who fast will be executed by a firing squad." They expected him to go on and continue to enumerate the benevolence and righteousness of the German army. But he stopped short and repeated his closing remark: "Violators will be executed by a firing squad."

On Yom Kippur, September 27, they worked as usual. It was an especially difficult day for it rained heavily and everything around them was turning into a muddy swamp. When food was distributed, all the men, as if by prior agreement, spilled the coffee into the running muddy gullies and tucked the stale bread into their soaked jackets.

Kalman Mann and another Jew, also from a Hasidic family, recited the Yom Kippur prayers, whatever they remembered by heart. All the others repeated after them while their tears mingled with the rain and their voices fought the noises of hammers, axes, and the constant downpour of the rain.

The battalion of converts approached the group of Jews. Their spokesman was one Sarwashi, a former Reform rabbi who had converted to Christianity. The rabbi told them that they too were fasting on this Yom Kippur and would like to join the others in prayer. He hoped they would accept them, for it says in the Yom Kippur prayer book:

By the knowledge of Almighty and sanction of this congregation; by the permission of the heavenly tribunal and of the earthly tribunal, we permit to pray with those who transgressed.

And so while demolishing telegraph and telephone poles in the heavy downpour, the men calculated the time to say the closing prayer of this holiest of holy days, the Neila prayer.

Night came and they fell exhausted at the foot of Mount Bornemissza, ready to break their fast. Just then the German commander and a group of soldiers emerged from their covered wagons and ordered them to line up for roll call. The Jews expected the worst. Fathers parted from their sons, brothers said good-bye to brothers, friends feared for their last moment together.

"I am a benevolent officer in the best German tradition." Their fears intensified for they knew what to expect when they heard one of these "generosity" speeches. It was usually followed by the most catastrophic aftermath. "I know that you fasted today, but I am not going to invoke the death penalty that you deserve according to law. Instead, you are going to climb that mountain and slide down on your stomachs. Those among you who would like to repent may say that they were wrong in disobeying army regulations and fasting today. Those who would like to do so please raise your hands." Not a single hand went up, neither from the Jewish battalion nor from the converts.

And so, tired, soaked, starved, the emaciated Jews climbed the wet, slippery mountain. When they reached the top, they were ordered to slide down on their stomachs. When they reached the bottom, they were ordered to line up again. They were asked if there were individuals who wanted to repent and be spared the ordeal. Mud-covered figures with feverish eyes looked at the clean-shaven German officer in silent defiance. And so ten times they repeated the humiliating performance, each time with more determination, each time with more strength, climbing and sliding from an unknown Polish mountain which on that soggy Yom Kippur night became a symbol of Jewish courage and human dignity.

At midnight, as the rains abated, the performance was stopped. The men were given food and drink. They lit small campfires, trying to dry their clothes and warm their shivering bodies. Their faces shone with a strange glow as they sat around the small campfires at the foot of Bornemissza. It seemed as if the campfires reflected the glow of their shining faces and burning eyes.

A young German officer of low rank walked over to the group where Kalman and his son Yitzhak were sitting and said, "I don't know who will win this war, but one thing I am sure of—people like you, a nation like yours, will never be defeated, never!"

*Based on my interview with Rabbi Yitzhak Mann, June 12, 1979.*

# TWO

## Friendship

When asked why his experiences during the war had not embittered him, one survivor said: "I learned about friendship in Auschwitz. When I was cold, strangers shielded me with their bodies from the blowing winds, for they had nothing else to offer but themselves."

*Arnŏst Lustig*

# Good Morning,
# Herr Müller

NEAR THE CITY OF DANZIG LIVED A WELL-TO-DO HASIDIC RABBI, scion of prominent Hasidic dynasties. Dressed in a tailored black suit, wearing a top hat, and carrying a silver walking cane, the rabbi would take his daily morning stroll, accompanied by his tall, handsome son-in-law. During his morning walk it was the rabbi's custom to greet every man, woman, and child whom he met on his way with a warm smile and a cordial "Good morning." Over the years the rabbi became acquainted with many of his fellow townspeople this way and would always greet them by their proper title and name.

Near the outskirts of town, in the fields, he would exchange greetings with Herr Müller, a Polish *Volksdeutsche* (ethnic German). "Good morning, Herr Müller!" the rabbi would hasten to greet the man who worked in the fields. "Good morning, Herr Rabbiner!" would come the response with a good-natured smile.

Then the war began. The rabbi's strolls stopped abruptly. Herr Müller donned an S.S. uniform and disappeared from the fields.[1] The fate of the rabbi was like that of much of the rest of Polish Jewry. He lost his family in the death camp of Treblinka and, after great suffering, was deported to Auschwitz.

One day, during a selection at Auschwitz, the rabbi stood on line with hundreds of other Jews awaiting the moment when their fates would be decided, for life or death. Dressed in a striped camp uniform, head and beard shaven and eyes feverish from starvation and disease, the rabbi looked like a walking skeleton. "Right! Left, left, left!" The voice in the distance drew nearer. Suddenly the rabbi had a great urge to see the face of the man with the snow-white gloves, small baton, and steely voice who played God and decided who should live and who should die. He lifted his eyes and heard his own voice speaking:

"Good morning, Herr Müller!"

"Good morning, Herr Rabbiner!" responded a human voice beneath the S.S. cap adorned with skull and bones. "What are you doing here?" A faint smile appeared on the rabbi's lips. The baton moved to the right—to life. The following day, the rabbi was transferred to a safer camp.

The rabbi, now in his eighties, told me in his gentle voice, "This is the power of a good-morning greeting. A man must always greet his fellow man."

*Based on my conversation with an elderly Hasidic personality.*

# Two Capsules
# of Cyanide (I)

AMONG THE MANY DEVILISH TORMENTS DEVISED BY THE S.S. MEN at the Janowska Road Camp was a ceremony at dusk at the camp's gate. The S.S. men formed two lines at the entrance to "welcome" the inmates upon their return from a day's slave labor. The pageantry at hell's gate began to unfold when the first working detachment reached the gate, pageantry which might aptly have been called Conquerors and Vanquished at Twilight. The Germans would shout gleefully: "Who is the most respected race on the face of the earth?" The inmates, exhausted from their labor, would respond hoarsely: "The Third Reich!"

"And who is the most accursed race on earth?" the S.S. men would continue the diabolic dialogue. Prisoner's caps would fly in the air and above them once more the Jewish voices would rise in unison: "The Jewish people!"

"Louder!" the German command would roar and the Jews would respond again and again: "The Jews are the most accursed race on the face of the earth." This they would repeat while filing through the gate, trying to protect their bodies from the blows of rubber truncheons swinging at them from all directions.[1]

In those days Rabbi Israel Spira, the Rabbi of Bluzhov, worked side by side with a distinguished lawyer from Borislav by the name of Hurowitz. One day the lawyer said to the rabbi, "Mr. Spira, I think that during the short time that we have worked together, I have come to know you quite well. How can you join in the diabolic choir and announce publicly that they are the chosen people and we are the accursed race?" He did not wait for the rabbi's response and continued, "I had two thousand dollars sewn into the lapel of my concentration-camp jacket so that when an opportunity came to redeem my life, I would have something with which to pay, or at least to bargain. Last night, I was a lucky man. For the two thousand dollars, I was able to buy two capsules of cyanide at a thousand dollars apiece—one for you and one for me."[2]

The Rabbi of Bluzhov touched his friend's shoulder with gratitude. "I envy you that you are able to do it, but I cannot. My father was a rebbe, my grandfather was a rebbe, and my great-grandfather was a rebbe. When my time is up, I will join them in the World of Truth. I will come then with the rest of the Jews. But I will not be able to enter the World of Truth and face my illustrious ancestors as a murderer, as one who has taken a life—even his own life. Thank you, my friend, for your friendship."

That day, at dusk, when the inmates returned to camp, the S.S. men were lined up in their usual manner at the entrance. On their well-fed faces were malicious smiles of anticipation as they awaited their regular evening entertainment. As the prisoners neared the gate, some of the Germans cleared their throats so that their evening performance would be worthy of their superior racial status.

The anonymous, faceless, gray column was at the gate.

"Who is the most respected race on earth?" thundered the S.S. men in their strong, clear-throated voices.

"The Jews!" proclaimed one voice that overpowered all the others. The German commander ordered the question to be repeated.

"The Jewish people are the most respected race on the face of earth!" proclaimed the same single powerful voice, and the echoes from what seemed like thousands of voices resounded from the surrounding hills: "The Jews, the Jews, the Jews."

The S.S. men rushed in the direction of the dissident voice. On the ground lay stretched out the body of Hurowitz, the Borislav lawyer. On his lifeless face was frozen a smile of victory, and his gaping mouth continued silently to proclaim the eternity and greatness of the Jewish people.

*Based on a conversation of the Grand Rabbi of Bluzhov, Rabbi Israel Spira, with Aaron Frankel, January 1974.*

# On the Waiting Bench at the Gallows (II)

THE INMATE AT THE JANOWSKA ROAD CAMP WHO HAD TAKEN cyanide lay stretched out on the ground. "Who worked with the dead dog?" inquired the S.S. commandant. The brigade leader jumped to attention and promptly replied, "Number 1236." "Number 1236, report here immediately," the S.S. man commanded. The Rabbi of Bluzhov stepped out of the column and stood near the commandant. "Who else worked with this tall dog?" continued the investigation. The brigade leader announced two additional numbers. The two men joined the rabbi and flanked him on both sides. "The punishment for treason is immediate death and you three dogs will be exterminated today," pronounced the commandant.

The three were ordered to undress, their hands were tied behind their backs, nooses were placed around their necks, and they were marched in the direction of "Death Square." The faceless gray column looked on in silence as the three inmates walked to their death.

When the three reached the gallows, bodies were swinging from all of them. One of the hangmen at the gallows, upon discovering that the bodies displayed some signs of life, was giving them food and water to prolong their agonies.[1] Upon noticing the new arrivals, the chief hangman walked over to the rabbi and his two companions. With a broad smile on his face, he welcomed them as if they had come for a social visit and asked them to make themselves comfortable, to sit on the waiting bench and await their turn patiently. He apologized for the delay and explained that it was beyond his control since it had been a very busy day.[2] The other hangman checked the bodies on the gallows. They were still clinging to life.

Just then an S.S. messenger arrived. He saluted the hangman and ordered him to release a few Jews for an hour since there were heaps of dead Jews on the other side of camp who needed to be thrown into ditches and covered up with dirt. The hangman checked the bodies again as he pushed some more water and food into their mouths, looked at his watch, and pointed with his lit cigarette in the direction of the waiting bench. He turned to the people there and said, "*Schnell, Schnell!* Run to work. In one hour you must be back right here!"

They buried the dead and covered the ditches.

"Run, *schnell, schnell!*" The young German soldier, no older than seventeen, pointed the gun and commanded the three men. "Run, *schnell, schnell!* Otherwise, you will miss your appointment." The men began to run in the direction of the gallows with the German lad trailing behind. Night was descending. The young German disappeared in the distance. The Rabbi of Bluzhov stopped running, paused for a minute, and said, "Wait, my friends, wait a minute. Why are we rushing? If we are late, what can they do?" One of the two young men, oblivious to the rabbi and the world, continued to rush as if in a trance in the direction of the gallows. The rabbi and the other Jew turned toward the barracks.

It was dark when they reached the blocks where the inmates slept. The rabbi suggested that they enter one of the barracks. "They won't allow us in," said the other Jew. "We have nothing to lose by trying," replied the rabbi. "The gallows are waiting for us anyway." They entered one of the barracks. The inmates attempted to chase them away. "I am the Rabbi of Pruchnik from the Bluzhov dynasty. Don't be afraid. I beg of you to let us hide here overnight, for otherwise we will hang from the gallows." The inmates huddled together, debated for a minute, then returned with their verdict. "We will hide you. For a Hasidic rebbe we are willing to take a risk, but not for the other Jew." "Without him I am not staying," the rabbi bargained as he moved toward the door. "Jewish blood will be on your conscience."

They remained in the block. That night no search and no head count took place. In the morning one of the inmates approached a Jewish policeman. He told them that in their midst they had one of the great Hasidic rabbis of Poland and he needed help. The Rabbi of Bluzhov and the other Jew were attached to a new working brigade and given new numbers.

"God manages a strange world; at times it is difficult to comprehend," the rabbi reflected as if to himself as he told the story some thirty years later in his Brooklyn home. "Yet it is our duty to tell the story over and over again. Telling the tales is an attempt to understand and come to terms with a most difficult reality."

*Based on a conversation of the Grand Rabbi of Bluzhov, Rabbi Israel Spira, with Aaron Frankel, January 1974.*

# A Sip of Coffee

AFTER A LONG AND EXCRUCIATING JOURNEY FROM LVOV, THE death train arrived at its final destination, the killing center of Belzec. It was October 1942.[1]

The doors of the cars were pulled open, a horde of Germans and Ukrainians rushed at the victims with whips, and a shrill voice blasted at them over a large loudspeaker. "He is only forty-five years old!" The Rabbi of Bluzhov heard the voice of his wife Perl cry out among the other voices as she tried to point out her husband to the S.S. officer who was looking for young, healthy men.

"I am fifty-six years old!" shouted the rabbi when he realized that his wife was being pushed in the opposite direction.

"You are forty-five years old." The S.S. officer smiled with malice as he dragged the rabbi by his collar to the other side of the platform. "You will join her later, I assure you." The S.S. man held on to the rabbi as he tried to run in the direction in which his wife had disappeared. Her last command was still lingering. "You must survive. One day you will be needed."[2]

Some time later, the rabbi was taken back to the railway station. Near the platform there were stacks of valises stamped with home addresses, neatly folded clothing, heaps of hair and gold teeth, jewels and gold coins—all that remained of the Lvov transport. Many new transports had since arrived at the Belzec station from Galicia and from all over Europe.

"You, tall dog, come over here!" the S.S. officer snapped at the Rabbi of Bluzhov in his steely cold voice. "You and two other dogs will accompany the clothing to Lvov. The Third Reich is in need of clothing. You Jewish warmongers caused World War II. Because of you, our women and children suffer from the bitter winter cold. Because of you, we had to convert civilian shops into munitions factories." A blow over the rabbi's head signaled the conclusion of the speech.

Dressed in a strange uniform, his head shaven, the lone survivor of his family, the rabbi made his way back to Lvov atop bundles of clothes belonging to the dead Jews of that town where he had once been a rabbi with a large Hasidic following. The trucks arrived in Lvov's Janowska Road concentration camp at midnight.[3] Shivering from cold, exhausted and starved, trying to comprehend the nightmarish days at the Belzec inferno, the rabbi searched for shelter in the shadows of the trucks. At dusk, the figure of a young man appeared. He was selling coffee from a soup pot. "A sip of coffee for twenty pfennig! A sip of coffee for twenty pfennig!" he was calling in a subdued voice.[4]

The rabbi walked over to the coffee vendor. "Young man, I am going to ask you a favor. Please give me a sip of coffee. It is a few days since a morsel of food or a drop to drink has passed my lips. I can't pay you. I have no money."

The coffee vendor examined the emaciated face of the man in the striped uniform and gave him a ladle full of coffee.

With one hand the rabbi held the ladle of coffee, while with the other he covered his head and recited the appropriate blessing. Upon hearing the blessing, the vendor burst into tears.

"Woe unto me. What ever happened to us? To what debased state have we fallen, that a person no longer recognizes his own rabbi? I am young Landau, the brother of Meyer Landau, your own Hasid."[5]

The rabbi comforted him. "There is no need to cry, my young friend. As long as one recognizes the voice of Jacob, the hands of Esau will have no power over us."[6]

There are only a handful of survivors of Belzec. The Rabbi of Bluzhov is one of them.

*Based on a conversation of the Grand Rabbi of Bluzhov, Rabbi Israel Spira, with Aaron Frankel, January 1974. I heard it at the rabbi's house on several occasions.*

# For the Sake
# of Friendship

WHEN ROCHELLE, THE DAUGHTER OF THE RABBI OF VISHNITZ, heard that the Rabbi of Bluzhov, Rabbi Israel Spira, was back in the Janowska Road Camp, near Lvov, she managed to smuggle in to him some coffee and bread.[1] This contact with the outside world gave the rabbi new hope and suggested the possibility of escape. Rochelle described to the rabbi in great detail the least guarded terrain between the camp and the town of Lvov, the abandoned buildings and the distance between them.

"What will happen if you are caught?" she asked the rabbi. "I have faced death tens of times before," the rabbi replied. "One must always try to save one's life."

At dusk, when his work detachment was marching back to camp from Lvov, the rabbi moved slightly away from the group, ducked, then began to crawl in the direction of the closest vacant building. He entered the building and stood flattened against the walls in a corner. He decided to wait for the darkness of night when people would disappear from the streets of Lvov. Then, dressed in his camp uniform with its two yellow rags affixed to the front and back and its broad stripe permanently affixed from collar to bottom of jacket, he would be able to walk outside at night undetected and try to reach the Jewish sector of the town.

A group of well-dressed young people passed near the rabbi's hiding place, laughing and conversing in German. He pressed himself even flatter against the wall and remained motionless.

How strange it is, he thought to himself, that people still lead normal lives and engage in friendly conversations in German, a German without orders, without commands. . . .

It seemed so long ago that the rabbi had loved demonstrating his perfect command of the German language. He usually had an opportunity to do so on his annual vacations at the springwater resorts in Germany. He particularly remembered the trips in the company of his wife and beloved daughter, whose beauty had dazzled all who saw her. He remembered his trip to Marinsbaad, a trip on which a friendship began with Helmut Müller.[2] It began on a train when a tall, well-dressed gentleman entered their first-class compartment. A conversation developed between the rabbi and the tall stranger, who introduced himself as Helmut Müller. The rabbi's daughter, who also spoke fluent German, joined in the conversation.

This casual meeting developed into a lasting friendship. Each time the rabbi planned a trip to the resorts, he would notify his friend and the latter would join him at a designated railway station. For the Jewish New Year, Rosh Hashana, Helmut Müller would send the rabbi a New Year's card wishing him, his family, the Jewish people, and all mankind a happy, peaceful year. Müller was a charming, gentle individual whom one felt fortunate in befriending.

The rabbi was so deeply immersed in his memories that he did not realize that darkness had descended upon the streets of Lvov. The German-speaking voices were no longer heard; all was quiet.

The rabbi went out to the street. As he walked on the cobblestones of Lvov he felt reassured. He had lived in Lvov before his deportation to the killing center of Belzec and had had a big Hasidic following. In Lvov some of his Hasidim were probably still living in the ghetto and would remember him, he thought. He walked toward the house of David Igra, whom he had met in Lvov some months ago. At that time, he had met Igra walking around the streets of the ghetto without the mandatory white armband with its blue Star of David. When asked for an explanation, Igra had replied that he was a foreign national and, as such, was not required to wear an armband. From that day a friendship developed between the rabbi and Igra. Now, as he was approaching Igra's house, he again met him on the street. He immediately informed him that he had just escaped from the Janowska camp and might cause him some trouble by associating with him. Igra paid no attention to the rabbi's warning.

Igra took the rabbi to his home, fed him, and gave him clothing so that he could get rid of his prisoner's uniform with the Janowska insignia that was meant to preclude escape. "Where is your South American passport?" asked Igra. The rabbi told him that after his only daughter and son-in-law were murdered in spite of being holders of South American passports, he had buried his own passport in the ground because he felt it was useless. But now, upon the advice of Igra, the rabbi went to his former place of residence and unearthed his passport in the backyard. The passport would not be valid, however, until it was stamped and signed by a Gestapo official in the Passport Division.

As the hour approached when the rabbi had to go to the Gestapo Passport Division, he felt a paralyzing fear come over him. The Nazi who approved foreign passports was reputed to be among the cruelest Nazi officials in Lvov. No one ever referred to him by name. When one said in the ghetto, "The dog, may his name be obliterated," it was clear to all to whom the reference was made: to the *Hauptsturmführer* (captain) in the Passport Division. When a person walked up to his office to have a passport validated, his chance of remaining alive was very slight. If ten people went up, one survived and the rest were shot on the spot in the Gestapo backyard. The chief's selections were made at random and defied any pattern.

Finally, the Rabbi of Bluzhov went to the Gestapo offices. From the moment he entered the building he searched for a plan to survive. He gave up his place in line several times, thus hoping to postpone his death sentence for a few additional minutes. Why should he rush to the fatal door? he thought to himself. Through the door the terrifying, brutal voice of the Gestapo man rang.

"Filthy dog, where did you buy this passport? Shoot him! Remove him to the courtyard!" The death sentence was repeated throughout the morning. Only two people walked out again through the same door they had entered earlier. Pale and frightened, they rushed to the stairway, fearing that the official would still change his mind and call them back.

The Rabbi of Bluzhov was the last one in the waiting room. The voice from the next room roared through the door, "Dog, come in!" The rabbi entered the room. The back of the Gestapo man was facing the rabbi.

The chief of the Passport Division turned sharply in his swivel chair and faced the rabbi. The rabbi was shocked. Wearing the Gestapo uniform was none other than his friend Helmut Müller.[3] Before the rabbi had a chance to utter a sound, Müller shouted his familiar phrase. "Dog, where have you purchased the passport?"

Rabbi Israel Spira gathered all his strength and said, "Your honor, may I ask you one question?" Müller was taken by surprise at this unexpected change in the by now familiar scenario. He motioned that the rabbi could speak. "But make it brief, dog," he added.

"My name is Rabbi Israel Spira," said the rabbi, trying to speak in the old, prewar, relaxed manner. Müller underwent a dramatic change. His face lost its harshness, a glimmer of compassion flickered in his eyes, and his voice became gentle and human.

"My God, my God," he began to whisper. "You are Rabbi Israel Spira, the elegant handsome Rabbiner? How is your beautiful daughter? She must be a blossoming woman by now." When Müller mentioned his daughter, the rabbi could no longer control himself and tears began to stream down his face. "She is no longer among the living; she was murdered."

"My God, my God," Müller whispered again. "Who could have killed such a charming, enchanting woman? What do you plan to do now?" Müller asked the rabbi. The rabbi smiled bitterly through his tears.

"Don't worry, my friend, don't worry, my friend, just don't worry." Müller got up from the chair, locked the door, sat next to the rabbi, and he too began to cry. "Don't worry," he comforted the rabbi. "As long as I am alive, nothing will happen to you in this town." They spoke for a while and recalled the old days. "Come, let's wash our faces. Everything will be fine," Müller comforted the rabbi again.

Müller calmed down and returned to his desk. He stamped and signed the rabbi's passport and the rest of his papers. "You need a nice, comfortable apartment," Müller, said, after validating the papers and rechecking them to make sure that all was in order and legal. "Just a place to live in. The sector for foreign nationals would be perfect," the rabbi replied.

Müller parted from the rabbi as from an old friend and again reassured him that no ill would befall him as long as he was in Lvov. But he made the rabbi promise that no one would know of their friendship because it would be disastrous for both of them.

The rabbi received an apartment in 36 Lwowska Street. A few hours after he moved in, a horse-drawn wagon stopped in front of the building. A delivery was made to the rabbi's apartment of bread, butter, chocolate, and coffee.[4]

The rabbi lived there till the liquidation of the Lvov ghetto in June 1943, when he was deported with the other foreign nationals to Bergen Belsen.

*Based on a conversation of the Grand Rabbi of Bluzhov, Rabbi Israel Spira, with Aaron Frankel, January 1974.*


# Under the
# Blue Skies of Tel Aviv

ON AUGUST 25, 1942, THE GREAT AKTION TOOK PLACE IN THE ghetto of Bochnia. Five hundred women, children, and elderly people were shot at a nearby forest.[1] At that time, Bronia was working at one of the ghetto's many workshops. When she heard about the impending Aktion, Bronia and the children took refuge in a bunker together with Dora and her small children. They were in mortal fear that the children would cry and their hiding place would be discovered by the Germans. Bronia kept little Yitzhak at her breast and Dora, by profession a nurse, gave her small child Luminal.

In the bunker they heard terrible cries from next door. Leah Grossman and her children had been discovered. They heard her pleas to be shot first. They could hear the earthshaking lamentations of a mother witnessing the death of her beloved children, then the terrible silence following the volley of fire that pierced the mother's heart. Leah Grossman was dead.

Early in the morning they crawled out of their bunker. Dora was carrying the body of her child, who had died from an overdose of Luminal. Bronia covered the eyes of her children so they should not see the dead covering the city streets.

When the ghetto returned to the strange normality that followed the Aktions, Bronia with a small pot of soup in her hands rushed to Feifush. As she neared his residence, her pulse quickened. Maybe he too was swallowed up last night by that beastly Aktion? But there, in his tiny cubicle, lying on a straw mattress on the bare floor, was Feifush.

Feifush was a young man from Palestine who had come to visit his parents in Poland. When the war broke out he was stranded in Poland. All his efforts to reach a port, or a neutral country, had ended in failure. His parents were now dead, murdered in their hometown. And Feifush, after much wandering and running from place to place, had found himself far away from his beloved Tel Aviv, dying from disease and starvation in the ghetto of Bochnia, where he had been befriended by Bronia. When Bronia brought him the soup, his only nourishment that day, he could hardly sit up. Bronia propped him up and fed him. As she fed him the soup, Feifush's face became relaxed, and the pain in his eyes was replaced by a strange tranquility, an expression of peace and restfulness, rarely seen those days in Jewish eyes.

"You know, Mrs. Koczicki, when I lie here on my mattress in this corner of the earth where the sun never shines, I see my sunny Tel Aviv, the blue skies, the blue sea, the golden sands. But in my visions of my beloved Tel Aviv, I never see myself. Instead I see you walking in the streets of Tel Aviv, under its majestic blue skies, with your two children. I sense that it is a vision of the future, that you and the children will live through this darkness and reach the promised land. Remember me when you arrive there."

A few days later, when Bronia arrived as usual with her little pot of warm soup, Feifush's mattress was empty. Neighbors told her that he had been taken away in the most recent Aktion. Bronia never saw him again.

In 1946, Bronia and her two small sons went to Palestine from Europe. One day as they were playing in the sand on Tel Aviv's seashore, little Yitzhak asked his mother if she knew anyone in Tel Aviv. She looked up at the beautiful clear-blue skies above the peaceful waves and said, "Yes, we have a very dear, close friend in Tel Aviv; his name is Feifush."

*Based on a conversation of Rebbetzin Bronia Spira with Dina Spira, April 26, 1979.*

# "What I Learned at My Father's Home"

IN BERGEN BELSEN, BRONIA'S DEDICATION TO THE EDUCATION of her two small sons, Zvi and Yitzhak, was viewed by some as an obsession bordering on insanity. She would deny herself food, bartering it for her children's education. For a piece of bread and a potato, Mr. Rappaport taught her children Jewish law and tradition. She herself taught the children the weekly portion of the Five Books of Moses. At times the children were so hungry that they could neither hear nor see. Words became muffled, distant sounds and the letters seemed like a colony of busy ants rushing in all directions.

When Passover approached, Bronia's program became more rigid. She insisted that the children learn all the laws and customs pertinent to the holiday, while she herself supervised their studies and hustled for food. A kind old German who worked at the showers gave her some beets and potatoes, and these she saved for the holiday so she and the children would be able to manage without bread.

Bronia did not rest until she got rid of her hametz, or leavened food and bread, as required by tradition. She sold it for the duration of the Passover to a Gentile woman from Prague, the wife of a famous Jewish lawyer. Both of them were now inmates in Bergen Belsen. Bronia's sale of hametz became a source of mockery, and people taunted her and asked if the sale of hametz were her only concern at this particular time and place.

"I learned the Jewish tradition in my father's home when I was a child. Now it is my duty as a Jewish mother to teach it to my children in my home."

"Some home, a Nazi concentration camp!" someone said, while glancing at the two children with pity for their sad lot, being children to a mother who had lost her mind in these troubled times.

On their way back to their barracks, Bronia and the children stopped at the infirmary. A long line of people were standing and waiting for treatment that would offer relief from their pain and discomfort. Two German doctors in white coats passed by on their way to the infirmary. One casually pointed to the people on line and said to his companion, "I don't know why God has punished me so severely by forcing me to witness daily such ugliness as these Jews."

Bronia glanced at the line. All around her were skeletons disfigured by disease and starvation, covered with boils, blotches, and sores.

"*Mutti* (Mommy), did you hear what the German doctor said?" asked Zvi of his mother.

"Yes, I heard," Bronia responded. "Just study and be good, for a time will come when we will once more be a great and wise nation. Remember the Ten Plagues that God brought upon Egypt?"

Zvi was comforted. In his mind he saw the Germans covered with sores, boils, and lice, while the Jews were marching to freedom through the open gates of Bergen Belsen.

Passover came and went, and the Jews of Bergen Belsen were still slaves behind barbed wire. On the evening when Passover ended, a woman by the name of Mindel Heller came running. "Bronia, it is a matter of life and death. The Rabbi of Pruchnik is almost dead.[1] He hardly ate during the Passover holiday, and now he refuses to eat hametz that was not sold prior to the holiday as required by law. I heard that you are the only person in camp who sold your hametz."

Bronia did not hesitate for a moment. She took out a loaf of white bread, her most precious possession, and gave it for the Rabbi of Pruchnik.

People around her nodded their heads in disbelief. "Woe to a woman who gives away her children's last bit to a stranger," said people in her barracks.

"What I learned and saw at my father's home, I want my children to see and learn in my home. I could not choose the home but I can preserve its spirit," said Bronia as she handed the bread to Mindel.

"*Mutti*, Passover is over and we are still slaves and the Germans eat plenty and are free and clean," said Zvi as Mindel Heller was rushing with the bread to the Rabbi of Pruchnik.

"My child, the Jews were slaves in Egypt for 210 years and then freed. We have been slaves for only the past four years," said Bronia.

Little Yitzhak, who was listening to his big brother's questions, said, "The Ten Plagues are here, so the Exodus to freedom will soon follow."

Zvi was tempted to point out to his younger brother that at present it was the Jews who were afflicted with the Ten Plagues and not the Germans, but he remained silent.

"Where are we going to be next year on Passover?" Zvi continued to ask.

"In Jerusalem," responded Bronia.

"How do you know?" Zvi continued to question.

"I learned it at my father's home," said Bronia.

Mindel Heller returned. The Rabbi of Pruchnik was improved. Bronia's bread had saved his life.

When Rebbetzin Spira finished her story, she said to me, "Do you know the value of the loaf of bread I gave Mindel Heller?"

I shook my head.

"Today a skyscraper on Times Square is less valuable than a loaf of white bread was in Bergen Belsen," said Bronia Spira.

*Based on a conversation of Rebbetzin Bronia Spira with Dina Spira, May 2, 1976, and my own conversation with the rebbetzin on April 26, 1979.*

# "The World Needs You"

NEAR THE END OF MARCH 1945, A HASIDIC WOMAN IN BERGEN Belsen dreamed about her father. In her dream her father came to visit her. He brought her food and told her not to worry, for all would end well. She should prepare to take a journey on the sixth or the seventh of April. She would be given tickets. "Be ready and do not lose faith," were his concluding words.

It rained heavily the following day and, without any warning, not even a rumor, they were all transferred from their barracks to another sector of the camp. People were sure that this transfer spelled doom. Behind the thin wall in the new barracks the Hasidic woman heard a rabbi tell his people to get ready for their last walk, since all was clearly lost. When the woman heard the rabbi's words she banged on the wall and shouted, "Shame on you, to discourage people! Is this what we need to hear from a rabbi?! We need faith and comfort, not despair."

"And from where does one glean his faith in these lean days?"

The dialogue between the woman and the rabbi continued through the thin barracks walls. "From heaven and its messengers. If my father told me that all will end well, it will be so."

Someone laughed. "Crazy woman," a faint voice whispered through the walls. "Even the heavens are lamenting our fate, with buckets of tears."

It was time to bring the "coffee" to the barracks. Six men were selected for this task. All the others stood and watched as the men walked into the gray, murky courtyard. One of the six men bent down; on the ground he had spotted some potato peels. Shots were fired. Blood began to stream from their knees. Two men fell into the puddles. A group of inmates were marched from another direction and trampled them to death.

"Faith! faith! faith!" Someone shook an angry fist at the woman's face.

It was dark and damp in the barracks. The children fell asleep, and the woman felt an urge to venture out into the cold Bergen Belsen night. Against the electrified fence she saw the silhouette of an inmate. Taking great care not to startle the man, the woman quickly made her way in the direction of the fence. As she approached, she recognized him. It was none other than Rabbi Israel Spira, who was well known in the camp. What could a man be seeking at this time of night before the electrified fence? It could only be his death, a death in the shadow of night, away from the questioning eyes of other inmates.

"Rabbi Spira, merciful Jew, what are you doing there? Please come back." She spoke to him in a voice in which anger and compassion were mingled.

He began to cry. "I am all alone in this world. My entire family is gone. I was left alone to witness all this suffering and shame. I am standing here at the electrified wires, at this horrible forbidden place, so that the angels of death who dwell in the watchtowers will put an end to all my misery and pain. It is forbidden to take one's own life; they will do it for me."

The woman held back her tears. In a voice that managed to suggest compassion, outrage, respect, and faith all at once, she said to the rabbi, "How could you even contemplate such a drastic step? You are the scion of such a prominent family in Judaism, that enriched our lives with saints, scholars, and righteous Jews. How can you stand here now and think of ending your life? A day will come and God will bless you once more; you will be grateful that your life was spared. And besides, the world needs you!" Rabbi Spira stepped away from the fence.

Moments later the cold, penetrating ray of the searchlight passed over the electrified fence, revealing nothing but darkness. The rabbi returned to his barracks, while the woman rushed back to her children to prepare for the journey.

*Based on interview by Dina Spira with the Hasidic woman, May 10, 1976.*

# The Yeshiva Student

RADIN WAS A SMALL LITHUANIAN SHTETL. ITS GREATEST PRIDE
was its most illustrious resident, a saintly man and world-renowned
scholar, Rabbi Israel Meir HaCohen (1838–1933), known as the
Chafetz Chayim, after his famous book. Jewish students the world
over came to the rabbi's yeshiva in Radin to seek wisdom and guidance. One of these students was Reb Hirsch Kamenitzer. Day and
night he studied the holy books of the Talmud. When he was close to
fifty, he married a much younger woman by the name of Rivka, from
the town of Brisk. The couple lived not far from the yeshiva in a
small frame house owned by Bashe and Israel Tocker. In the summer
of 1941 the Germans occupied Radin, and Reb Hirsch and Rivka
were blessed with a son, their first child. The parents' joy knew no
limit.

When the ghetto was formed, Hirsch and Rivka's house was the
last house in the ghetto and stood on the border. It became a shelter
for many illegal ghetto residents. One of them was sixteen-year-old
Zvi Michalowsky, a fugitive from the neighboring shtetl of Eisysky,
which had been destroyed by the Germans. In the same house there
also lived a young, pretty Jewish girl. The burgermeister of Radin,
Mr. Kolkowski, a former officer in the Polish Army and the head of
the Polish police, took a fancy to the girl. She spent the day in his residence, cleaning the house and taking care of his needs. She knew no
hunger or cold. The burgermeister showered her with clothes, eggs,
butter, milk, and delicacies unheard of in the ghetto.

As May 10, 1942, approached, Kolkowski warned his Jewish girl
friend that the ghetto would be liquidated. Thursday night, the eve
of the ninth, Kolkowski came to the girl's house and arranged for her
safe passage from the ghetto. Rivka learned from the girl about the
impending doom, and together with her husband, Reb Hirsch, and
the baby, they managed to escape under the cover of night.

They hid in the forest of Mischantz. During the summer they survived on berries and mushrooms. In the winter, when there was no vegetation in the forest and the snow covered the ground, Rivka would go out to nearby villages and beg food from the local farmers. The farmers of Tatar origin were the most generous ones. Meanwhile, Hirsch and his beloved son would stay in the underground shelter that they had managed to dig. While eagerly waiting for his wife's return, he would try to teach his child the wisdom of our sages. Thus they survived for nearly a year, till one day Polish farmers killed Rivka and the child as they were begging for food.

Zvi Michalowsky, by then a young partisan, heard that Reb Hirsch Kamenitzer was still alive and about the tragic fate of his family. He took eggs, butter, bread, cheese, warmly lined pants, boots, and other items and began to search for Reb Hirsch in the Mischantz forest in the vicinity of Dochishok. When he found him he could not believe his eyes. There was a living corpse: an emaciated pale face covered with sores and a body clad in rags. Zvi thought to himself, when the dry, dead bones described by the prophet Ezekiel arise and come back to life, they will surely look like Reb Hirsch.[1] Only his eyes were shining like two burning coals. Zvi gave Reb Hirsch the food and warm clothing. Hirsch looked at him and asked: "My dear friend Zvi, tell me the truth. How did you obtain these items? Forgive me for my question. Did you take them by force from the Polish farmers? Our holy law strictly forbids us to steal from our fellow men."[2] Zvi assured him that he had robbed no one and had not used force to obtain the food and clothes. Only after Zvi's assurance was Reb Hirsch willing to place a morsel of food between his parched lips, and put the warm boots on his frozen feet.

Weeks later, Zvi and his fellow partisans found Reb Hirsch's naked body. He had been killed by local farmers. His clothes and boots had been stolen.

*Based on my interview with Zvi Michalowsky, November 11, 1979.*

# Stars

MICHAEL SCHWARTZ ARRIVED IN AUSCHWITZ-BIRKENAU IN August of 1944 with one of the last transports from the Lodz ghetto. Though a veteran of this first and last ghetto of Nazi Europe,[1] Michael was in a state of shock when he was shoved out of the cattle car into the Auschwitz kingdom. The railway platform with its barking dogs, screaming S.S. men, kicking Ukrainians, and the sorrowful eyes of quick-moving prisoners in striped uniforms inspired terror, hopelessness, and a strange wish to get it over and done with as quickly as possible. Before he realized what was happening, he was separated from his family and was led away in the opposite direction with a group of young men. The men marched beneath a barrage of leather truncheons, near the edges of flaming pits where people were tossed alive. The air was filled with sulfur and the stench of burning flesh.

A few hours later, his hair shaven, his body stinging from disinfectants, wearing a striped, oversized uniform and a pair of skimpy, broken clogs, Michael along with hundreds of young men was led off to a barracks. There in the barracks, he found a cousin from whom he had been separated earlier at the platform. Only after looking at his cousin did Michael realize the transformation that he himself had undergone since his arrival on that accursed platform. That night in the barracks the cousins promised each other never to part again. It was the first decision Michael had made since his arrival in Auschwitz.

Michael quickly learned the realities of Auschwitz. Survival depended on one's ability to "organize" anything and everything, from an additional sip of coffee to a better sleeping place on the three-tiered wooden planks, and of course one had to present a healthy and useful appearance if one hoped to pass selections.

One day rumors spread in Michael's barracks that the impending selection was of particular importance, for those selected would be transferred out of Auschwitz to work at another camp. Michael was especially anxious to pass that selection. In the few months he had been in Auschwitz he had learned that Auschwitz would eventually devour everybody, even those who deciphered its survival code.

Dr. Joseph Mengele himself was supervising the selection. It was apparent to Michael that Mengele was using what was known among the Auschwitz old-timers as the "washboard" criterion. Each inmate was ordered to lift his hands high above his head as he approached Mengele. If his rib cage protruded and each vertebra was clearly visible, Mengele would smile and motion with his snow-white glove to the left.

The moment came. Michael and his cousin stood in front of Mengele, whose clean, shaven face glittered in the sun and whose eyes shown. The angel of death was in his moment of bliss. Michael's turn came and Mengele's finger pointed: "Right!" Then Michael heard Mengele's death sentence on his cousin: "Left!"

A moment later Michael stood before a table where three people sat dressed in white coats. One was holding a stamp pad, one a huge rubber stamp, and the third a pen and a white sheet of paper. Michael felt the cold rubber stamp press against his forehead and saw a pen mark a line on the white sheet of paper.

Michael moved on to a group of young men, all naked like himself, wearing only a huge ink star on their foreheads. Michael realized that this star was the passport that would take him out of the camp, and that his cousin in the other group just a few meters away would be taken to the chimneys.

In the commotion of the selection Michael decided to act. He walked briskly over to his cousin, spat on his cousin's forehead, pressed his own forehead against his cousin's, took his cousin by the hand, and led him to the group marked with stars. Only then did he dare look at his cousin. There in the middle of his forehead was the imprint of the lucky star, the passport that would lead them out of the Auschwitz hell.

From Birkenau, Michael and his cousin were transported to Neuengamme, Braunschweig, Watenstadt, Beendorf, Ravensbrück, and Ludwigslust, where they slaved in the Hermann Goering works in private German companies engaged in the war industry.

On a May day in 1945 a tank entered a camp near Ludwigslust.[2] On it was painted a huge white star and inside tank sat a black-faced soldier wearing a steel helmet. After six years in the Nazi slave kingdom, Michael and his cousin were once again free men.

*Based on interview by Ellen Blakfein with Michael Schwartz, March 31, 1979.*

# The Mosaic Artist's Apprentice

JACOB (JACK) GARFEIN WAS ONLY THIRTEEN YEARS OLD WHEN HE was deported to Auschwitz with a transport of Hungarian Jews. As the men were separated from the women and children upon arrival on the platform, Jacob was clinging to his mother's skirt. Suddenly he felt his mother's hand tearing him away from her and pushing him in the direction of the men's column. Jacob ran back to his mother, pleading with her to let him stay with her. "Mommy, I love you, please let me stay with you, please, Mommy, don't send me away."

His mother had a strange look in her eyes that he had never seen before. She did not look at him; her glance was fixed far away on the distant glow of the chimneys. Her teeth were clenched and she looked as if she was holding back her tears, but Jacob was not sure. Jacob tried again to plead with her. Once more her firm hand pushed him away.

Feeling betrayed and abandoned by his beloved mother, Jacob, with tears in his eyes, was pushed into a stream of men amidst dogs and S.S. men that carried him in an unknown direction.

"Boy," he heard from behind him a voice in a distinct Polish-

Yiddish accent, "when you reach the man on the podium, stretch yourself out as tall as you can."

"How old are you?" Jacob now heard the voice of the man on the podium.

"Sixteen," said the voice from behind him.

"What is your occupation, young lad?" Mengele continued to question him. Before he had a chance to reply "student," the Polish Jew behind him hastily replied, "Your honor, he is my apprentice. The two of us are among the world's greatest mosaic artists." Jacob turned his head, and only then, for the first time in his life, did he see the face of the Polish Jew; his big, deep-set eyes, his white, stubby beard, and his long, delicate, almost transparent fingers. "His fingers must have turned thousands of Gemara pages," thought Jacob when he saw those exquisite hands. Mengele lifted his own glove-clad hand and motioned to the right.

Jacob's face was burning with insult and shame. First he had been rejected by his beloved mother and now he was guilty of being an accomplice to a lie. He was not an apprentice to a mosaic artist, he did not even know what the word *mosaic* meant. He was a student, a yeshiva bocher. And he had never seen that man before in his life. He turned back to complain to the Polish Jew, but the man was gone, lost in the crowd. Jacob tried to go back to the nice, elegant man on the podium to tell him that he had been party to a lie and to ask for his forgiveness. But as he was trying to push his way against the streaming mob of men, a Kapo kicked Jacob in the stomach and ordered him to turn back.

All that night Jacob searched for the old Polish Jew with the white beard. All the men had been shaven, all were bald, all were wearing striped camp uniforms, but Jacob was sure that he would recognize the man's voice and his long delicate fingers.

For months, during his stay at Auschwitz, Jacob searched in vain for the old man, wishing to thank him for saving his life on the selection line. He never saw him again.

One day, at dusk, as the chimneys were spitting out thousands of lives in strange red clouds, Jacob was searching for his old savior. Suddenly it occurred to him that he would never find him, for the old man must have been Elijah the Prophet who was sent by his mother's prayers to save him, a mother's last prayers to save her only beloved son.

*Based on a talk by Jacob (Jack) Garfein at the opening of the Jack Eisner Institute at the Graduate School and University Center of the City University of New York, March 15, 1979.*

# A Girl Called Estherke

IT WAS THE NEW MONTH OF SIVAN, 5704, SPRING 1944. IDA, HER father, mother, brothers, and sisters were ordered to the train station with the rest of the Jewish community of their Czechoslovakian town. Jews had lived there for generations, but their history was all coming to an abrupt end with a single train ride to Auschwitz.

The cattle cars were sealed. More than eighty people were squeezed into a single wagon. Ida and her family managed to stay together, and they comforted each other amidst the choking heat, filth, and fear of the unknown. "Papa, where are they taking us?" Ida asked. "My children, once there was an altar on Mount Moriah in the holy city of Jerusalem. God commanded a father to take his only, beloved son and sacrifice him upon that altar, in order to test his faith in God. As the father was about to fulfill God's command and lifted the knife, the Lord God spoke to Abraham and said, 'Lay not thy hand upon the lad.'[1]

"Today, my children, there is another huge altar, not on a sacred mountain but in a profane valley of death. There, man is testing his own inhumanity toward his fellow man. The children of Abraham are again a burnt offering, this time by the command of men. But man, unlike God, will not stop the knife. To the contrary, he will sharpen it and fan the altar flames so that they may totally consume their sacrifice. A man-made fire, a knife held by man, must be stopped by man, by a human voice, a human hand. My children, be human in this inhuman valley of death. May the merit of our Father Abraham protect you, for whoever saves one Jewish soul, it is as if he saves an entire universe.''

On the eve of the holiday of Shavuot, Ida and her family arrived in Auschwitz. The skies above Auschwitz were red. Ida's father spoke as if to himself: "On this day, millenniums ago, God came down to man in fire and smoke and gave his commandments. Today, man is commanding in fire and smoke, 'Thou shalt kill!' ''

The Auschwitz platform separated Ida forever from her father, mother, young sisters, and brothers. Ida and her older married sister passed the selection and were put to work for the German civilian population and the Reich's war machine. Ida sorted the clothes of the gassed, folded them neatly, and placed them in symmetrical piles according to size and quality, ready for shipment to Germany to be used by the German people.

One day, as Ida was sorting the clothes, an S.S. officer walked over to her and said: "Why do you smile, Jewish pig?" Before Ida had a chance to respond, she saw a black boot flying into her face, felt a piercing pain and the gush of blood, and looked down to behold her front teeth on the floor in a puddle of blood. "Pretty white teeth look better on the floor than in a filthy Jewish mouth," said the S.S. officer. He commanded Ida to wipe the blood off the boot that knocked out her teeth and cheerfully walked away, humming a tune.

Ida quickly assessed her condition. She realized that a gaping hole in her mouth was a sight that an S.S. officer at a selection would not cherish. She walked over to the pile where thousands of dental bridges were thrown and hastily selected one. She placed it in her swollen mouth and returned to her assigned spot.

That night in the barracks it was especially difficult to fall asleep. Heartbreaking screams were piercing the night, mingled with the wailing of children and mothers as they were torn away from each other. Slowly, the screams subsided and gave way to the usual deadly sounds of the Auschwitz night. Most of the girls in Ida's barracks fell asleep.

Then there was a noise under Ida's three-tiered bunk bed where thirty-six girls slept, twelve per bed, packed together like sardines. "All we need are rats, just to give them another reason to shoot us," someone said. "Shut up, I am tired," another voice complained. The noise persisted. "Ida, you are the brave one, go down and see what it is." All the other eleven girls had to turn so that Ida could move from the spot where she had wedged herself in.

Under the bed, in a corner, curled up like a frightened porcupine, was a little girl. She told them that when the children's Aktion[2] began, she managed to run away and hide in the latrine among the piles of chlorine cans. When it became dark, she ran into the barracks and hid under the bed.

The girl's name was Estherke. She had big, blue frightened eyes, beautiful blond curls, and two deep dimples. Ida became instantly attached to the child and kept showing her off to all the others girls, exclaiming: "Doesn't she look like a little actress?" The blockhova told Ida that she must give up the child, otherwise she, her sister, and maybe all the girls in the barracks would pay with their lives for harboring a little criminal. Ida stood there clutching the child. "I will never give her up," she said with determination. She walked over to the blockhova and asked to speak to her privately. "I know that your boyfriend is Jewish and assumed a false Aryan identity. Killing me, my sister, and others will not help. Other girls, and even men outside of this barracks, know it too. We will all keep quiet if you will help to save Estherke. During the day when we are at work, you must keep Estherke in your private room." The blockhova agreed. Ida had won her first battle for Estherke's life.

Ida loved the child. All her thoughts focused on Estherke. To save that child became her obsession and purpose for living. Rumors began to circulate that *Lager* (camp) C, in BII, Ida's camp, would be evacuated. Ida became frantic. She knew that Estherke would not pass the selection for transfer from one *Lager* to another. With the help of her older sister, whom Estherke called Grandma, and men from the nearby *Lager*, Ida worked out a plan.

When the evacuation materialized, Ida wrapped Estherke in a blanket and threw her over the electrified fence into the waiting arms of a male inmate in the adjacent men's camp, BIId. Later that afternoon, a package flew once more over the fence into Ida's waiting arms. She got back her Estherke. Ida was now in BIIe, *Zigeunerlager* (gypsy camp).

During that selection, however, Ida was separated from her sister, who, with a group of other girls, was taken away to an unknown destination. Again rumors spread in the camp that the eastern front was nearing and the entire camp was going to be evacuated. Ida began to plan once more how to save her little Estherke. On January 18, 1945, the camp was evacuated. Ida put Estherke into a knapsack that she had "organized" for this purpose. With Estherke on her back, she set out with the others on the dreadful death march.[3]

The winds blew, the frost bit, the snow fell, and her stomach growled from hunger, but Ida marched on. At night she shared with Estherke whatever stale bread she had managed to conceal. She comforted the little girl, warmed her tiny frozen hands, and promised her that one day they would be free. After many days of marching and travel in open cattle cars, a few of the original group that began the death march on January 18, 1945, reached Bergen Belsen. Ida and her beloved Estherke were among them.

In Bergen Belsen, Ida found conditions even more difficult than in Auschwitz. With the evacuation of camps in the east, thousands of evacuated inmates were driven into Bergen Belsen. Absorbing all the evacuees was far beyond the camp's capacity. Water was scarce; a few crumbs of stale bread and inadequate toilet facilities made life almost impossible. Filth, lice, starvation, and epidemics took over. Ida managed to find a job, for which she was given a piece of bread and a warm drink that they insisted on calling coffee. One day, as Ida was cleaning the latrines, she heard a familiar voice calling her name. She looked around, but saw no one she knew. A face covered with blotches and lice, a body covered with rags, was coming closer to her while calling her name. Ida stepped backward. "Ida, don't you recognize your own sister?"

Estherke was overjoyed. "Grandma" was back, the three of them were once more together, just like in Auschwitz. While Ida was out searching for food, Estherke and "Grandma" stayed together. But their happiness did not last long. "Grandma" succumbed to typhus. Estherke did not leave her side and tried to ease her suffering. One day, while Ida was trying to get some coffee for her dying sister, the squad that came daily to collect the dead took the sister away with the other corpses. Estherke protested, insisting that her "grandma" was still alive. She pleaded, but to no avail. Estherke followed the squad, and when "Grandma" was dumped on the big pile of corpses, Estherke managed to pull her out from under the corpses and did what she could to warm her body with her own.

When Ida returned with the coffee and discovered that Estherke and her sister had been taken away with the dead, she felt her knees giving way as if she would collapse, but her weakness did not last long. Ida was not one to give in to despair. She took the coffee and began to search for Estherke and her sister, and there, near a pile of corpses, she found them. Ida wasted no time. She gave the coffee to Estherke to guard. After mouth-to-mouth resuscitation, massage, and a few drops of coffee on her sister's parched lips, Ida revived her. Thousands were dying, but with Ida's and Estherke's love, "Grandma" recovered. Their joy knew no limit.

On April 15, 1945, Bergen Belsen was liberated by the British Army. The two sisters and Estherke made their way back home to Czechoslovakia, together with throngs of other refugees. They were all trying to go home, all hoping that perhaps other relatives had also survived and families could be reunited.

After finding a temporary shelter in Prague, the three set out in different directions to search for other surviving members of their families. Estherke traveled to Bratislava hoping that her father, mother, or some of her eight brothers and sisters had survived. Ida and her sister left with similar hopes for their family. The parting was painful for Ida. She and Estherke had not been separated since that fateful night in Auschwitz. The three agreed upon a time and place to meet no matter what the outcome of their search might be.

The two agreed-upon weeks passed. Ida and her sister returned to Prague as planned. But Estherke failed to return. They waited a few more days, but still there was no trace of her. Then Ida launched an intensive search. She traveled to Bratislava, but no one recalled seeing a child who matched Estherke's description. Ida then contacted all children's homes and refugee centers, but to no avail. Estherke had vanished without leaving behind a single trace or clue. After months of search, Ida gave up. She met and married a young man, a survivor like herself. Her sister was fortunate too, for her husband had managed to survive the camps and one day they ran into each other on a street in Prague.

The sisters parted once more. Ida and her husband went to America. Her sister, her husband, and their newly born baby became part of the illegal immigration to Israel. They outmaneuvered the British blockade and finally reached the shores of Palestine.

In the early 1950s, Ida traveled to the young state of Israel to visit her sister. One very hot day, Ida fainted on the street. Two young Israeli soldiers who happened to pass by picked her up from the pavement and took her in their jeep to the nearest hospital. The following day, the soldiers came in to see how their patient was doing. A friendship developed between Ida and the two soldiers, who continued to visit her daily. As Ida was about to be discharged from the hospital, she asked the two young men how she could repay their kindness. The taller of the two, Yossi, told Ida that he was getting married in a few days. The biggest reward would be if she would come to his wedding.

"But I don't know anyone!" she protested. "You know me, and I am a pretty important man at this wedding," Yossi said with his good-natured smile.

It was a beautiful dusk in Jerusalem. A gentle summer breeze scented with Jerusalem pine provided relief from the summer heat. The sun, like a huge orange, hung low above the Judean hills, which glowed in a beautiful pink-gray light. Ida was standing among the other guests hoping to find a familiar face. "The bride is coming," someone near her said. Ida made her way to the front so she could see the bride whom Yossi had described so lovingly. The door opened, the bride walked in. It was none other than her own long-lost Estherke! Under the bright stars shining above the eternal city and the Judean hills, Ida stepped forward and led her beloved Estherke to the bridal canopy.

There was a strange presence in the air. Ida was sure that her father was present at this very holy moment in Jerusalem. She could even see the smile on his face and hear his gentle voice: "Whoever saves a single soul, it is as if he saves an entire universe."[4]

*Based on interview by Marcy Miller with Mrs. Ida Hoenig, April 16, 1976.*

# In the Image of God

IT WAS NEW YEAR'S DAY, 1945. THE STREETS OF HANOVER, GERMANY, were covered with pure white snow. Windows were gleaming with holiday decorations, church bells were tolling, families and soldiers, bundled up in warm winter coats, were walking in the streets.

"We appeared into those festive streets like evil spirits from another world," recalled Margaret, some thirty years later. "A long gray column of starved young women with shaven heads, dressed in shabby gray summer dresses, and on our frozen, numb feet, wooden clogs. Even the Hanover snow produced a strange hollow sound under our slippery clogs covered with ice." It was bitter cold and the girls had been traveling in open cattle cars for days. Now they were marching on foot to the nearby camp of Bergen Belsen.[1] They begged for food from the people strolling on the street, for a piece of bread, a sip of water. But people just looked at them in disgust, or ignored them as if they did not exist at all. "Why don't you pray to your

God?'' a man dressed in a fur coat told the girls. ''He helped you in the past, he split the Red Sea for you and gave you manna from heaven for forty years. Ask him, he can surely spare a few crumbs of bread and a few drops of water. There are only a few of you Jews left by now. Where is your God? Why doesn't he help you?'' The remarks cut into Margaret's flesh deeper than the biting snow, frost, and cold winds. Each of his words was like a stab in her heart, for she too had been asking these questions since her arrival in Auschwitz some months ago. But to hear the questions from German lips, from a man with warm boots on his feet, was too much for Margaret. She pleaded with the girls next to her to stop begging for bread and water. She herself clenched her chattering teeth as if to assure that no plea would escape her blistered lips. She straightened her torn gray dress and walked with her head held high, taking an even greater beating from the wind. She was going to show the Germans that human dignity was not yet dead.

From a side street a group of Wehrmacht soldiers appeared. It was clear that they saw the girls as they turned in the direction of the gray marching column.

The soldiers were very young, some of them already crippled and scarred by war. They came close to the girls and wished them a Happy New Year, adding that they hoped that next year the girls would celebrate the New Year back home together with their loved ones. The fear in the girls' huge staring eyes diminished; a faint expression of gratitude appeared on their frozen faces.

A warm feeling came over Margaret. The winds seemed gentler and the hunger pangs less piercing. It was the first human gesture she had witnessed in a very long time. ''Maybe there is still some hope. If man is indeed made in the image of God, as I believed in the pre-Auschwitz days, maybe there are still some godly sparks left in men and some humanity in God,'' Margaret thought to herself as the column slowly entered the gates of Bergen Belsen.

*Based on interview by Judy Offen with Margaret Schwartz, November 29, 1976.*

# The Merit of
# a Young Priest

IT WAS JUNE 1942; THE MURDER OF JEWS IN THE CRACOW GHETTO was at its height. About 5,000 victims were deported to the Belzec death camp. Hundreds were being murdered in the ghetto itself, shot on its streets on the way to deportation. Among them were Dr. Arthur Rosenzweig, head of the Judenrat, the famous Yiddish poet Mordechai Gebirtig,[1] and the distinguished old artist Abraham Neumann.

The Hiller family realized that their days in the Cracow ghetto were numbered; they too would soon be swept away in one of the frequent Aktions. Yet there was still a glimmer of hope. They were young and skilled laborers; if they were deported to a labor camp, perhaps they would still have a chance of survival. But the fate of their little son Shachne was a different matter. Small children had become a rare sight in the ghetto; starvation, disease, and the ever-increasing selections took their constant toll. Helen and Moses Hiller began feverishly to plan the rescue of their little Shachne. After considering various possibilities they decided to contact family friends on the Aryan side in the small town of Dombrowa, childless Gentile people named Yachowitch.

Helen Hiller, with the help of the Jewish underground, made her way to Dombrowa.[2] She went to Mr. and Mrs. Joseph Yachowitch and begged them to take care of her little son. Although they could do so only at great risk to their own lives, the Christian friends agreed to take the child.

Despite the ever-increasing dangers of the ghetto, the young parents could not bring themselves to part from their only child. Only after the large Aktion of October 28, 1942, when 6,000 additional Jews were shipped to Belzec and the patients at the Jewish hospital, the residents of the old-age home, and 300 children at the orphanage were murdered on the spot, did the Hiller family decide to act.[3]

On November 15, 1942, Helen Hiller smuggled her little boy out of the ghetto. Along with her son, she gave her Christian friends two large envelopes. One envelope contained all the Hillers' precious valuables; the other, letters and a will. One of the letters was addressed to Mr. and Mrs. Yachowitch, entrusting them with little Shachne, and asking them to bring up the child as a Jew and to return him to his people in case of his parents' deaths. The Hillers thanked the Yachowitch family for their humanitarian act and promised to reward them for their goodness. The letter also included the names and addresses of relatives in Montreal and Washington, D.C.

The second letter was addressed to Shachne himself, telling him how much his parents loved him, that it was this love that had prompted them to leave him alone with strangers, good and noble people. They told him of his Jewishness and how they hoped that he would grow up to be a man proud of his Jewish heritage.

The third letter contained a will written by Helen's mother, Mrs. Reizel Wurtzel. It was addressed to her sister-in-law Jenny Berger in Washington. She wrote to her of the horrible conditions in the ghetto, the deportations, the death of family members, and of the impending doom. She wrote: "Our grandson, by the name of Shachne Hiller, born on the 18th day of Av, August 22, 1940, was given to good people. I beg you, if none of us will return, take the child to you; bring him up righteously. Reward the good people for their efforts and may God grant life to the parents of the child. Regards and kisses, your sister, Reizel Wurtzel."[4]

As Helen was handing the letters to Mrs. Yachowitch, she once more stated her instructions: "If I or my husband do not return when this madness is over, please mail this letter to America to our relatives. They will surely respond and take the child. Regardless of the fates of my husband or myself, I want my son to grow up as a Jew." The two women embraced and Mrs. Yachowitch promised that she would do her best. The young mother hurriedly kissed her little child and left, fearing that her emotions would betray her and she would not be able to leave her little son behind in this strange house, but, instead, would take him back with her to the ghetto.

It was a beautiful autumn day. The Vistula's waters reflected the foliage of a Polish autumn. The Wavel, the ancient castle of the Polish kings, looked as majestic as ever. Mothers strolled with their children and she, the young Jewish mother, was trying to hold back her tears. She slowed her hasty, nervous steps so as not to betray herself and changed her hurried pace to a leisurely stroll, as if she too were out to enjoy the sights of ancient Cracow. To thwart all suspicion, Helen displayed a huge cross hanging around her neck and stepped in for a moment to the Holy Virgin Church in the Old Square.

Smuggling little Shachne out from the ghetto to the Aryan side was indeed timely. In March 1943, the Cracow ghetto was liquidated. People in the work camp adjacent to the ghetto were transferred to nearby Plaszow and to the more distant Auschwitz. Anyone found hiding was shot on the spot. Cracow, the first Jewish settlement on Polish soil, dating back to the thirteenth century, was Judenrein!

Mr. and Mrs. Joseph Yachowitch constantly inquired about the boy's young parents. Eventually they learned that the Hillers had shared the fate of most of Cracow's Jews. Both of them were consumed by the flames of the Holocaust.

The Yachowitches, too, faced many perilous days. They moved to a new home in a different town. From time to time, they had to hide in barns and haystacks. When little Shachne suffered from one of his crying spells, calling for his mother and father, they feared that unfriendly, suspicious neighbors would betray them to the Gestapo. But time is the greatest healer. Little Shachne stopped crying. Mrs. Yachowitch became very attached to the child and loved him like her own. She took great pride in her "son" and loved him dearly. His big, bright, wise eyes were always alert and inquiring. She and little Shachne never missed a Sunday service and he soon knew by heart all the church hymns. A devout Catholic herself, Mrs. Yachowitch decided to baptize the child and, indeed, make him into a full-fledged Catholic.

She went to see a young, newly ordained parish priest who had a reputation for being wise and trustworthy. Mrs. Yachowitch revealed to him her secret about the true identity of the little boy who was entrusted to her and her husband, Joseph, and told him of her wish to have him baptized so that he might become a true Christian and a devout Catholic like herself. The young priest listened intently to the woman's story. When she finished her tale, he asked, "And what was the parents' wish when they entrusted their only child to you and your husband?" Mrs. Yachowitch told the priest about the letters and the mother's last request that the child be told of his Jewish origins and returned to his people in the event of the parents' death.

The young priest explained to Mrs. Yachowitch that it would be unfair to baptize the child while there was still hope that the relatives of the child might take him. He did not perform the ceremony.[5] This was in 1946.

Some time later, Mr. Yachowitch mailed the letters to the United States and Canada. Both Jenny Berger, from Washington, D.C., and Mr. and Mrs. H. Aron from Montreal responded, stating their readiness to bring the child to the U.S.A. and Canada immediately. But then a legal battle began on both sides of the Atlantic that was to last for four years! Polish law forbade Polish orphan children to leave the country. The immigration laws of the United States and Canada were strict, and no visa was issued to little Shachne. Finally, in 1949, the Canadian Jewish Congress obtained permission from the Canadian Government to bring 1,210 orphans to the country. It was arranged for Shachne to be included in this group, the only one in the group to come directly from Poland. Meantime a court action was instituted in Cracow, and Shachne was awarded, by a judge in Poland, to the representatives of the Canadian American relatives.

In June 1949, Shachne Hiller boarded the Polish liner *MS Batory*. The parting from Mrs. Yachowitch was a painful one. Both cried, but Mrs. Yachowitch comforted little Shachne that it was the will of his real mother that one day he should be returned to his own people.

On July 3, 1949, the *Batory* arrived at Pier 88 at the foot of West

48th Street in New York City. Aboard was little Shachne, first-class
passenger of cabin No. 228. He was met by his relatives, Mrs. Berger
and Mrs. Aron.[6] For the next year, Shachne lived in Montreal.[7] On
December 19, 1950, after two years of lobbying by Jenny Berger,
President Harry S. Truman signed a bill into law making Shachne
Hiller a ward of the Berger family. When Shachne arrived at the
Bergers' home on Friday, February 9, 1951, there was a front-page
story in the *Washington Post*.[8]

It was more than eight years since Shachne's maternal grandmother Reizel Wurtzel, in the ghetto of Cracow, had written the letter to her sister-in-law (his great aunt) Jenny Berger, asking her to
take her little grandson to her home and heart. Her will and testa-
ment were finally carried out.

Years passed. Young Shachne was educated in American universi-
ties and grew up to be a successful man, vice-president of a company,
as well as an observant Jew. The bond between him and Mrs.
Yachowitch was a lasting one. They corresponded, and both Shachne
and his great aunt Jenny Berger continually sent her parcels and
money, and tried as much as possible to comfort her in her old age.
He preferred not to discuss the Holocaust with his wife, twin sons,
family, or friends. Yet all of them knew about the wonderful Mr. and
Mrs. Joseph Yachowitch who saved the life of a Jewish child and
made sure to return him to his people.

In October 1978, Shachne, now Stanley, received a letter from
Mrs. Yachowitch. In it she revealed to him, for the first time, her in-
clination to baptize him and raise him as a Catholic. She also went on
to describe, at length, her meeting with the young parish priest on
that fateful day. Indeed, that young parish priest was none other than
the man who became Cardinal Karol Wojtyla of Cracow, and, on October 16, 1978, was elected by the College of Cardinals as
Pope—Pope John Paul II!

When the Grand Rabbi of Bluzhov, Rabbi Israel Spira, heard the
above story, he said, "God has mysterious, wonderful ways unknown to men. Perhaps it was the merit of saving a single Jewish soul

that brought about his election as Pope. It is a story that must be told.''

*Based upon several of my conversations with Shachne Hiller (Stanley Berger), his family, and his mother-in-law, Mrs. Anne Wolozin. September 1977–October 1, 1981.*

# THREE

## The Spirit
## Alone

There is nothing more wholesome in the entire world than a broken Jewish heart.

*Rabbi Menachem Mendl of Kotsk*

# Circumcision

"I WILL TELL YOU ANOTHER STORY," SAID RABBI ISRAEL SPIRA TO his student Baruch Baer Singer, "a story that took place in the Janowska Road Camp. Janowska was one of those camps about which, if one is to recall the events that took place during one year, one can fill the pages with tales of heroism, suffering, and death. Not one book, but ten volumes. And even then, it would just be a drop in the ocean.

"Many have asked me to publish the stories of Janowska in a book. I told them I am not writing new books. It would be sufficient if we read and studied the existing books. But this particular story is a duty to record. It is a mitzvah to tell it, for it is a tale about the devotion and sacrifice of a daughter of Israel.

"One morning in Janowska, I was standing and sawing wood with another katzetnik (camp inmate). To humiliate us as much as possible, I was given as a partner a very short man. As you see, thank God, I am not among the short ones. It made the wood sawing both a difficult task and a laughable sight. With each pull of the saw my partner would stretch out and stand on the tips of his toes, and I would bend down till my aching, swollen feet were bleeding. And the Germans stood by and watched our misery and suffering with delight.

"One morning, on Hoshana Rabbah, as we were sawing wood, the wind carried in our direction piercing, tormented cries such as I had never heard before, even in the Janowska hell. The desperate clamor was coming closer and closer as if the weeping was filling up the entire universe and drowning it with painful tears.

" 'It is a children's Aktion, little angels from the entire vicinity of Drohobycz, Borislov, Lvov, Stryj, Stanislav, and others were brought here to meet their maker,' " said a katzetnik who passed by, pushing a wheelbarrow, without even glancing in our direction. I thought the cries would shake the world's foundation. We continued sawing the wood as our eyes became heavier and heavier with tears.

151

"Suddenly, just next to us, I heard the voice of a woman. 'Jews, have mercy upon me and give me a knife.' In front of us was standing a woman, pale as a sheet. Only her eyes were burning with a strange fire. I thought that she wanted to commit suicide. I looked around, and since I saw no Germans in sight, I said to her, 'Why are you in such a rush to get to the World of Truth? We will get there sooner or later. What difference can one day make?'

" 'Dog, what did you say to the woman?' A tall young German who appeared from nowhere demanded an answer, while swinging his rubber truncheon above my head. 'The woman asked for a knife. I explained to her that we Jews are not permitted to take our lives. For our lives are entrusted in the hands of God.' I hastily added, 'And I hope that you, too, will spare our lives.' The German did not respond to my words. He turned to the woman and demanded an explanation from her. She answered curtly, 'I asked for a knife.'

"As she was talking, she kept examining the German with her feverish eyes. Suddenly her eyes stopped wandering. Her gaze was fixed on the top pocket of the German's uniform. The shape of a knife was clearly visible through the pocket. 'Give me that pocket knife!' she ordered the German in a commanding voice. The German, taken by surprise, handed the knife to the woman.

"She bent down and picked up something. Only then did I notice a bundle of rags on the ground near the sawdust. She unwrapped the bundle. Amidst the rags on a snow-white pillow was a newborn babe, asleep. With a steady hand she opened the pocket knife and circumcised the baby. In a clear, intense voice she recited the blessing of the circumcision. 'Blessed art Thou, O Lord our God, King of the Universe, who has sanctified us by thy commandments and hast commanded us to perform the circumcision.'

"She straightened her back, looked up to the heavens, and said, 'God of the Universe, you have given me a healthy child. I am returning to you a wholesome, kosher Jew.' She walked over to the German, gave him back his blood-stained knife, and handed him her baby on his snow-white pillow.

"Amidst a veil of tears, I said to myself then that this mother's circumcision will probably shake the foundations of heaven and earth. Next to Abraham on Mount Moriah,[1] where can you find a greater act of faith than this Jewish mother's?"

The rabbi looked at his student with tear-filled eyes and said, "Since liberation, each time I am honored at a circumcision to be a Sandak (godfather), it is my custom to tell this particular story."

*Based on a conversation of the Grand Rabbi of Bluzhov, Rabbi Israel Spira, with Baruch Singer, January 3, 1975. I heard it at the rabbi's house.*

# Slain with Hunger

TOGETHER WITH RABBI ISRAEL SPIRA IN JANOWSKA, THERE WERE twin brothers. The rabbi felt especially close to the two boys. They had been born after thirteen years of a childless marriage. Their circumcision was celebrated joyfully by the entire shtetl of Worshtein and its vicinity. The boys' father was a devout Polish Hasid. It was his custom to travel to Israel Spira's father, Rabbi Joshua Spira of Ribatich, on every holiday. The Hasid was sure that it was the merit of the rabbi's blessing that gave him his twin sons. After the death of Rabbi Joshua Spira of Ribatich, the Hasid began to travel to the son, Rabbi Israel Spira, who was later to become known as the Rabbi of Bluzhov.

When World War II engulfed European Jewry in flames of destruction, the family was separated. The twins, then about eleven years old, found themselves in Janowska, along with Rabbi Israel Spira. The three helped each other whenever it was possible. The rabbi constantly assured the guards and the Askaris that the boys were older than they appeared to be. And the twins kept the secret that the tall, shaven inmate with the comforting voice was a Hasidic rabbi. In Janowska, being a child or a Jewish leader was a crime punishable by immediate death.

One day all the inmates were taken out to work. Three people were left behind to sweep up the barracks: one of the twins, Rabbi Israel Spira, and a third Jew. The German guard ordered the young boy to bring him water. In no time, the boy returned with the water. The German took out his revolver and shot the child in the leg. The boy fell, the water spilled. "Get up, dirty Jew!" shouted the German. The boy managed to stand up. He was shot in the other leg. The boy collapsed and fell once more. "Up, up, dirty Jew!" The boy made an attempt to get up, but to no avail. The German walked over and emptied his revolver into the child's body. "Take him away!" the guard now roared at the rabbi. Rabbi Spira took the boy into his arms and carried him to the pile of bodies while his tears washed the lifeless boy's face.[1]

How will he tell the other twin about his brother's death? Rabbi Spira began to ponder. How will he break the terrible news to one of two souls that were so close to each other? "Tell him that his twin brother is very sick," the other Jew advised the Rabbi.

Evening came. The inmates returned to camp. "Chaim'l, your brother is very sick, his life is in danger. It is quite possible that he is no longer alive," said the Rabbi of Bluzhov, trying to avoid the boy's eyes. The brother began to cry: "Woe unto me! What am I going to do now?" The rabbi tried to comfort the boy, but he refused to be comforted. "Today was his turn to watch over the bread. I left all the bread with him, now I don't have a single piece of bread left," lamented Chaim'l. The rabbi was shocked but continued his ruse, saying that the other twin had sent Chaim'l's share. With a trembling hand, he took from under his jacket a small piece of bread which was his ration for the day and gave it to the boy.[2] Chaim'l glanced at the stale piece of bread and said, "It's missing a few grams. The piece I left with him was a much larger one." "I was hungry and ate some of it. Tomorrow I will give you the rest of the bread," replied the Rabbi of Bluzhov.

When Rabbi Israel Spira finished telling the story, he said, "Only on that day in Janowska did I understand a verse in the Scriptures: 'They that are slain with the sword are better than they that are slain with hunger.' "[3]

*Based on a conversation of the Grand Rabbi of Bluzhov, Rabbi Israel Spira, with Baruch Singer, January 3, 1975.*

# Even the Transgressors in Israel

"THIS PARTICULAR STORY IS ONE OF THOSE STORIES THAT DE-serves to be published in a book," said the Rabbi of Bluzhov to his Hasidim as he was telling about his experiences during the concentration-camp era.

In the Janowska Road Camp, there was a brigadier (a foreman of a brigade) from Lvov by the name of Schneeweiss, one of those people one stays away from if he values his life. He had known Rabbi Israel Spira in Lemberg (Lvov), but was not aware that the latter was an inmate at the Janowska Road Camp. Only a handful of Hasidim who were close to the rabbi knew the rabbi's identity and they kept it a secret.

The season of the Jewish holidays was approaching.[1] As the date of Yom Kippur was nearing, the fears in camp mounted. Everyone knew that the Germans especially liked to use Jewish holidays as days for inflicting terror and death. In Janowska, a handful of old-timers remembered large selections on Simhat Torah and Purim.

It was the eve of Yom Kippur. The tensions and the fears were at their height. A few Hasidim, among them Mendel Freifeld and others, came to the Rabbi of Bluzhov and asked him to approach Schneeweiss and request that on Yom Kippur his group not be assigned to any of the thirty-nine main categories of work, so that their transgression of the law by working on Yom Kippur would not be a major one.[2] The rabbi was very moved by the request of his Hasidim and despite his fears, for he would have to disclose his identity, went to Schneeweiss. He knew quite well that Schneeweiss did not have much respect for Jewish tradition. Even prior to the outbreak of World War II, he had publicly violated the Jewish holidays and transgressed against Jewish law. Here in Janowska, he was a cruel man who knew no mercy.

With a heavy heart, the rabbi went before Schneeweiss. "You probably remember me. I am the Rabbi of Pruchnik, Rabbi Israel Spira." Schneeweiss did not respond. "You are a Jew like myself," the rabbi continued. "Tonight is Kol Nidrei night. There is a small group of young Jews who do not want to transgress any of the thirty-nine main categories of work. It means everything to them. It is the essence of their existence. Can you do something about it? Can you help?"

The rabbi noticed that a hidden shiver went through Schneeweiss as he listened to the rabbi's strange request. The rabbi took Schneeweiss's hand and said, "I promise you, as long as you live, it will be a good life. I beg you to do it for us so that we may still find some dignity in our humiliating existence."

The stern face of Schneeweiss changed. For the first time since his arrival at Janowska, there was a human spark in it.

"Tonight I can't do a thing." said Schneeweiss, the first words he had uttered since the rabbi had come to him. "I have no jurisdiction over the night brigade. But tomorrow, on Yom Kippur, I will do for you whatever I can." The rabbi shook Schneeweiss's hand in gratitude and left.

That night they were taken to work near the Lvov cemetery. To this very day, the rabbi has scars from the beatings of that night. They returned to their barracks at one o'clock in the morning exhausted, beaten, with blood flowing from fresh wounds. The rabbi was trying to make his way to bed, one level of a five-tiered bunk bed made of a few wooden planks covered with straw. Vivid images from the past, of Yom Kippur at home with his family and Hasidim, passed before his tear-filled eyes that wretched night at Janowska.

Suddenly the door opened and into the barracks came a young Hasid named Ben-Zion. "Rabbi, we must recite Kol Nidrei."

"Who can say Kol Nidrei now?" the rabbi replied. "The people can't even stand on their feet."

"Rabbi, I used to pray in your shtibl. Do you remember the tune?" In the darkness of the barracks, among tens of hungry, beaten, exhausted Jews, a melody was heard, the soothing, comforting melody of Yom Kippur, as Ben-Zion chanted a prayer:

And pardon shall be granted to the whole congregation of Israel and to the stranger who sojourneth among them. . . .

"Rabbi, the heart wants to hear a prayer. We must say Kol Nidrei. . . ." As Ben-Zion was talking to the rabbi, about twenty men gathered around them. How could he refuse? He took out his prayer shawl, which he kept well hidden underneath the straw on his bunk bed, and was about to begin to chant the Kol Nidrei.

No one knew how, but the news spread fast: In barracks number 12 they were chanting the Kol Nidrei. In the dark shadows of the Janowska barracks one could see dark shapes against the barracks walls as they made their way to barracks number 12.

They recited with the rabbi whatever they could recall from memory. When they reached the prayer "Hear our voice, O Lord our God; have pity and compassion . . ." the voices were drowned in tears.[3]

In the morning, the rabbi and a small group of young Hasidim were summoned to Schneeweiss's cottage. "I heard that you prayed last night. I don't believe in prayers," Schneeweiss told them. "On principle, I even oppose them. But I admire your courage. For you all know well that the penalty for prayer in Janowska is death." With that, he motioned them to follow him.

He took them to the S.S. quarters in the camp, to a large wooden house. "You fellows will shine the floor without any polish or wax.

And you, rabbi, will clean the windows with dry rags so that you will not transgress any of the thirty-nine major categories of work." He left the room abruptly without saying another word.

The rabbi was standing on a ladder with rags in his hand, cleaning the huge windows while chanting prayers, and his companions were on the floor polishing the wood and praying with him.

> All of them are beloved, pure and mighty, and all of them in dread and awe do the will of their Master; and all of them open their mouths in holiness and purity, with song and psalm, while they glorify and ascribe sovereignty to the name of the Divine King.[4]

"The floor was wet with our tears. You can imagine the prayers of that Yom Kippur," said the rabbi to the Hasidim who were listening to his tale while he was wiping away a tear.

At about twelve o'clock noon, the door opened wide and into the room stormed two angels of death, S.S. men in their black uniforms, may their names be obliterated. They were followed by a food cart filled to capacity. "Noontime, time to eat bread, soup, and meat," announced one of the two S.S. men. The room was filled with an aroma of freshly cooked food, such food as they had not seen since the German occupation: white bread, steaming hot vegetable soup, and huge portions of meat.

The tall S.S. man commanded in a high-pitched voice, "You must eat immediately, otherwise you will be shot on the spot!" None of them moved. The rabbi remained on the ladder, the Hasidim on the floor. The German repeated the orders. The rabbi and the Hasidim remained glued to their places. The S.S. men called in Schneeweiss. "Schneeweiss, if the dirty dogs refuse to eat, I will kill you along with them." Schneeweiss pulled himself to attention, looked the German directly in the eyes, and said in a very quiet tone, "We Jews do not eat today. Today is Yom Kippur, our most holy day, the Day of Atonement."

"You don't understand, Jewish dog," roared the taller of the two.

"I command you in the name of the Führer and the Third Reich, *fress!*"[5]

Schneeweiss, composed, his head high, repeated the same answer. "We Jews obey the law of our tradition. Today is Yom Kippur, a day of fasting."

The German took out his revolver from its holster and pointed it at Schneeweiss's temple. Schneeweiss remained calm. He stood still, at attention, his head high. A shot pierced the room. Schneeweiss fell. On the freshly polished floor, a puddle of blood was growing bigger and bigger.

The rabbi and the Hasidim stood as if frozen in their places. They could not believe what their eyes had just witnessed. Schneeweiss, the man who in the past had publicly transgressed against the Jewish tradition, had sanctified God's name publicly and died a martyr's death for the sake of Jewish honor.

"Only then, on that Yom Kippur day in Janowska," said the rabbi to his Hasidim, "did I understand the meaning of the statement in the Talmud: 'Even the transgressors in Israel are as full of good deeds as a pomegranate is filled with seeds.' "[6]

*Based on a conversation of the Grand Rabbi of Bluzhov, Rabbi Israel Spira, with Baruch Singer, January 3, 1975. I heard it at the rabbi's house.*

# The Last Request

AS THE GERMAN EINSATZGRUPPEN WERE ABOUT TO EXECUTE THE Jewish population in a small Ukrainian town, a Hasidic Jew walked over to the young German officer in charge and told him that it was customary in civilized countries to grant a last request to those condemned to death. The young German assured the Jew that he would observe that civilized tradition and asked the Jew what his last wish was.

"A short prayer," replied the Jew.

"Granted!" snapped the German.

The Jew placed his hand on his bare head to cover it and recited the following blessing, first in its original Hebrew, then in its German translation:

Blessed art thou, O Lord our God
King of the Universe, who hath not made me heathen.

Upon completion of the blessing, he looked directly into the eyes of the German and with his head held high, walked to the edge of the pit and said: "I have finished. You may begin." The young German's bullet struck him in the back of the head at the edge of the huge grave filled with bodies.

*I heard it from a speaker who was addressing a Hasidic group in April, 1978.*

# The Ritual Bath

AN AKTION TOOK PLACE IN THE BOCHNIA GHETTO. AMONG THE people caught that day was an especially large number of young women. The women knew full well what would happen to them. They discussed something among themselves and selected a spokeswoman. She was a very attractive young woman in her early twenties. She walked over to the German officer in charge of the Aktion and said: "We know the inevitable. You will murder us as you murdered the other innocent Jews before us. We demand that you grant us our last wish." "Granted," snapped the German as his hand lovingly caressed his pistol. "And what is it, may I ask?" he said in a derisive tone. "We demand that the ritual bath house, closed since your occupation of our town, be reopened, heated, and cleaned, and that we be permitted to take our ritual bath of purification,'' said the young woman.

For more than half a day the women cleaned the ritual bath house and filled it with water. Then they cleaned themselves and immersed themselves in water as prescribed in the Laws of Purification.

As they were led off to be shot, the German officer asked for the young lady who had approached him earlier in the day. When she stood before him, he said: "You are a filthy race, the source of all disease and vermin in Europe. Suddenly, before your death, you wish to be clean. What spell did you cast in that ritual bath house of yours?'' "Cleanliness and purity of body and mind are part of our tradition and way of life. God has brought our pure souls into this world in the pure homes of our parents, and we wish to return in purity to our Father in Heaven.''

The German officer took out his pistol from his holster and at close range shot the woman between the eyes. Most of the other women were also killed that day.

*Based on my conversation with Rebbetzin Bronia Spira, June 1976.*

# Death
# of a Beloved Son

ON JULY 8, 1941, GERMAN SOLDIERS AND A UKRAINIAN MOB SET ablaze the famed synagogue of Przemysl, Galicia. Any Jew caught on the streets was tossed alive into the burning synagogue. More than forty Jews sanctified God's name in the synagogue's flames and died a martyr's death.

Since arriving in Przemysl some months before, it had become the custom of the Rabbi of Belz, Rabbi Aaron Rokeach, to pray daily in that synagogue. When the rabbi's eldest son, Moshele, saw the blazing synagogue, he thought that his father, the Zaddik of Belz, was trapped inside the building. Instantly he ran outside and raced in the direction of the synagogue, calling to his father and reassuring him that he was on the way to save him. "Father, Father, I am coming to save you, Father, I am on my way. Where are you?"

Near the synagogue he was caught by Ukrainians and thrown into the leaping flames.

One of the rabbi's close Hasidim came to the father to bring him the tragic news. When the Hasid entered the rabbi's room and told him what had happened, the rabbi lifted his sorrowful eyes to heaven and said, "God is merciful; I, too, offered a sacrifice."

That is all the Zaddik of Belz said, never again mentioning the death of his beloved son.

Despite the fact that the date of his son's death (July 8, the thirteenth day of Tamuz) was known, the rabbi's close associates tell that he never observed the yahrzeit, the anniversary of his son's death, nor did he ever publicly mourn the death of thirty-three members of his immediate family, all consumed by the flames of the Holocaust.[1]

The Zaddik of Belz was known for his boundless love and compassion for the Jewish people. "How can one mourn the death of an individual," he said, "even a beloved son, when one is overwhelmed by the collective pain of a nation mourning its six million dead!"

*I recorded this story from Belzer Hasidim, January 1979.*

# Satan's Altar

WHEN THE JEWS OF BOCHNIA LEARNED THE WELL-KEPT SECRET that the world-famous Hasidic master the Rabbi of Belz, Rabbi Aaron Rokeach, and his brother the Rabbi of Bielgory, Rabbi Mordechai, were living in their midst, a ray of hope appeared in the ghetto. Day and night, despite tight security, people flocked to the tiny overcrowded cubicle where the rebbe and his brother had found a temporary shelter. The ghetto residents came to seek the rabbi's advice and blessing.

One day, two people came to the rabbi. It was apparent that the wretched conditions in the ghetto had taken their toll of the two: they were emaciated skeletons, more bone than flesh, with hollow cheeks and patched clothes. One of the two was covered with blotches from bites and malnutrition. Yet it was the healthier one who walked over to the rebbe and in a trembling voice asked for a blessing that would restore him to good health and a promise that he would survive this deluge of blood and once more be a free man, able to worship his God.

His companion, who looked the embodiment of misery and poor health, did not approach the rebbe for a blessing. The Rabbi of Bielgory, who during the war never left his illustrious brother's side, was standing nearby. He was puzzled by the man's behavior and said, "Can a Jew explain to me why he does not want relief from his misery? Why does he not ask for a blessing?"

Sad eyes filled with pain and suffering looked at the Rabbi of Bilgoraj, and the man spoke: "We Jews are commanded that when we offer a sacrifice on God's altar, the burnt offering must be a whole one, without any blemish or defect.[1] But now, when we are being sacrificed on Satan's altar, the command for a burnt offering without a defect is no longer binding. The debased flames of the crematoria will not reject me because of sores, ill health, and a broken Jewish heart."

*I heard it from a former resident of the Bochnia ghetto, February 19, 1980.*

# The Grandson
# of the Arugat Ha-Bosem

DAVID WAS A YOUNG HUNGARIAN JEW WHO SHARED THE FATE OF his brethren. He, too, was deported to the kingdom of death camps. In the winter of 1945 he was slaving for the German war industry in Gusen, Austria. An epidemic of typhus broke out there and David was one of its victims. For some time his friends were able to shield him from the searching eyes of the Kapo and the S.S. men and save him from the certain doom awaiting the sick and dying. Every morning they dragged him out from the barracks to the Appell, and propped him up against a board, its base anchored into the ground and its top concealed under David's striped jacket, thus creating the impression that David was well and standing on his own two feet. At work his friends placed him near his machine and worked alternately on their own machines and on David's, thereby completing his daily quota in addition to theirs. When the German overseer passed by, David moved his hands to give the impression that he was working at full speed.

But David's body could not take the strain; his fingers became numb and his feet could not move. One morning, as his friends were about to drag him to work, they discovered that his body was cold. He did not respond to any of their attempts to revive him. They begged forgiveness for being unable to save his life, though they had tried to the best of their abilities. They walked out to the Zeilappell without David, and from there they marched to their daily jobs at the ammunition factory.

At night, when they returned to their barracks, David's body was gone. It had been taken away with all the other corpses and placed in the death shack where the bodies were collected for disposal.

That night David's closest friend, who shared the top of the three-tiered bunk bed with him and others, had a dream. In his dream he saw a man with a long beard. The man told him, "Go to the death chamber and wish David a full and speedy recovery." The friend woke up. Although the dream made a strong impression upon him, he did not consider it anything more than a dream and he fell asleep again. Once more he dreamed the identical dream. He woke immediately, as before, but this time he was very frightened.

The dream was in fact a command to go to the death shack which was located at the other side of the camp. To go there at this hour meant his own death, for to leave the barracks at night was a violation that carried the death penalty. The fear for his own life was stronger than the dream and David's friend decided not to leave for fear of being shot by the German guards. Once more he fell asleep.

He dreamed again. This time the old man with the flowing beard said, "I am the Arugat Ha-Bosem, David's grandfather.[1] Go and tell David that I say that he will have a speedy and complete recovery. To you no evil will happen and your merit will be very great."

This time the friend jumped out of bed in great fear and without thinking ran in the direction of the death shack. Miraculously, there were no German guards around and no one noticed him.

The death shack was filled with corpses stacked together like logs of dry wood. He located his friend David's corpse and placed it on the floor, stood next to it, and said as he had been commanded in his dream: "Your grandfather, the Arugat Ha-Bosem, lets you know that you, David, will have a complete and speedy recovery." Suddenly David lifted his hand, grabbed the hand of his friend, and said: "Repeat what you just said."

"Your grandfather, the Arugat Ha-Bosem, lets you know that you will have a speedy and complete recovery!" The friend wanted to run away from the death shack, but David did not let him. His frozen fingers were intertwined with his friend's and he would not let go.

"Tell me once more!" David commanded his frightened friend. The friend repeated the same sentence about twenty times. Finally David eased his grip and released his friend's hand. Frightened to death, the friend ran back to his barracks with all his strength.

In the morning the German in charge of the death shack arrived.

David, shivering with cold, was sitting up amidst the corpses. A spark of humanity flickered in the Nazi's heart. He took David to the camp's hospital.

David recovered fully and was liberated by the American Army in the spring of 1945. Today he is a pious Hasidic Jew who lives with his family in Williamsburg, Brooklyn, a few doors away from his friend's home.[2]

*I heard it from a Zeilemer Hasid, April 15, 1978.*

# "He Hath Delivered Me Out of All Trouble"

GEZA WAS A PIOUS HASIDIC JEW, THE PROPRIETOR OF A GROCERY store. He lived with his wife and son in the small Hungarian town of Adevande near the metropolis of Miskolc. Suddenly, their peaceful life was disrupted and Geza was taken into a Hungarian labor battalion.

Geza found himself at the center of the destruction of Byelorussian and Ukrainian Jewry by the Einsatzgruppen and their local collaborators.[1] In Zhitomir his battalion saw thousands upon thousands of murdered Jews dressed in their Sabbath finery. In the destroyed synagogue, which they were commanded to clean up, they found desecrated Torah scrolls and an open Megillah (Scroll of Esther) telling how the Jews in ancient Persia were delivered from the hands of their enemies. In Brest-Litovsk, all the Jews were dead and buried. Only two synagogues remained standing, with broken windows and doors like gaping wounds. Near Kiev the battalion felled trees and built foxholes for the German Army. Every day they marched about forty kilometers. In Skanowitz, they camped and were permitted to pray on Rosh Hashana and Yom Kippur. However, the Hungarian officer in charge permitted prayer only for those individuals who had prayed daily prior to the High Holidays.

An especially cruel man, aptly named Stinko, this officer was ever eager to find new punishments for his laborers. Those who ate kosher food held on to their meager rations. Stinko soon discovered this and ordered them to be beaten severely for hoarding. When it was Geza's turn before the whip, something caught Stinko's attention. "What are you concealing in your breast pocket?" he roared at Geza. It was a small prayer book that Geza kept with him throughout the war.

"My most precious possession, a prayer book," he told Stinko. Somehow Stinko was moved by Geza's reply and Geza was spared the beating.

Despite the fact that they had mail privileges, since they were officially part of the Hungarian Army, Stinko did not distribute the Jewish laborers' mail. Even after he took out of their parcels whatever was of any value, such as clothing, food, and old newspapers (their only source of news), he held on to their mail. From time to time, he would flash opened letters before their eyes. He would read a few lines, in the familiar, dear handwriting, stop at the most informative spot in the letter, and then tear up the letter in front of the onlooker's eyes. The torture was unbearable. But they were helpless.

On his birthday, the battalion decided to give Stinko a present—a watch—in the hope that some of his cruelty would abate. He was very pleased with the gift and their mail was distributed. But the new harmony did not last long. As a matter of fact, life became even more difficult after the birthday present. "So, you steal watches? You are thieves! You must all hand in your watches. Those who refuse will be placed on the tracks when the evening train passes here." Six people refused. That evening they buried six mutilated bodies near Kharkov.[2]

In 1944 they were returned to Hungary and from there sent directly to German labor and concentration camps.[3] Geza, along with a large segment of his former labor battalion, found himself in Borenhauser. Now that they were no longer part of the Hungarian Army they lost even their pseudoprivileges. They were simply Jews in the Holocaust kingdom. Selections became a fact of life—or death. Conditions grew more difficult with each passing day. It was obvious that fewer and fewer of the original group would pass the next selection and witness liberation.

Geza remembers one selection in particular. Twenty-five men were very ill. Despite help and care from their fellow inmates, they were in such a deteriorated state that all hope of saving them was lost. However, a German S.S. man was very moved by the expressions of friendship and care among the men. He took the twenty-five sick inmates and marched them to a nearby hilltop, pretending they were urgently needed to dig foxholes. Meanwhile, the selection took place down below in the camp. He was able to save twenty-three of these people; two died on the way.

From Borenhauser, what was left of the battalion was marched to Mauthausen. Despite the fact that Geza and his friends had survived the horrors of war for four years, Mauthausen was beyond anything even they could imagine. That it existed in the middle of the twentieth century, near cultured Vienna, was beyond belief. About one hundred emaciated skeletons slept on a bare filthy barracks floor. A kilo of bread was thrown in once a day to be divided among ten starving men, men who had labored from dawn to darkness in German factories.

Geza's best friend, a man by the name of Mendel, with whom he had shared the odyssey of horror since the Hungarian labor battalion, could not go on any longer. His will to live just left him. "What for?" he kept asking. "We will never make it. Why prolong the agony?" Another friend kept telling him that liberation was close. "Mendel, I feel it in my blood; I hear it flow with the special sound of freedom." Mendel just stared with big empty eyes and did not respond. Geza somehow managed to get food from the Swedish Red Cross, and fed the starving Mendel.[4] But he too began to doubt that they would survive, for the Germans' commitment to murder seemed to be stronger than ever.

That night Geza dreamed about his mother. She told him, "All my sons are dead except you. All my grandchildren were murdered. You are the last living member of the family. My son, open Psalms chapter 54, verse 9.'' She disappeared as if in smoke.

Geza opened the small prayer book that he had managed to conceal ever since his labor battalion days. The verse said, ''For He hath delivered me out of all trouble; and mine eye hath gazed upon mine enemies.''

Later in the day, a group of tormented bodies arrived, remnants of a death march. Some of them were from Geza's hometown. They told him that his mother, wife, and children had perished in Auschwitz.

The Allied forces were nearing Mauthausen. Geza, with a group of other dying people, was hastily evacuated to Gunskirchen. A few days later they were liberated by the American Army.[5]

*Based on interview by Suzanne Kletzel with Geza S., November 27, 1979.*

# No Longer Husband and Wife

AFTER LIBERATION, IN THE SPRING OF 1945, GEZA RETURNED TO HIS hometown of Adevande. In his home lived a Hungarian family, other children played with his son's toys, his wife's clothes were worn by another woman, strangers dined at his table. It looked as if nothing but the faces had changed. It was as if reality were a strange dream from which he would awake any moment and everything would be just the way it used to be. He will close his grocery store, his son will run to welcome him, and they will go together to the synagogue to chant the evening prayers. They will return home. His wife will be there, standing near the set supper table.

But the strange reality continued to linger on. It refused to fade away, and strangers continued to stay in his house, his wife and child did not come back.

Other Jews returned to town, survivors like himself, hoping that some members of their family had also survived. People kept telling Geza that his hopes were in vain, that his wife and son were murdered in Auschwitz.

One night he dreamed about his wife. She was all dressed in white in a strange outfit, which looked like both a wedding gown and a shroud. She told him that they could no longer be husband and wife since she was murdered in Auschwitz. He must get married and start a new life.

A few days later his wife's three unmarried younger sisters returned from the concentration camp. They confirmed what his wife had told him in his dream about her tragic fate. Months later, Geza married one of his wife's sisters. In 1947, they boarded a ship for New York to start a new life.

*Based on interview by Suzanne Kletzel with Geza S., December 20, 1979.*

# A Prayer and a Dream

"IT WAS A PRAYER AND A DREAM THAT KEPT ME ALIVE IN BERGEN Belsen," said Sheila Gamss. "It was a very special prayer and a dream, a dream in which reality overshadows dreams, and dreams overpower reality.

"Rabbi Gross, a Hasidic Jew from Slovakia, taught us the prayer in camp. I don't know if the prayer is written down in any prayer book, or if it existed before the concentration-camp era—a time when the living were the walking dead and the dead the only link with a normal world that was gone forever. It was a prayer that seemed created from crematoria ashes—a prayer from the valley of death that kept the soul alive. We prayed it every minute of our wretched existence. It gave us so much hope, so much strength, so much light. But one day after the war the words of the prayer just left me, one by one. And till today, I can't remember them. I hope that somewhere, Rabbi Gross is alive and he remembers that prayer.

"When liberation was nearing the gates of Bergen Belsen, I became ill with typhoid. Delirious and near death, I kept repeating the prayer Rabbi Gross taught, but its words were moving further away from me till I heard only the faint echo like the fluttering of wings in the distance. Suddenly, in the vacuum left by the prayer, I distinctly heard my mother's voice. 'We are all God's children. He can do with us whatever he pleases.' She repeated the phrase over and over again.

"I was walking toward my mother's voice. We were all marching, a women's work detachment. Heads shaven, dressed in gray with wooden shoes on our swollen feet, six abreast, we walked through the camp's main gate. We marched toward my mother's voice. We walked through snow-covered fields and frozen roads, through peaceful villages where blue smoke from house chimneys was gently making its way to the sky. We begged for bread, but no one heard us. The villagers looked through us as if we were transparent as thin air, and went on about their business as if we didn't exist.

"We reached my hometown. There it was springtime and the lilac bushes were in full bloom. It was Friday night. Sabbath candles were glowing in each window. Fathers and sons, dressed in their Sabbath attire, were rushing to the shtiblach, the small Hasidic prayer houses, and to the synagogue. They, too, did not notice us. I knew them all and called them by their names. But my words were voiceless, just soundless movements of my mouth. I could hear the clatter of our wooden clogs on the cobblestones. I could hear the sound of their leather shoes as they rushed to pray. But no one heard us or saw us.

"My mother's voice was very near. Around the corner, at the doorway, she was standing—awaiting us with outstretched arms. She was dressed in her Sabbath finery, with a snow-white apron. I fell into her awaiting arms. 'Mother!' I cried, 'I can't go on anymore!'

My mother hugged me, caressed me, and her gentle touch made my hair grow. In her soft voice she told me, 'My child, don't worry. Everything will be all right. You will recover and soon be liberated. Here, my child, here is food which I prepared for you.' She gave me gefilte fish, chicken soup, and freshly baked hallah.

"When I opened my eyes I saw my friends on the wooden planks around me staring with amusement. They couldn't believe I was alive and hadn't succumbed to the typhoid. I felt strong and sat up. I could still feel the warm, gentle, kind hands of my mother supporting me. The taste of the fish and the aroma of the freshly baked hallah filled the stench-ridden Bergen Belsen barracks.

"A few days later we were liberated."[1]

*Based on interview with Sheila Gamss by her son, December 1, 1976.*

# The Third
# Sabbath Meal
# at Mauthausen

IGNAC OF LIPSHE, CZECHOSLOVAKIA, WAS ONE OF THE TENS OF thousands of concentration-camp inmates who were chased on foot across the frozen landscapes of Europe during the winter of 1945. They were driven into the inner lands of Germany and Austria ahead of the advancing eastern front. It seemed as if heaven too had no mercy and unleashed its winter fury with blowing snows and gusting winds on the rag-covered, emaciated bodies of the people on the death marches.

Ignac, though only in his teens, was already a veteran of many camps. He was quick to assess the march and its awesome, deadly rhythm. He knew that luck and faith alone could not assure one's survival; that winter and S.S. guards could only be outmaneuvered by the determined will of a Jewish lad. Ignac knew that as long as his feet would carry him and as long as he did not attract attention, life would cling to his wretched body. If his feet failed, the road would be his grave. All his will to live, all his determination to survive now concentrated on his two legs. He commanded them not to stop, not to slip, not to stumble. He became oblivious to the rest of his body as if it had ceased to exist, as if it had dissolved into the biting winds and drifting snows. There was nothing to him but two frostbitten feet, two skinny bones that kept conquering life, meter after meter down the endless, white-shrouded roads. Bodies were slumping and falling to the ground all around him, but Ignac kept on marching.

When the Germans realized that winter and hunger were making their own "selection" on the march as to who should die and who should live, they were upset. As sons of the superior race they felt deprived of their innate right to command life and death. So they decided to assist the elements in their deadly chores. Those who marched with a steady step were commanded to carry on their weary backs the staggerers and the stumblers. Now inmates were returning their souls to their Maker in pairs—one inmate facing the white barren land, the other gaping with open frozen mouth at the gray skies above. But Ignac continued to march. It was as if his legs were separate from his aching back and its human cargo.

After two weeks, a few thousand marchers reached their final destination—the infamous concentration camp of Mauthausen. Ignac was among them. Some time later at Mauthausen a selection took place. Stripped to their waists, the newly arrived inmates were lined up on the roll-call grounds. Protruding rib cages and stomachs sunken into triangular hollow pits lined the roll-call square. A young S.S. officer began to select his prey.

Ignac followed intently each movement of the S.S. man. He tried to figure out the criteria for life and death. He noticed that the man quickly bypassed the more healthy-looking inmates and lingered for a moment near the emaciated ones, just long enough to record their number, never raising his eyes above the inmate's sunken chest. Ignac understood that skilled laborers were not among the privileged. The only passport to life was a few pounds of flesh on one's body, and he was a mere bundle of bones. He knew that he stood no chance of passing this selection. He would be taken away with the other "musselmen," fuel for the chimneys.

An idea flashed in his mind. His lips started to move and frantically he began to whisper something. With each movement of his lips his heart beat faster and faster! Color was returning to his pale lips and determination filled his eyes. He looked as if he were reciting an ancient rite of life, a magic spell that could change darkness into light, and beasts into men. The S.S. man stood in front of him. He never looked at Ignac's face, as though his eyes were drowned in the hollow pit that once was Ignac's stomach. "Your number," the German hissed between his clenched teeth. Ignac recited a number with the same self-assurance and ease with which one responds to one's own name. The Nazi recorded it on his list and moved on to pick his next victim. Hours later all were dismissed.

At the edge of the roll-call grounds, trucks were lined up. Zeilappell was called again. The inmates, dressed in the concentration-camp uniform, lined up again in the huge square. Ignac saw his life and death hanging in the balance, for the number he had given earlier that morning to the S.S. man was not his present number, 7327, but one of his numbers from a previous camp.

The same S.S. man from the morning roll call appeared with list in hand. Each time he called out a number, an unfortunate man would step out from the line and march to an assigned section near the waiting trucks. Some ran, others walked as if in a trance. Still others lingered for a while, knowing that they were taking their last steps on this blood-stained earth.

A number was called. No one responded. The S.S. officer repeated the number again; no one stepped forward. With each repetition of the number, the anger in the officer's voice mounted until it became a raging scream. But to no avail: not a single inmate took a step. The S.S. man began to run from one man to another staring into their gray faces, checking their numbers. He stopped in front of Ignac. His bloodthirsty eyes searched for his elusive prey. "Your number!" the German screamed. Ignac looked straight into his eyes and calmly said, "7327." The S.S. man moved on and continued to search in vain for the missing number. No number on the roll-call square matched the one on his morning list.

The camp commander appeared. A paralyzing fear came over the inmates. Though new at Mauthausen, they had heard about the cruelty of Franz Ziereis.[1] The camp commander whispered something to the young S.S. officer. Only Ignac knew what the experienced henchman of Mauthausen was telling the young S.S. man, that the number given to him that morning was not a Mauthausen number.

Roll call ended. The lucky ones returned to their barracks. The trucks pulled out, the engines letting out a strange, weeping shriek. Roll-call square was empty, except for the smoke that trailed behind the departing trucks.

That night, Ignac dreamed that World War II had not yet begun. He was a young yeshiva student, going to visit his grandfather, the Dolha Rabbi, Rabbi Asher Zelig Grunsweig.[2] It was Sabbath afternoon at dusk. The little house was filled with twilight shadows and the special, tranquil Sabbath spirit permeated each corner of the sparkling room. It was time to eat the third Sabbath meal. While Grandmother set the table, he and Grandfather washed their hands from the special big copper cup with two huge handles. Grandfather made the blessing over the two loaves of hallah. It was warm in Grandfather's home. They were singing zemirot, traditional Sabbath songs. Grandfather was stressing the importance of the third meal, telling him that it is the most spiritual and mystical of the Sabbath meals. He who becomes imbued with its spirit will be spared the battles of Gog and Magog. "Remember what our sages say, Whoever observes the three Sabbath meals will be saved from the suffering to precede the coming of the Messiah, the rule of Purgatory."[3] Grandfather was caressing Ignac's head while he spoke to him in his good and gentle voice. "You will grow up, my child, and will survive the suffering that precedes the coming of the Messiah and the rule of Gehinnom (Purgatory). But you must always attempt to observe the third Sabbath meal, for its merit will protect you."

Ignac woke up, still feeling his grandfather's warm hands upon his shaven head, hearing that reassuring voice and tasting the aroma of Grandmother's Sabbath hallah. Ignac did not permit himself the luxury of dwelling too long on his pleasant dreams. Camp reality demanded every iota of his strength and concentration. But the dream did not allow itself to be forgotten. It did not fade away into the deadly realities of Mauthausen. Night after night he kept dreaming the same dream, until his Grandfather's house became a reality and Mauthausen a nightmare.

From his meager rationed food, his starvation diet, Ignac began to hide crumbs of bread, a crumb of bread per day. He concealed it well inside his concentration-camp uniform so that no one could steal it from him even when he was asleep. Despite the terrible, constant hunger pangs, Ignac did not touch the crumbs of bread. Even when he felt that hunger was going to triumph over life, he would not eat his precious crumbs.

On Sabbath, at dusk after a long day of backbreaking slave labor, Ignac would manage to wash his hands, seek a corner where he would not attract too much attention, and celebrate his third Sabbath "meal." Slowly he would chew his six crumbs of bread, tasting in them his grandmother's delicacies, hearing his grandfather's soothing melodious voice singing the zemirot.

The peace and tranquility of the Sabbath would be upon him and the hell of Mauthausen would be overpowered by the Sabbath bliss.

On May 6, 1945, Mauthausen was liberated by the Americans, the 21st Armored Infantry Battalion and Combat Command B of the 11th Armored Division of the Third Army. Ignac was among the lucky inmates to be liberated that day.

*Based on interview by Leila Grunsweig with Ignac Grunsweig, December 1978.*

# A Hill
# in Bergen Belsen

ANNA WAS AMONG THE TENS OF THOUSANDS WHO SUCCUMBED to the typhus epidemic in Bergen Belsen.[1] Her friends gave her up for dead and told her that her struggle with death was useless. But Anna was determined to live. She knew that if she lay down, the end would come soon and she would die like so many others around her. So, in a delirious state, she wandered around camp, stumbling over the dead and the dying. But her strength gave way. She felt that her feet were refusing to carry her any farther. As she was struggling to get up from the cold, wet ground, she noticed in the distance a hill shrouded in gray mist. Anna felt a strange sensation. Instantly, the hill in the distance became a symbol of life. She knew that if she reached the hill, she would survive, but if she failed, the typhus would triumph.

Anna attempted to walk toward the hill which continually assumed the shape of a mound of earth, a huge grave. But the mound remained Anna's symbol of life, and she was determined to reach it. On her hands and knees, she crawled toward that strange mound of earth that now was the essence of her survival. After long hours passed, Anna reached her destination. With feverish hands she touched the cold mound of earth. With her last drop of strength, she crawled to the top of the mound and collapsed. Tears started to run down her cheeks, real human, warm tears, her first tears since her incarceration in concentration camps some four years ago. She began to call for her father. "Please, Papa, come and help me. I know that you, too, are in camp. Please, Papa, help me, for I cannot go on like this any longer."

Suddenly, she felt a warm hand on top of her head. It was her father stroking her just as he used to place his hand over her head every Friday night and bless her. Anna recognized her father's warm, comforting hands. She began to sob even more and told him that she had

177

no strength to live any longer. Her father listened and caressed her head as he used to. He did not recite the customary blessing but, instead, said, "Don't worry, my child. You will manage to survive for a few days, for liberation is very close."

This occurred on Wednesday night, April 11, 1945. On Sunday, April 15, the first British tank entered Bergen Belsen.[2]

When Anna was well enough to leave the hospital in the British Zone where she was recovering from typhus, she returned to Bergen Belsen. Only then did she learn that the huge mound of earth in the big square where she spent the fateful night of April 11 in her combat with typhus was a huge mass grave. Among thousands of victims buried beneath the mound of earth was her father, who had perished months earlier in Bergen Belsen. On that night when she won her battle with death, Anna was weeping on her father's grave.

*Based on interview by Kalia Dingott with Anna, May 1976 (family name withheld by request).*

# A Father's Blessing

BLACK TYPHUS BROKE OUT IN HIDEGSEG, THE NOTORIOUS CAMP near Sapron, Hungary. Of 1,200 young men between the ages of twenty and twenty-five, only about 500 survived at the beginning of March 1945. But the stronger the epidemic raged in camp, the stronger grew Adolf Hershkowitz's will to live. "I want to live!" he repeated over and over to himself, trying constantly to avoid shovels and other tools which were flung directly over his head by the Hungarian guards at those who were staggering from the typhus and exhaustion and could no longer work at the required speed. With each blow of the shovel, they would inform victim and survivor alike that bullets were too expensive for Jews.[1]

In the middle of March, Adolf first felt the symptoms of black typhus. He became dizzy, his vision blurred, and he began seeing double images. He asked a Jewish doctor from Poland named Zolte, whom he had met in the labor battalion, for help. But the doctor told him that he too was helpless; the only thing he could give was advice: to go on moving and not lie down because that would bring on the end.

But Adolf could not heed the good doctor's advice, for he collapsed one morning and could no longer move. Fortunately, no guards were around. He was saved from a shovel blow and was thrown instead into a shack where people were dying of typhus. Adolf looked around him and counted the men. He decided that if the majority lived, he would live too, and if the majority died, that would be his fate also.

At night he lost his blanket and shivered from the cold and sickness. He was too weak to sit up and look for his blanket, but all he felt around him were cold dead bodies. Without food, warmth, or medicine, he knew that his end was near. Awaiting death, he wanted to say the Vidduy, the confession before one's death, but he was too weak to utter the words or move his lips. Instead, he feverishly thought the words of the prayer until he felt a pleasant, deep sleep descend upon him and engulf him completely.

He dreamed that he was back home. It was Friday afternoon and his entire family—sister, brothers, mother, and father—were polishing their shoes in honor of the Sabbath. The table was set with a white tablecloth. On it were the two beautiful polished candlesticks, and his mother was lighting the Sabbath candles. Next to his father's place was the crystal wine bottle used only on the Sabbath and holidays. The father, his three brothers, and he all went to shul. The synagogue was filled to capacity; no one was missing, and all prayed with great devotion. Upon returning home, they went into the kitchen where a big bowl was hanging on the wall. It was the bowl in which Adolf's mother used to prepare the Sabbath babka, his favorite cake. Father and mother took down the babka and gave him a piece of babka and a drink of wine. His father told him, "Drink it and you will be an honest Jew. You will be a healthy Jew and you will live."

Adolf woke up. He felt as if he were still drinking, as if his parents were close by. He regained enough strength to sit up, find his blanket, and cover himself. He was sure that his dream was a reality, that indeed he was back home with his family. He looked around, but he was still in the same shack with the dead and dying. Yet Adolf could still taste the drink his parents had given him. At that time Adolf was unaware that his parents were no longer among the living.

It was March 28, 1945, Passover, and Adolf felt much stronger but he remained in the shack and did not go back to work. The Russian front was approaching Hidegseg, and the camp administration broke down. The warehouses were open, and someone managed to get some flour for Adolf. Adolf baked it on an open flame and something resembling matzot resulted.

The camp was evacuated. His friend the doctor helped him escape and cared for him. As a result of the typhus, Adolf could not hear well or think clearly. They crossed a deep river. For three days they sat in a leaky boat among the weeds in the marshes. The doctor had some bread with him which he wished to share with Adolf, but Adolf refused to eat it because it was Passover. Adolf told the doctor, an assimilated Jew, the story of Passover for the first time in that leaky boat in the marshes while the skies were lit with "Stalin's candles."

Turning to Adolf, the doctor said, "If Passover is indeed what you have told me, the holiday of Exodus from slavery to freedom, you must eat in order to live and see that freedom. I am sure that if God is looking from heaven this very moment, He would approve." He sliced the bread very thin, like matzot, and gave it to Adolf and urged, "Eat, so you may be alive to see the fall of the Pharaohs of our time and your freedom."

Three days later they were liberated.

*Based on interview by Sharon Silverman with Adolf Hershkowitz, April 24, 1978.*

# A Sign from Heaven

DURING THE SUMMER OF 1944 THE INFERNO OF AUSCHWITZ WAS AT its height. Dr. Joseph Mengele, the elegant "Angel of Death," was smilingly directing hundreds of thousands of newly arriving Hungarian Jews to his favorite kommando, the "Himmel (Heaven) Kommando," at the crematoria, the place of no return.

That summer the chimneys were burning day and night; a low haze constantly hung over the camp, filling the air with the stench of burning human flesh.

Among the newly arrived victims was Elaine Seidenfeld from Chust. She began to learn the realities of Auschwitz at the station's huge platform where she was forcibly separated from her husband and all the male members of her family in the Chust transport.

On her first night in Auschwitz, on the top of a three-tiered bunk, squeezed like a sardine among twelve other young women, she was initiated into the hell of Auschwitz. The old timers of *Lager* C did not spare Elaine. They explained to her the horrifying realities of Auschwitz. "Today it is them, tomorrow it will be us," said one emaciated girl from Poland as she was pointing her bony finger in the direction of the glowing skies.

"Not I," protested the horrified Elaine, "I will survive: I want to live and find my husband."

"You are new here," replied the girl from Poland. "Once upon a time we all wanted to live, but it is useless."

"I want to live." Elaine was pleading with the girl. "I must live, I must find my husband." No one responded to her plea. In the distance someone was screaming and then it was silent again. Only Elaine was still whispering, "I want to live, I want to live."

From May to August, Elaine passed numerous selections. At times, they took place twice a day, at the morning Zeilappell and at the evening roll call. Most of all she feared Dr. Mengele and a woman Kapo, rumored to have been the daughter of a famous Slovakian

181

rabbi. And then it happened. Her fears materialized. She was selected, the only one from her immediate group. She pleaded with an acquaintance from Chust who had risen to a minor position in *Lager* C to switch her and place her back in her former group, but to no avail.

And so on a hot, humid August day in 1944, while the women's orchestra played and the S.S. men lined the route with German shepherd dogs, Elaine was marched out from *Lager* C with about 3,000 other women inmates. They were marched in the direction of the gas chambers. The closer they got to the gas chambers, the more feverishly Elaine repeated the only plea she had uttered since she came to Auschwitz: "I want to live, I want to find my husband." They reached the gas chambers. The march halted.

Someone blew a whistle and they were taken into a huge empty hall. They were told to undress, fold their clothes neatly, and walk into the showers. Elaine closed her eyes. Real cold water came pouring down. The water shut off automatically and they were taken to a second hall. Each girl was given a straight grey dress with a number sewn onto its sleeve and a pair of shoes. Again they were marching, this time passing *Lager* C on the other side, closer to the train station.

They were loaded on sealed cattle cars, about 150 girls to a wagon. Elaine managed to press herself against the wagon's wall in hopes that she would find a crack between two boards that would allow her to figure out the direction of the train, and her fate. This was to no avail. The train was tightly sealed. It was dark in the train and the girls stood close together like vertical boards of lumber.

"I want to live," she kept repeating. "I want to live. If only I could find some promising sign, something I could believe in, something, just anything, something that will indicate that I will live."

The train jolted, the boards near Elaine were groaning, a slit of light appeared. Between two boards a crack was formed. Through the tiny crack she saw the clear blue sky, a sky that belonged to the world outside the Auschwitz kingdom of death. And there in the bright blue skies was a straight pure-white line. Joy overcame Elaine.

She felt that her prayer was answered, that heaven had given her a sign that she would indeed survive and live. This was the sign she was praying for. The pure-white line was a verdict, a decision made in heaven as to who shall die and who shall live. All the blood, all the burning skies above Auschwitz were transformed especially for her into one pure, single white line—the line of life. "O God, you have given Noah a rainbow and me this white line in heaven. I too will survive this deluge of blood, for this is a sign from heaven that you have inscribed my name in your Book of Life."

The train arrived at Stutthof.[1] Soon the girls were to learn that Stutthof was no improvement over Auschwitz. Many died from hard labor, hunger, and lack of water; others were taken to the gas chambers. But not Elaine; she was lucky. She clung to her invisible white line, to the promise from heaven, with all her strength, and did not succumb to the deadly realities of Stutthof. In the last months of 1944, 4,000 women were deported from Stutthof and its satellite camps to Dachau, Buchenwald, Neuengamme, and Flossenburg. Elaine was miraculously spared.

As the Russian front was nearing Stutthof in January 1945, Elaine and 26,000 other women were evacuated. Many were drowned in the Baltic Sea, others were sent on the long death march. Thousands fell along the road. The frozen earth, the deep snows, the biting winds, hunger, and thirst took their toll. But Elaine marched on. Dressed in a single summer dress with a pair of shabby clogs, she held on to her white line of life. She could see it guiding her bleeding feet through the trampled snow. She could see it in the black skies above, laden with smoke and ashes. She saw her straight, unfaltering white line and she held on to it with each breath of her soul.

Then it was all over. The war ended, the guns were silenced; corpses lined the face of the earth. The Germans fled and the Red liberators began to demand the rewards of victory: men's minds and women's bodies. Elaine was holding on to her white line, the line that would lead her back home to Chust and to her husband.

Lone survivors, all that was left of an entire family or an entire town, made their way through a devastated Europe. They were going

home to search for remnants from a vanished past. They passed
through the same train stations, traveled on the same tracks that just
months before led to the gas chambers and fed the chimneys. Now
they were heading "home." Elaine was on her way to Chust. Then,
on a crowded train platform, she saw her husband board a train to
Chust also.

"What do you suppose that white line in the sky that you saw from
the crack in the cattle car on your way to Stutthof really was?" the
interviewer asked Elaine some thirty years later in her Brooklyn
home.

"You see, in order to survive you must believe in something, you
need a source of inspiration, of courage, something bigger than yourself, something to overcome reality. The line was my source of inspiration, my sign from heaven.

"Many years later, after liberation, when my children were growing up, I realized that the white line might have been fumes from a
passing airplane's exhaust pipe, but does it really matter?"

*Based on interview by Sharon Lynn Perris with Elaine Seidenfeld, April
1978.*

# A Bobov Melody

AMONG THE TENS OF THOUSANDS OF SLAVE LABORERS AT
Mauthausen and its many satellite camps was a young lad named
Moshe. He was brought there in 1944 together with thousands of in-
mates from Auschwitz as the eastern front approached.

Moshe was fourteen years old, son of the head of the Bobov
Yeshiva, and the sole survivor of a large family. Young Moshe was a
fervent Hasid, a devout believer in and follower of the grand Rabbi of
Bobov, Rabbi Ben-Zion Halberstam. The rabbi's wisdom and saintly
appearance, and the beautiful melodies that he composed, attracted
many Hasidim to Bobov.[1] The rabbi had a special interest in young

people, and they responded with unlimited admiration and youthful enthusiasm.

Each Friday night young Moshe with all the male members of his family would walk to the rabbi's house and welcome the Sabbath there with dance and song. Moshe's favorite melody was the one to which the rabbi chanted the holy Zohar, the mystical Book of Splendor. Moshe was convinced that when the angels sing before the Lord, they sing the rabbi's Zohar melody.

When Moshe was torn away forever from his mother's arms and separated from his father, he had no idea that his beloved rebbe was no longer among the living and his holy lips would no longer chant the beautiful melodies. For on "Black Friday," July 25, 1941, Aktion Petliura was unleashed in Lvov. The Grand Rabbi of Bobov, Rabbi Ben-Zion Halberstam, and his family were among the 2,000 Jews who were arrested. Four days later, on Monday, the fourth day of the month of Av, Rabbi Ben-Zion Halberstam, dressed in his silk Sabbath kapote and his tall shtraiml (fur hat), marched to his death. He was urged to escape. "One does not run away from the sounds of the Messiah's footsteps," replied the Rabbi of Bobov and continued to walk in his dignified stride in the direction of Janow, where the open pits in the forest were waiting. He was murdered by the Nazis and their Ukrainian collaborators. May his sainted memory be blessed.

In the misery of Mauthausen, young Moshe never lost faith in the rabbi. He was sure that the rabbi was guiding him and watching over him even amidst the intolerably harsh realities of the camp. The image of the rabbi as he had seen him on many Friday night visits to the rabbi's house was constantly before Moshe's eyes. In the bleakest moments in camp, in spite of physical exhaustion from his slave labor at the granite quarry or at the subterranean aircraft factory, in moments of despair and hunger, he felt the presence of the rabbi next to him. The rabbi's soothing voice comforted him and commanded him to live.

Wherever Moshe went, he felt the Bobover Rabbi guiding his steps, almost as if the rabbi were pulling him and pushing him, often in directions opposite those he would have chosen to follow. When Moshe's strength failed, he would try to concentrate and remember the beautiful melody with which the rabbi chanted the holy Zohar. The memory of that melody would fill him with courage and determination to go on. At times Moshe wanted to cry, to weep, to express his pain and anguish, but his tears would not respond; all the wells of tears had dried up together with all other signs of humanity. Moshe would then concentrate on the rabbi's Zohar melody, and tears, warm, human tears, would fill his eyes and stream down his hollow cheeks. The melody of the rabbi filled his being and momentarily dispelled the harsh realities of Mauthausen.

A bitter cold Austrian winter descended upon Mauthausen. Many of the inmates died of exposure, disease, and starvation, but not Moshe, by then a fourteen-year-old bundle of skin and bones. He was clinging to life with all his fervor and belief.

It was a cold December day in 1944, "delousing day." The prisoners' tattered striped uniforms were exchanged for clean ones and they were all chased to the showers across the camp's huge square while the Kapo took the eternal head count. While the inmates were in the showers they heard the sudden, familiar order: "Zeilappell!" Roll call! Kapos with truncheons and clubs began to chase the still wet prisoners into the camp's square, into the howling winds of the subzero December winter. Naked, wet living human skeletons lined the square. The ritual of the head count began. There was a discrepancy between the list in the Kapo's hand and the number of prisoners in the square; one was missing. The head count began again but the discrepancy persisted. An hour passed. The naked people began to be covered with a thin layer of white frost; breathing became more and more difficult and people began to fall on the snow like frozen laundry dropping from a clothesline. The search for the missing man continued. The ranks of standing prisoners became sparse, while the rows of bodies on the trodden snow grew longer and longer.

Young Moshe tried to move his feet and his hands, but his body no longer responded to his will. He felt that he too was slowly freezing into a pillar of ice, being drawn and pulled to the white snow on the ground beneath him.

Suddenly he felt the Rabbi of Bobov, Rabbi Ben-Zion Halberstam, supporting him. The rabbi's reassuring voice rang in his ears: "Don't fall, my young friend, don't stumble! You must survive! A Hasid must sing, a Hasid must dance; it is the secret of our survival!" The rabbi's melody was burning in his head, ringing in his ears, but his frozen lips could not utter a single sound. Then slowly his lips began to move. A note forced its way through the colorless lips. It was followed by another and another, individual notes strung together into the rabbi's niggun, his melody. Like burning coals the tune scorched his lips and set his body aflame. One foot began to move, to free itself from its chains of frost. The ice crackled; one foot began to dance. The other foot tore itself away from the clinging ice. The snow became red as skin from the sole of Moshe's foot remained grafted to the ice. Bones, muscles, and sinews began to step in the snow, to dance to the rabbi's niggun. Moshe's heart warmed up, burning tears streamed down his face as his body and soul sang the Bobov melody.

The Zeilappell was over. The Mauthausen camp square was strewn with scores of bodies. But Moshe's red footprints burned the white snow with the glow of a Bobov melody.

In his Monsey, New York, home Rabbi Moshe and his wife, six children, and grandchildren sing the rabbi's niggun every Friday night at the Sabbath table. Amidst the warmth of his family, the glow of the Sabbath candles, and the guiding gaze of the Bobover Rabbi's portrait, tears glitter in Rabbi Moshe's eyes. His bones and sinews are covered anew with flesh. The trail from Mauthausen to Monsey was blazed by burning faith.

*Based on interview by Brenda Glatt with Rabbi Moshe, a Bobover Hasid, May 1977.*

# Rudolf Haas Is Human!

ONE PARTICULAR SELECTION IS STILL FIXED IN ZVI KOCZICKI'S mind. Thirty-five years later it is as vivid as the day he witnessed it in Bergen Belsen at age seven. A transport of people had been brought to the adjacent camp facing the windows of his barracks. The camp was nearly vacant since the Kasztner Transport had just left for Switzerland.

The new arrivals did not stay long. But they were not as fortunate as the previous occupants of the barracks. Their bodies never left Bergen Belsen.

One morning, before each other's eyes, the new inmates were clobbered to death with sticks, truncheons, and lead pipes. Only occasionally was a shot fired. The pile of dead bodies kept growing taller and taller until it became a mountain of torn human flesh with streams of blood.

The German faces were shining with a strange glee as each fresh victim was transformed by their hands from a human being into broken bones, torn flesh, and sinews. Even Rudolf Haas, the camp commander, came to inspect. He was meticulously dressed, with shining boots, a beautiful, warm, well-tailored coat, white gloves, and an officer's cap. He looked the very symbol of perfection as he stood there watching the inmates being destroyed. Zvi was sure that Haas would not permit such brutality. He watched his face, handsome, composed, powerful, like a strange god of blood and power. Just then another victim was brought. Zvi thought he recognized his own father whom he had last seen in the death train. Haas remained motionless as the man was battered to death. Little Zvi passed out.

When he was revived, there were new piles of martyred Jews. "*Mutti, Mutti,* will it ever end? Are we going to die too?" Zvi demanded an answer from his mother. His mother reassured him that they would survive for so she had been promised by a sainted man. But Zvi was scared. A strange, paralyzing fear that he had never known before came to dwell in his little heart. People told him that all would be well, that their camp commander, Rudolf Haas, was a kind man, that people in his camp would survive the war. But Zvi had watched Haas during the horrible selection. His eyes did not shed a single tear, his mouth did not utter a single sigh. He stood there like Satan in Hell. "Nothing will ever be the same," Zvi confided to his baby brother Yitzhak. "Only if Haas is human, as people say, do we stand a chance of coming out alive from this hell on earth."

And then, one day, Zvi received a sign in a very unexpected manner. He saw the camp commandant running. Haas was half dressed, in a state of disarray. His eyes were filled with terror and he was looking for cover from the British planes that were flying overhead. The planes were flying very low. One plane even knocked down the kitchen chimney near Zvi's barrack. The British planes were strafing and Rudolf Haas tried to outmaneuver the bullets.

That day Zvi knew that the Germans would lose the war. They were human, like the Jews—frightened in the face of death. Even Rudolf Haas was human!

*Based on interview by Dina Spira with Rabbi Zvi Spira, May 12, 1976.*

# A Miracle
# in a Potato Field

DAVID JUNGER HAD JUST PASSED ANOTHER SELECTION IN Auschwitz. The criterion for passing was "Young Jewish men not born in Poland." David qualified. He was born in Kralova Nad Tisou, Czechoslovakia, on May 23, 1925. "Does it really matter in this pipe factory where one is born? Eventually, we all will go up in smoke," remarked a young fellow standing nearby.

Polish Jews remained on one side and a huge detachment of young

Jewish men from all over Europe, with a significant number of Hungarians and Czechs, on the other. The latter group was loaded into sealed cattle cars and taken to an unknown destination.

They arrived in Warsaw at a camp that had been built a year earlier by Dutch and Greek Jews brought to Warsaw from Auschwitz to clean up the rubble of the destroyed Warsaw ghetto.

David's newly arrived group was placed in the same camp and given the name the Berlin Building Brigade. Their task, like that of their predecessors, was to sort out the whole bricks and pile them in stacks for shipment to Germany to rebuild factories destroyed by Allied bombing. Breaking a whole brick was a severe crime. Many young Jewish men paid for it with their lives. When the bricks were ready for shipment, Poles carted them away in huge trucks.

Food was scarce in the Warsaw concentration camp, even by Auschwitz standards. The portions of rationed food became smaller and smaller as the Russian bombing raids became more frequent. To survive long on camp rationing was impossible. Despite the fact that Polish Jews were not supposed to be selected for this assignment, many young Polish Jews did somehow manage to get on Warsaw transports. Their knowledge of the Polish language and local vegetation was a crucial factor for survival. They could barter with the local Poles and they knew how to make tea from local flowers and evergreens.

As the eastern front was nearing the gates of Warsaw, spirits in camp ran high, but not for long. The front halted and the slave laborers were ordered to dig huge graves. The message was clear: in case the German retreat is a hasty one, the Jews will remain in Warsaw forever.

Then, on July 28, 1944, came the order to evacuate the concentration camp which had been set up amongst the ruins of the Warsaw ghetto on Gesia Street. About 4,000 Jewish inmates, with David among them, began their death march. They marched along the banks of the river Vistula. It was a hot July day and they were thirsty. Drinking from the river was forbidden. Anyone who broke ranks and drank was shot. Thirst, hunger, and the heat were just too much to bear and many ran to the river. Moments later, the gentle waves of the Vistula would carry their bodies downstream. The marching continued. Soon the name Dachau was heard on more and more lips.[1] Their destination was Dachau, but first they must reach a train station from which German trains operated. The column of marchers continued to shrink, the blazing sun to beat down upon them without mercy.

It was Tishah Be'Av, a fast day, marking the destruction of the first and second Temple in Jerusalem centuries ago. Fasting was no problem. It was several days since they had been given their last food rations. Their thirst was unbearable. The cool Vistula was so close and its cool waters looked so inviting. Then the march took a turn. They turned sharply to their left. The distance between the marching men and the Vistula grew greater and greater until the soothing waters could no longer be seen.

Late at night they reached a huge open field. Unexpectedly, they were given orders to camp. Exhausted, they threw their dehydrated bodies on the cool ground and fell asleep. Someone started to dig with his bare hands, and after digging to the depth of a half a meter, behold—there was water! Water, muddy brown water, but nevertheless water. The word spread quickly. As though rising from the dead, the bodies that resembled corpses lifted their heads from the ground and began digging frantically and chanting "Water, water, water," in a strange orchestra of all languages. Slowly, the Polish field was covered with hundreds of water holes, small wells in which a pale moon and emaciated faces were reflected. Not only did the field yield water but small, fresh potatoes as well.

And so, around small water puddles in a potato field between destroyed Jewish Warsaw and the waiting death camps in Germany, Jewish slave laborers broke their fast commemorating the destruction of the Temple in Jerusalem centuries ago.

Near David's group, at the edge of the field, German officers were watching the Jews in amusement and admiration as they determinedly dug for water and food, and miraculously the field yielded to them. One tall German officer, considerably older than the rest, remarked: "Now I understand that our effort is in vain. The Jews will never be destroyed. For their will to live is unmatched by any other people. They, indeed, must be the eternal people."

*Based on interview by Eva Slomovics with David Junger, November 28, 1979.*

# FOUR

## At the
## Gates of Freedom

The biggest miracle of all is the one that we, the survivors of the
Holocaust, after all that we witnessed and lived through, still believe
and have faith in the Almighty God, may His name be blessed. This,
my friends, is the miracle of miracles, the greatest miracle ever to
have taken place.

*The Rabbi of Klausenburg,*
*Rabbi Yekutiel Yehuda Halberstam*

# The Plague
# of Blood

IN FEBRUARY 1946, RABBI ISRAEL SPIRA ARRIVED IN NEW YORK.
Among the people who welcomed him in the New York harbor was
an American G.I. from the Ninth Army, which had liberated the
rabbi and others when they were fleeing from a death train in a German forest near Magdeburg.

The G.I. from Philadelphia pointed out with great pride the Statue
of Liberty, which welcomes the immigrants to shores of freedom. He
told the rabbi: "On its pedestal is an inscription written by a Jewish-
American poet, Emma Lazarus: 'Give me your tired, your poor,
your huddled masses yearning to breathe free.' " The G.I. translated
the words into Yiddish for the rabbi's benefit.

The rabbi listened intently and wiped a tear from his eye. There he
was, the lone survivor of his family; his beard was burnt off, his head
and body still covered with open wounds from beatings with truncheons, iron rods, and boots. He was a lonely man at the portals of
freedom. He placed his hand on the G.I.'s shoulder and said, "My
friends, the words you have just translated to me are indeed beautiful. We, the few survivors coming to these shores, are indeed poor,
tired, and yearning for freedom. But there are no longer masses. We
are remnants, a trickle of broken individuals who search for a few
moments of peace in this world, who hope to find a few relatives on
these shores. For we survived, 'One of a city, and two of a family.' "[1]

Soon after his arrival in New York, a group of prominent American rabbis organized a welcoming reception for the Rabbi of Bluzhov
at the Bialer shul on the Lower East Side. Because the rabbi was one
of the first survivors to arrive in America after the war, he was asked
to tell about his wartime experiences.

At the end of the evening there was not a dry eye in the audience.
The people were shocked when they heard the extent of death, de-

struction, and suffering, and when they realized how limited their own knowledge of the tragedy had been while it was taking place.

Rabbi Jacob Rosenheim (1870–1965), founder and president of Agudat Israel, who was aware of the rabbi's destitute position, told him that it was an American custom to pay an honorarium to a speaker. "It is a fine custom," replied the Rabbi of Bluzhov, "for a man should indeed be rewarded for his labor. But for this particular labor of mine, recalling the suffering in the ghettos and camps, telling you about the biggest blood deluge in history, for this type of labor I cannot accept money.

"When our God Almighty brought upon the Egyptians the plague of blood, when all the water in the Nile, in ponds, reservoirs, and in drinking utensils at home turned to blood, a strange thing occurred. The Midrash tells us that the only way an Egyptian could obtain water was to go to the Jewish quarter where the plague was not effective.[2] But then an even stranger phenomenon occurred. When a Jew offered water to an Egyptian, the water turned to blood even when the Jew had just drunk from the same cup. Only when the Eygptian paid for that water did it not turn to blood. It was a golden opportunity for Jews to become rich, and some did. But the majority refused to make money from other human beings while they were afflicted with the plague of blood.

"I came here to tell you about the biggest plague of blood, about the greatest affliction suffered by the Jews and so many others in Europe. How can I accept payment when the rivers in Europe are flowing with ashes and blood? Never will my hands touch such money."

And so it is the rabbi's custom, until this very day, never to accept any kind of reward for his efforts to memorialize the suffering during the Holocaust.

*I heard it at the house of the Grand Rabbi of Bluzhov, Rabbi Israel Spira, April 26, 1979.*

# "I Envy You"

RABBI AARON KOTLER, THE FOUNDER OF THE LAKEWOOD (NEW
Jersey) Yeshivah, was one of the last major opponents of the Hasidic
movement. After his death, his son Rabbi Schneur Kotler became
the rosh yeshivah, head of the academy.

Today the yeshiva is a Talmudic center for many students from
both Hasidic and non-Hasidic backgrounds. There is no trace there
of the old animosities that marked the rift between Hasidism and its
Lithuanian opponents, the Mitnaggedim.

When Rabbi Schneur Kotler lost his young beloved son, the Rabbi
of Bluzhov, though advanced in years, traveled with his devoted student Baruch Baer from Brooklyn, to New Jersey to pay the customary condolence call during the Shivah.

When they entered Rabbi Schneur's house, the Rabbi of Bluzhov
was shocked at what he saw. Rabbi Kotler, according to law, was sitting on a low mourner's stool. Around him were sitting about sixty
men, rabbis and yeshiva students, and no one uttered a single word
or sound.

The flickering candles played with the lingering shadows on the
walls, while a deadly silence hung over the room. As Rabbi Spira entered, a chair was immediately placed for him next to that of Rabbi
Kotler. All remained silent, despite the fact that it is prescribed by
the mourners' law that the mourner must open the conversation.[1]
When Rabbi Kotler continued in his silence, the Rabbi of Bluzhov
decided to speak.

"I envy you, Rabbi Schneur. Your son passed away, yet he left a
young wife and child to carry on his name. You know the place where
your son is buried. God blessed you with other children, and so many
people are coming to comfort you in your sorrow. I had one daughter
whose face brightened the world, a son-in-law who was a most promising young scholar, and a grandchild, the delight of my heart. Then
came the Holocaust. I don't even know the day they were murdered

197

or the site of their graves, if they have one at all. No one came to comfort me because we were all being murdered. How can I not envy you?

"It's said that 'sorrow shared is sorrow halved.' So many people, rabbis, students, friends, neighbors, have come to share your sorrow; you must be comforted. I beg of you, please be strong, for in a strange way you are privileged."

A few days later, after the Shivah, Rabbi Schneur Kotler called the Rabbi of Bluzhov and thanked him for giving him so much courage and strength to overcome the most difficult days of his life.

*I heard it at the house of the Grand Rabbi of Bluzhov, Rabbi Israel Spira, April 26, 1979.*

# "Pray for Us!"

EZEKIEL, SON OF RABBI RUTTNER OF TARGUMURES, WAS ORdained as rabbi at a very young age, and hoped to continue in the family's rabbinic tradition. But the Third Reich had different plans for young Ezekiel. He was taken into a labor battalion. Then, in the summer of 1944, together with other Czech, Hungarian, and Greek Jews, he was deported from Auschwitz to the camp on Gesia Street in Warsaw, to clean up the site of the former ghetto.

Conditions in the camp were difficult. Food was scarce, the summer days were long and hot, and the nights brought with them more terror and death. The skies would light up with "Stalin's candles," as Russian bombers dropped their deadly cargo. The inmates at the camp were both delighted and fearful. They knew that liberation was at hand, but they were not sure that they would be privileged to witness it. German cruelty increased with each bombing raid, and the huge, freshly dug graves were a reminder that the Germans were totally dedicated to the Final Solution, even during the last, critical stages of the Third Reich.

One night, Russian bombing was especially heavy. Frightened Germans ran for cover. They took shelter together with the Jews, certain that the Russian pilots knew exactly where the inmates' shelter was and were being particularly careful not to harm the Jews. A young German S.S. officer, visibly shaken, followed the drama in the skies intently. There were numerous explosions, and sand and chips of wood and stone began to pour into a nearby shelter. It looked as if their shelter might be hit at any moment.

"Is there a rabbiner among you?" asked the young German officer. No one responded. There were indeed a few young rabbis in the group, but anonymity in the camp was the most prudent policy.

"Is there a rabbiner among you?" repeated the German officer, attempting to conceal a tremor of fear in his voice. Ezekiel Ruttner decided to identify himself. He stood up. His concentration-camp uniform hung loosely on his tall frame, and a bit of blondish-reddish hair had begun to grow on his shaven head.

"I am a rabbiner," he said in a low, steady voice.

"Pray for us! Pray that we should be saved from the Bolshevik-Jewish dogs," ordered the S.S. man as he pointed to the planes zooming overhead.

The young rabbi from Targumures was overwhelmed by surprise. This was the last thing he expected to hear from an S.S. officer. He composed himself and replied, "I will pray. But the prayers of a group are more effective. In Judaism, unity of the people is essential. A quorum of ten is needed for prayer."

The S.S. officer agreed. And so, by German request, traditional Jewish prayers were offered among the ruins of destroyed Jewish Warsaw. The bombs kept falling but the German S.S. men were relaxed, confident that the young rabbi's ancient Hebrew chant had drawn around them a magic circle. He was chanting Psalms:

> They are bowed down and fallen;
> But we are risen, and stand upright. Save, Lord.[1]

Miraculously, the Russian bombs hit neither Jew nor German. It was the last communal Jewish prayer held in Warsaw.

A few days later, the Jewish prisoners were evacuated on the death march to Germany. Among the survivors who witnessed liberation was young Rabbi Ruttner.

*Based on interview by Perry Shulman with Rabbi Ezekiel Ruttner, 1974.*

# A Kvitl on the Frankfurter's Grave

RABBI ISRAEL PERLOW (1869–1922), KNOWN AS THE BABE OF KARLIN-Stolin, was one of the most famous Hasidic rabbis of Lithuanian Hasidism. He became a Hasidic leader at the age of four when his father, Rabbi Ascher of Karlin, passed away. Rabbi Israel was a scholar, a fine composer, and had a commanding knowledge of the sciences. He died in Frankfurt an Main during one of his many travels and was buried there. After his death he was sometimes referred to as the Frankfurter. Despite the desecration of many Jewish cemeteries in Nazi Germany, the rabbi's grave was never vandalized.

After liberation, Germany became the center for displaced persons. Most of them were people who had been liberated from the concentration camps; the others were those who came to seek possible survivors of their families and ways to emigrate to Palestine and America. Among the many refugees were a handful of Hasidim from Karlin-Stolin. For them, the Frankfurter's grave was a source of strength and solace.

One day a Hasid of Karlin-Stolin who, along with his son, had been fortunate enough to survive the horrors of the war, came to pray at the rabbi's grave. He placed a pebble on the gravestone as is customary, and said a few chapters of Psalms. Then he poured out his heart before the holy grave, begging the Frankfurter that his holiness would intercede with the Almighty so that his son would find a proper mate, befitting a pious young man. As is also customary, he wrote his son's name and his request on a piece of paper, folded the kvitl neatly, and placed it in one of the crevices of the tombstone. The Hasid left the Frankfurter's grave in high spirits, sure that his prayers and request would be answered.

A few days later another Hasidic Jew, also a Karlin-Stolin Hasid, made his way to Frankfurt to the Babe of Stolin's grave. Like the thousands before him, he told his bitter tale and asked the rabbi's blessing. He too was fortunate, more than many others. Though he had lost almost his entire family, one daughter of marriageable age survived. He prayed now on his daughter's behalf, that she should meet a Jewish boy who would find favor in the eyes of God and men, and if possible, also be a Hasid of Karlin-Stolin. As he was about to write his request, he realized that he did not have anything to write on. Just then a gentle wind blew and a piece of paper fluttered to his feet. He picked up the paper and wrote his request in the customary manner. As he was about to fold the kvitl, he noticed that the other side also had writing on it. It was the kvitl of none other than the first Hasid of Karlin-Stolin who had appeared earlier.

A few days later, a wedding took place in a D.P. camp in Germany. The two young people whose fathers had prayed on the zaddik's grave were united in matrimony. And so you see that the miracles of the Frankfurter Rebbe do not cease unto this very day.

*I heard it from my brother-in-law, Rabbi Zvi Yehiel Eliach, a Hasid of Karlin-Stolin, February 24, 1980.*

# The Grip
# of the Holy Letters

YOAV KIMMELMAN, A NATIVE OF SOSNOWIEC, WAS BORN INTO A
pious Jewish home. Both parents were Hasidim, ardent followers of
the Gerer dynasty and its famed zaddikim. At the age of sixteen,
Yoav was deported to the Nazi concentration camp kingdom. Four
years later he was liberated by the American army at Buchenwald.[1]
He was soon to find out that he was the sole survivor of his once
large, pious Hasidic family. Yoav, like many other religious Jews,
stopped practicing Judaism in the face of Nazi brutality and its aftermath.

Today, thirty-seven years after liberation from Buchenwald, he
still vividly remembers the first Friday night after freedom. He and
some other survivors found some bacon. They fried it with onions in
honor of their first Sabbath meal as free men. They chanted the
Kiddush, and lingered at the table singing zemirot and talking. "Our
zemirot singing that Friday night in liberated Buchenwald was not
necessarily directed to God; it was primarily against the Nazis—to
spite them and show that they had not crushed us," Kimmelman recalled in his comfortable home in Melbourne, Australia, not long
ago.

"During the first weeks following our liberation we were drunk
with freedom, we could go as we pleased and take whatever we
wanted from the nearby town. During four years of minute-to-
minute existence in the camps, we could not allow ourselves the luxury of thinking about the future, even about the next minute; now
that we were free we thought only of experiencing the present to the
fullest. At that point we could have stayed in Germany forever and
enjoyed the 'good life' there."

Working with these young survivors was an American chaplain,
Hershel Schachter.[2] He understood that the first step in the long pro-

cess of their spiritual rehabilitation was for them to leave Germany. Working through international relief organizations, Rabbi Schachter succeeded in making an arrangement with the Swiss government, which grudgingly allowed the Red Cross to bring the youngsters to Switzerland for rest and recuperation.

Yoav Kimmelman had no interest in joining the group traveling to Switzerland and told the chaplain he wanted to stay in Germany. Rabbi Schachter asked Yoav only to accompany the group who were leaving to the railway station to say good-bye. Yoav joined the group reluctantly. As the train was about to pull out of the station, Schachter arranged with an American soldier to grab Yoav from the platform and lift him up into a compartment on the moving train. Yoav resisted, but to no avail. He too was now on his way to Switzerland with the other young men. As much as he did not want to go, he could not help but appreciate what the chaplain had done for him. Schachter's genuine concern and interest moved Yoav. It was a feeling he had not experienced in a long time.

It took a few days for the train to reach the Swiss border at Rheinfelden near Basel. The engineer was not too keen on taking the refugees into Switzerland. An American soldier had to be posted with him in the cabin to make sure that he cooperated.

Once in Switzerland, the group was welcomed by the Red Cross. But the sight of the camp at Rheinfelden, where they were going to stay, stunned and frightened them. The camp was surrounded by barbed wires! The young people began to shout and scream at the top of their voices, "What have you done to us! Taken us back to German concentration camps?" ("Just as the Jews complained to Moses after he delivered them out of Egypt," Yoav now comments wryly.) But by then the train had left and the group had no choice but to quiet down.

Soon the camp in Rheinfelden became a center for many Jewish organizations, from Agudat Israel on the right to Hashomer Hatzair on the left, each trying to influence the youngsters to accept their particular ideology. Yoav was apathetic to the "soul hunt" that was going on around him. Even when Rabbi Moshe Soloveichik came from Lucerne to the camp one Sabbath, Yoav was walking around smoking a cigarette. That Saturday afternoon, someone approached Yoav, telling him that a tenth man was needed for a minyan. "Even though I was an Epicorus (skeptic), I was not going to deprive the others of a minyan; so I went inside," recalls Yoav of his deliberations on that Sabbath afternoon. They started to pray, Mincha, the afternoon prayer.

It soon became apparent that they could not continue the services because no one knew how to read the Torah with the proper cantillations and accents.[3] For some reason, Rabbi Soloveichik would not read the Torah during that Mincha prayer. "Is there someone who can read the Torah?" it was asked. Yoav did not respond. Requests for someone who could read the Scriptures continued for quite a while. Finally, Yoav stood up and said that although he had not seen a Sefer Torah for a long time, he could probably still remember how to read it. Yoav looked over the reading in a *chumash* (Pentateuch), walked over to the bimah, stood in front of the open scroll of the Sefer Torah, and began to chant the ancient melody and words. As he stood before the holy scrolls, he felt the letters reach out from the parchment, fixing him in their grasp, riveting him to the spot in front of the Torah. He finished reading and wanted to step down, but the letters would not let him go; their grip on him was firm.

Years later, an observant Jew once more, he said to the interviewer: "As you see, the letters have not relinquished their grip on me, to this very day."

*Based on interview by Dr. Joel B. Wolowelsky with Yoav Kimmelman on August 9, 1981.*

# Puff . . .

ONE DAY IN THE WINTER OF 1946, IN THE D.P. CAMP AT NEUFREI-man, the door to the Fischelbergs' apartment opened. In the door-way stood a well-dressed man with a tall, formidable looking blond woman.

"Hello, *shalom aleichem*, Mr. Fischelberg! Do you remember me?" There was a familiar ring to the man's voice, but Wolf Fischelberg could not recall where and when he had first heard it. I probably met him in Bergen Belsen when he was a bundle of bones, Fischelberg thought to himself.

"Well, actually, you will have difficulty remembering me, for the person who stands before you is a new man. In my previous life, as one refers to it, I had a wife, six children, one hundred and fifty years of Hasidic ancestors, and hundreds of years of illustrious rabbinic grandfathers, but, puff . . . all went up in smoke." He burst into wild laughter, stood on his tiptoes, and kissed the stout woman on her lips which were heavily smeared with bright red lipstick.

"See this shikse, this German woman? She is the future; the past went up in smoke!" He forcefully grabbed the tall blond woman by the hand and once more burst out in wild laughter. "Puff, the past went up in smoke! Puff . . . puff . . . puff . . ." He slammed the door and left.

Fischelberg remained motionless in his seat, still trying to remember where he had met this strange visitor. Suddenly he turned pale. He remembered. The man had been one of the most pious Hasidic shohatim, ritual slaughterers, from his hometown.

*Based on interview by Bella Linshitz with Miriam Lesser, née Fischelberg, May 1975.*

# To Marry a Baker

THE BAR MITZVAH AT THE APERION MANOR IN BROOKLYN, NEW York, was a beautiful celebration. The boy's father was from the Shanghai group[1] and his mother a survivor of Auschwitz. Next to me sat a vivacious blond with a delightful sense of humor who introduced herself as Tula Friedman. I soon learned that Tula could tell stories in perfect German, Hebrew, Yiddish, English, Hungarian, Czech, and no doubt in a couple of other languages we did not get around to. When the music interfered with our conversation, she asked me to raise my voice since her hearing was impaired in one ear. "A souvenir from an Auschwitz beating," she explained to me while pointing to her ear.

She recalled the event, blow by blow, in German, Yiddish, Hebrew, and English, telling it in the appropriate language with direct quotations, describing various episodes related to that beating and its aftermath.

A waiter came to the table with a basket of assorted breads. Tula closed her eyes and inhaled the aroma of freshly baked bread as one inhales the sweet smells of a bouquet of freshly cut flowers. She passed the basket to me without taking any. "Thank you," she said to the waiter, "but I am on a diet." She then turned to me. "You know, in camp I used to dream a lot about bread. There was especially one recurring dream that one day I would marry a baker and in our house there would always be an abundance of bread."

"For this basket of bread," another woman across the table said, "you could buy in camp all the jewelry you see at this Bar Mitzvah. Once in Bergen Belsen, I exchanged a diamond ring for a thin slice of white bread."

The bread on the table was still untouched. The waiter came again to the table. "Ladies, I see that you are not hungry today."

"Not today," replied Tula, "and not ever again."

The waiter was about to remove the bread. "Leave it on the

table," said another woman. "There is nothing more reassuring in this world than having a basket of freshly baked bread on the table in front of you."

*I attended the Bar Mitzvah of Aharon Feigelstein on September 13, 1977.*

# The Road to Mother

I HAVE KNOWN MRS. GROSS FOR MANY YEARS. SHE IS THE OWNER OF a successful food store in Brooklyn. Her black hair is always neatly piled in back of her head, her big gray eyes welcome you with a warm smile, and two deep girlish dimples dot her cheeks. During the summertime, when the sleeves of her white overcoat are rolled up, her blue Auschwitz number stares at you.

Early in the morning of Mother's Day, 1978, as Mrs. Gross was waiting on me, another customer rushed into the store, a well-groomed woman with flaming red hair. While puffing on her cigarette and blowing kisses to her equally well-groomed French poodle, she handed her written order to Mrs. Gross. As Mrs. Gross was reading the order back to her, the woman said: "I could never believe that my mother would turn into a useless, nagging old woman, a burden on all of us and especially on me. I am the only one who still lives in New York. Make sure that the order is delivered at noon." She left the store and drove away in her sleek, silver-toned car.

Tears appeared in Mrs. Gross's eyes. "If only I had my mother. She would be the crown of my head, the apple of my eye! There is not even a grave, a place where I could go and whisper that wonderful word: 'Mother.' For years she has not even visited me in my dreams. Perhaps it is because I get up at dawn to be here at the store," she said.

"Right after my liberation I used to dream about her a lot. Actually, it was always the same dream. Mother is standing near our home in our small Czech town. But the road leading back to mother and home is very muddy, filled with huge puddles and bomb craters. It is very hot and humid and a strange cloud hangs very low. Mother is calling to me to come back home. She tells me that she has prepared all my favorite dishes and baked my favorite cakes. While mother speaks to me, I am standing at the other end of the road. I am trying to go toward her, but my feet are glued to the ground and I cannot take a single step in her direction.

"When I married and became pregnant, I dreamed the same dream at a much greater frequency. It was a difficult pregnancy, and the dream made it almost unbearable. After the dream I would wake up covered with sweat, and the stickiness and humidity would linger into my waking hours. One night as I entered the ninth month of my pregnancy I dreamed it again. But that night there were slight variations. The muddy, bombed-out road was still there between Mother and me, but this time my feet moved and I could walk. I started to walk, and fell into my mother's awaiting arms. There was no end to my joy as we hugged and kissed each other. I ate all the delicacies my mother prepared for me and they tasted just the same as before the war. Mother begged me not to leave, to stay home with her. 'I can't, Mama,' I told her. 'I must go back to my husband. I must go back. He is waiting for me at the other end of the road.' I tore myself away from my mother's arms and walked away. I saw her standing with outstretched arms begging me to return. But I kept running faster and faster, to my husband. I reached him at the other end of the road and fell into his waiting arms.

"I woke up covered with sweat, with terrible pains. My husband was standing at my side. That day our first child was born. He was stillborn. I never dreamed the dream again, but each detail of that dream is engraved on my mind. The heat and humidity in that dream were like the first day in Auschwitz in June 1944, the day Mengele separated me forever from my mother, sister, and other members of my family. That night, my first night in Auschwitz, I asked the Czech stubhova about my mother. The healthy-looking stubhova grabbed me by the hand, pulled me to the door of the barracks, and pointed to the chimneys: 'There is your mother!'

"For some it is Mother's Day today. For others, it will never be," she said, and began to work on orders for Mother's Day.

I drove back home. The kitchen was especially decorated. The table was set, breakfast was ready, and my favorite flowers were on the table. "Happy Mother's Day!" my children and husband greeted me. Mother's Day had never meant as much.

*I heard it from Mrs. Gross, Mother's Day, May 1978.*

# "The Happiest Day of My Life"

MY FATHER SUFFERED A MILD HEART ATTACK IN ISRAEL. SOME time later I was informed of his illness. By then, my father had recovered and was back home from the hospital. Angry that I had not been notified by telephone or cable, I demanded an explanation.

"It is very simple, my child," my father said. "The day that I had my heart attack was the happiest day of my life. As you so well know, I am a veteran of Hitler's ghettos, Stalin's camps, and Arab wars. I have witnessed so much death and suffering and survived it all. At times I wondered if I had a heart at all. This heart attack reassured me that I indeed have one. For how can a man without a heart have a heart attack?!"[1]

*I heard it from my father, Moshe Sonenson, in June 1975.*

# Hans and I
# at the Rema's Grave

IT WAS A BEAUTIFUL SUMMER DAY. OUR BUS WAS DRIVING through luscious fields dotted with buttercups, past green pastures, with farmers waving to us. It was August, 1979, and we were traveling from Auschwitz to Cracow as members of President Jimmy Carter's Commission on the Holocaust.[1]

My memory was ablaze like the boiling sun on the peaceful horizon. These were the same roads, the same countryside. Nothing was changed, except for the souls of my dead people hovering above the clouds, and their ashes which fertilize the peaceful fields below.

Cracow, the first capital of Poland, is a jewel of medieval and Renaissance architecture. The town stands intact. Nothing was touched during World War II. It was the seat of the Governor General of Poland, Hans Frank. For those who do not know Cracow's history, ignorance is a blessing, for they can enjoy its magnificent sights.

As I walk down the streets of Cracow I feel as if I am stepping on the dead. Each cobblestone is a skull, a Jewish face. Cracow's violated synagogues are habitations of ghosts. Cracow, the first Jewish settlement on Polish soil, the center of Jewish creativity, of law and Hasidic lore, is now a town with virtually no living Jews. Only a handful remain here, more dead than the clouds above Auschwitz and neighboring Plaszow.

We make our way to the Rema synagogue, built in memory of the wife of a famous Polish Jewish scholar.[2] We walk among the headstones. The tombstones, overgrown with tall wild grass, bear inscriptions that tell a glorious tale of scholars and saints, mystics who spoke to Elijah the Prophet, doctors who cured kings. Lucky Jews! I think to myself. Their death is remembered. They have a grave, a tombstone that tells a tale.

In the direction of Auschwitz I see black clouds, above Plaszow

crows are flying. No tombstone for the dead of Auschwitz, no monu-
ment for the souls of Plaszow. We, the living, must tell 6 million
tales.

I stand before the grave of the Rema, the pride and glory of Polish
Jewry. "I see you read the ancient language of the Jews," a voice said
to me in German. In back of me stood a tall young man with long,
straight, blond hair. Under one arm was a rolled-up bundle of post-
ers. His other hand held the hand of a young woman dressed in a long
Indian skirt.

"May I ask you a favor?"

"I will be more than happy to help you," I said.

"I am an artist. I am about to exhibit in Germany. My Polish
friends in Cracow told me that if one writes a wish on a piece of paper
and places it in a crevice of the tombstone of this saint, the saint will
grant his wish. Can you please write my wish for me in Hebrew?" He
gave me a piece of paper with his name and a pen.

I decided to write the kvitl in the customary manner. "Your
mother's name?" He nervously gave me the names of both of his parents, adding, as though I had asked for his confession, "My father
was in the Wehrmacht!" I smiled. "I am not investigating, but the
format of a kvitl requires your mother's name. What is your wish?"

"I am about to exhibit in Germany and I would like the saint's
blessing." I wrote the request.

Hans folded the piece of paper neatly and placed it in a crevice of
the Rema's tombstone. He and his girl friend stood with closed eyes
before the saint's tombstone. Hans crossed himself, kissed his girl
friend, then slowly walked away as if from a magic rite.

The sun was setting. The fast of the Ninth of Av began, and we
entered the Rema's synagogue to mourn the destruction of the Temple in Jerusalem. We chanted Lamentations: "How doth the city sit
solitary, that was full of people!"[3]

*From the diary I kept during a fact-finding mission for President Carter's
Commission on the Holocaust, August 1, 1979.*

# "God Does Not
Live Here Anymore"

ON AUGUST 1, 1979, THE EVE OF TISHAH BE'AV, AFTER OUR RETURN
from Auschwitz, members of President Carter's Commission on the
Holocaust, held evening services at the ancient Rema Synagogue in
Cracow. Just as we were about to chant Lamentations, Miles
Lerman, a former partisan and the sole survivor of a large family,
stepped forward to the center of the synagogue, walked up to the
beautiful bimah with its magnificent ironwork, banged on the table,
and announced that he was calling God to a Din Torah, summoning
God to court. Without further ado, Miles started to speak in English,
stating his grievances against the accused.

"God! How could you stay here when next door are Auschwitz and
Plaszow? Where were you when all over Europe your sons and
daughters were burning on altars? What did you do when my sainted
father and mother marched to their deaths? When my sisters and
brothers were put to the sword?"

Miles's voice echoed from the thick ancient walls of the Rema's
synagogue. A red sky listened in through the arched windows. The
holy ark remained sealed like the faces of the old people, remnants of
Cracow's Jews, listening to the foreign language that they did not understand.

Miles stepped down and walked over to me. "Do you want to say a
few words?" he asked me. Was I being called as a witness by the
prosecution? I declined. No, not I. I have no quarrel with God, only
with men! I, too, want a trial, but not at the Rema's Synagogue, not
at Nuremberg nor at Frankfurt. I would put on trial each Western
university and library, for harboring millions of malicious words
written against an ancient people, words like murderous daggers hiding beneath the cloak of science and truth—the propaganda of con-
ceited little men. I want to bring to trial the pulpits of countless

212

churches where hate was burning like eternal lights. I want to try the music of Bach and Beethoven for allowing itself to be played while my brethren were led to their deaths. I want to try the botanist for cultivating flowers under the Auschwitz sun, the train conductors with their little red flags for conducting traffic as usual. I want to bring to trial the doctors in their white coats who killed so casually, who exchanged with such great ease the Hippocratic Oath for sheer hypocrisy.

I want to bring to trial a civilization for whom man was such a worthless being. But to bring God to trial? On what charges? For giving men the ability to choose between good and evil?

As we walked out of the synagogue, an old Cracow Jew asked me, "What did your American friend say in the language of dollars?" I told him. "Tell him," he instructed me, "this is not God's synagogue. This is the Rema's synagogue. God likes, these days, big concentrations of Jews, congregations with many quorums. God now dwells in Plaszow, Auschwitz, Sobibor, Treblinka, Majdanek, and many other such 'synagogues'! God does not live here anymore."

*From the diary I kept during a fact-finding mission for President Carter's Commission on the Holocaust, August 1, 1979.*

# Two Funerals

AS A MEMBER OF PRESIDENT CARTER'S COMMISSION ON THE HO-locaust, I traveled during the summer of 1979 on a fact-finding mission to Eastern Europe, to the sites of former ghettos, concentration camps, and locations of open-air killings.

On August 2, 1979, during the fast of Tishah Be'Av, a few of us on our own initiative and under the guidance of Benjamin Meed, a native of Warsaw and a resident of the ghetto during the war, searched in rebuilt Warsaw for remnants of its illustrious Jewish past. It was a painful day; Jewish Warsaw existed only in our tormented memories.

The visit to the Warsaw cemetery was overwhelming: tombstones to a vanished past, with no relatives ever to come to pay respects to their dead. For the relatives were even less privileged: their bones are scattered across the face of Europe in unmarked graves; their ashes and smoke fill the rivers and sky of Europe. Not far from the grave of Rabbi Chaim Brisker,[1] I met an acquaintance, a rabbi from Brooklyn, New York, who has made it his life's mission to look after the graves of prominent Jewish personalities in Eastern Europe.

Among the ancient, crumbling tombstones covered with moss and beautiful Hebrew inscriptions, he told me the following story:

"Recently the municipal government of Kaunas, Lithuania, a Baltic republic of the Soviet Union, decided to relocate the Jewish cemetery. Kaunas—or Kovna, as it was called by the Jews—was until World War II a center of Torah, Hebraism, and Jewish activism. In the Jewish cemetery stand tombstones of many famous men who in the past brought so much fame to this beautiful town: Abraham Mapu, Rabbi Elchanan Spector, and the last Rabbi of Kovna, Rabbi Schapira, who died in the ghetto.[2] At the outbreak of World War II, Rabbi Schapira was in New York visiting the Jewish community and his son Leon, a successful New York lawyer. When the war broke out his son and daughter-in-law begged him to remain. Despite their pleas, he rushed back to Lithuania. 'A shepherd's place is with his flock, especially in troubled times,' he said, and left for Nazi Europe.

"When his grave was about to be moved, the son in New York was consulted as to whether his father's remains should be taken to Israel or reinterred in the new location in Kovna. After much deliberation and consultation with rabbinic authorities, both in America and Israel, it was decided to relocate the grave to the new Jewish cemetery in Kovna with the remains of the other once prominent personalities of Kovna.

"On November 27, 1978, a funeral took place in Kovna as Rabbi Schapira's remains were moved to the new location. Jews from Kovna, Vilna, and as far away as Riga, remnants of past centers of bustling Jewish life, came to pay their respects to the last Rabbi of Kovna, who had died thirty-six years earlier.

"The same day another funeral took place, this one in Brooklyn, New York. People came from all over to pay their last respects to a dear friend, scion of a prominent family, Hebraist, and active member of the Jewish and New York community—Leon Schapira, the last surviving son of the Rabbi of Kovna. He died of a heart attack."

The Warsaw cemetery was a strange place in which to hear a story of that magnitude. It was a bright summer day. The beautiful willow trees bending over us and the tombstones seemed to be listening with us to strange Jewish tales.

Upon my return to New York, I called Henrietta Schapira, the widow of Leon Schapira. No one answered the phone. On February 18, 1980, I was at the Tel Aviv Museum on opening night of the traveling exhibit of Twentieth-Century American Art from the Museum of Modern Art in New York. I was standing in front of a painting entitled "The Face of God" when I heard someone call my name. It was Henrietta Schapira! She told me the full story of that fateful day, November 27, 1978. As we were parting in the rainy Tel Aviv night she said to me, "We must get together very soon. We are now working here in Tel Aviv on a huge family tree. Our grandchildren are already included there. The Kovna tree has many young branches."

*Based on the stories I heard in Warsaw, August 2, 1979, and from Henrietta Schapira on February 18, 1980.*

# The Telephone Operator

IT WAS A BEAUTIFUL, CRISP WINTER EVENING IN JERUSALEM. BIG bright stars were hanging low above the Judean hills and above the miniature model of Jerusalem in back of the Holyland Hotel. I was sitting with my daughter Smadar in the hotel's dining room waiting for our dinner guest. Punctually at 7:30, the time we had set, he arrived, a distinguished personality from Germany. After a fascinating conversation, in which we discussed art, theater, and literature, the inevitable came up: World War II. "You were probably not yet born during the war," he said. "I just managed not missing the event of the century," I told him. "You must have been just a baby—do you have any recollections?" "I do."

Yet somehow I did not want to speak about the Holocaust that night in Jerusalem, although our entire meeting had been arranged to discuss precisely that. "Did you ever witness an actual killing?" he continued to question me, almost interrogating me. "Yes, I did, one particular day. . . ."

Before my eyes stood pictures of a small Lithuanian town, an empty street strewn with Jewish bodies dressed in their Sabbath finery. "Did you see Germans kill on that particular day?" "Only Lithuanian collaborators." "And Germans?" he continued to question me. "Yes, there was one German, but he did not shoot." I stopped short. Again, pictures kept flashing before my eyes, like slides projected on a screen: a small Jewish child dressed in a powder-blue velvet dress with a white lace collar crying for her mother; a Polish friend wrapped in a big shawl holding her by the hand; Grandma's house; a smiling German sitting in a window blowing the little girl a kiss while talking on the telephone. The big Polish woman picks up the little girl and covers her with a large woolen shawl. All is dark. The Polish woman whispers to her: "He is probably calling to report that all the Jews in Eisysky are dead. But we fooled him, my little one, you are alive."

"And what did you do during the war?" I asked him. He smiled, a good-natured smile. "Nothing exciting. I served in the Wehrmacht. I was a telephone operator. . . ."

*Conversation took place on January 20, 1980.*

# Tipping the
# Scales of Justice

THE PHONE RANG IN BEN MEED'S OFFICE; BEN PICKED UP THE RE-
ceiver. A restrained, sorrowful voice asked to speak to the president
of WAGRO.[1] "Speaking," responded Mr. Meed.

The gentleman's voice continued: "My father, Mr. Abraham
Bachner, asked me to call you. The name won't mean anything to
you; you didn't know him. My father just passed away. During one
of my last visits to the hospital, he requested of me that when his time
came you would attend his funeral. You see, Mr. Meed, my father
attended all the annual Warsaw ghetto memorial services at Temple
Emanuel, the ones that your organization sponsors. It was his wish
that you attend his memorial service. My father was a Holocaust survivor." He gave Meed the place and time of the funeral.

Just as Ben Meed entered the chapel, he met Rabbi Fabian
Schonfeld of Young Israel of Kew Garden Hills. "I didn't know you
knew the deceased." "I didn't," responded Meed, and told Rabbi
Schonfeld about the telephone conversation with Bachner's son.
"Ben, I am really grateful that you came. You don't know how
meaningful it is to all of us who knew Abraham."

The casket was brought in, covered in black with a Hebrew inscription saying "He maketh death to vanish in life eternal." Rabbi
Schonfeld began to officiate. "As you know, it is prohibited, according to Halakha (law), to deliver a eulogy on a holiday, and we are now
in the midst of Hanukkah. Instead, I will share with you a conversation I had with Abraham Bachner during one of my visits to the hospital. 'Rabbi,' he said to me, 'I have been a member of your congregation for the past thirty years. I tried to be an honest, observant
Jew. I attended services regularly on Saturdays and weekdays, no
matter what the weather. I know that my time is up and I will soon be
summoned before the heavenly court. I want to be buried not in

217

tachrichim (a shroud), as required by Jewish law, but rather in my concentration-camp uniform, the one I wore in Auschwitz, the one in which I was liberated.'

"I could not understand his strange request and asked for an explanation. Abe said to me, 'You see, Rabbi, when I reach the seat of justice on high, the heavenly prosecutors probably have a list of grievances against me upon which they will base my guilty verdict. When they place my transgressions on one side of the scales of the heavenly court, I will place on the other side my concentration-camp uniform. The hunger, the fear, the humiliation I suffered each minute for years while I was a katzetnik (inmate) will surely tip the scales of justice in my favor. I hope, Rabbi, that you understand. I must be buried in my uniform. It is my defense case, my *melitz yosher* (champion of right).' "

At the conclusion of the services, as the casket was being taken out of the chapel, Ben Meed walked over to Rabbi Schonfeld and asked him, "And what was your decision, Rabbi?" "The concentration-camp uniform is there with him, in the coffin," responded Rabbi Schonfeld.

In Temple Emanuel, on May 3, 1981, the thirty-seventh commemoration of the uprising of the Ghetto Warsaw took place. Ben Meed told the story about Abraham Bachner's last request.

In this gathering, here on earth, there was no doubt that the scales tipped in favor of Abraham Bachner when he stood before the heavenly court. For there is nothing more wholesome in this world than a broken Jewish heart in a concentration-camp uniform.

*Based on the story Ben Meed told me on April 3, 1981, and a letter by Rabbi Fabian Schonfeld in* Martyrdom and Resistance, *March-April 1981, p. 8.*

# Grandfather Avrumche Backenroth's Table

SCHODNICA WAS A SMALL, PICTURESQUE TOWN IN THE CARPA-thian mountains in Galicia, Poland. In the winter the rolling hills instantly became skiing slopes. In the summer the town stood window-high in wild flowers, grass, and vegetable gardens. Winter or summer, the brothers Backenroth's wells pumped oil from the rich Carpathian soil in a steady cadence, for oil was Schodnica's heartbeat and lifeline. Many of the townspeople and residents of the vicinity were employed there. To them, the steady sound of the pumping motors was a constant reassurance that as long as the Backenroth pumps kept turning, their livelihood was as certain as the seasons of the year.

Avraham Yosef—or Reb Avrumche Backenroth, as he was known to all—took great pride in his oil empire and in his large family of seventeen living children. The oil company was managed by his oldest son, Yehuda Leib Backenroth. Leibele was tall and handsome, a former yeshiva student, well versed in secular knowledge and several foreign languages. He had married the very beautiful and well-to-do Sarah Tenzer. They were the parents of two children, Stella (Esther Rachel) and Zygus (Yitzhak Isaac), who were the pride and joy of their parents as well as of grandfather Backenroth.

Among the Backenroths, no business, big or small, private or public, was done without first consulting a Hasidic rebbe, sometimes the Husatyner, at other times the Rizhiner, and above all the Tchortkover Rebbe. One day when geologists recommended drilling for oil at a certain site, it was Rabbi Israel of Tchortkov (1854–1934) who was consulted. The rebbe advised against drilling at the site recommended by the geologist. Somehow, contrary to the Tchortkover's advice, drilling began, but instead of reaching oil they hit abundant water! Despite a substantial financial loss, Grandfather

Avrumche was delighted. It proved beyond any shadow of a doubt that his rebbe understood not only heavenly decrees but also the secrets locked in the depths of the earth.

The biggest and most memorable events of each year for the Backenroths were the Jewish holidays. Twice a year, for the High Holiday season and for Passover, Grandfather Avrumche's seventeen children from his two marriages would come to Schodnica from Baden near Vienna, Cracow, Czernowitz, Bolechow, Drohobycz, and other cities throughout Europe. They came with their spouses, children, governesses, and maids.

The holidays that are especially engraved in Stella's memory are Yom Kippur and Passover. Days before Yom Kippur, Grandmother Backenroth and all her granddaughters would stand around the huge family dining room table rolling long wax candles. Each member of the family, regardless of age, was given a *Gezunt Licht*, a health candle. Others were given an additional candle, a *Neshome Licht*—a soul candle, a candle lit for the souls of the departed members of the family.[1]

The maids were not allowed to partake in this sacred family ceremony. Grandmother Backenroth spared no words in telling her granddaughters the great significance and privilege of participating in the candlemaking for Yom Kippur. On the evening before the holiday, the big dining room was filled with pure-white hens, their legs tied together with a string, their beaks clucking incessantly. Then the ceremony of kapparot began. Each female held a white hen over her head. For the little ones, the hen was held by their mothers or relatives. The hens were swung around the head three times while the following was pronounced: "This is my substitute, my vicarious offering, my atonement; this hen shall meet death, but I shall find a long and pleasant life of peace." After the ceremony, the fowl were slaughtered by the shohet and all donated to the poor, except for the intestines which were thrown outside to the birds. The pure-white cocks waited outside in a shack with their big red combs for their turn, for the men would perform their own ritual of kapparot just at daybreak, at the coming of dawn.

Stella remembers the great terror that seized everyone one time when she made a mistake and during the ceremony of kapparot reversed the order of the sentence *"Mir zum leben, dir zum toit"* (I shall go to life, you to death). Grandfather Avrumche was immediately informed, rebbes were consulted, and large additional sums of charity were distributed to help correct and atone for the child's mistake. Little did they dream on that October day in Schodnica that this slender, beautiful girl with green captivating eyes and delicately sculptured features would one day be the sole survivor of her large, aristocratic family.

On Yom Kippur eve, after the final meal, Grandfather Backenroth would immerse himself in the mikveh (ritual bath). He then put on his snow-white kittel, entered his study lined with holy books, buried his head among the books, and cried as he asked for forgiveness. One by one his sons and daughters, with their spouses and children, all dressed like himself in pure white, approached him and asked him for forgiveness. Forgiveness was granted; then he would place his hands above their heads and bless them with the traditional blessing. They, in turn, blessed their own children and asked one another for forgiveness for any wrongdoings they might have committed during the year. In the background of each family room flickered scores of tall wax candles.

At the big synagogue one could sense the great awe of the hour as the time of Kol Nidrei approached. All the men wore white robes and stood in white socks on the ground which was covered with individual small carpets. In the women's gallery above, all were dressed in white without a trace of makeup, lipstick, or jewelry. Married women covered their heads with white scarves. Grandfather Backenroth stood with the other men for the entire duration of the prayers, for the next twenty-four hours, until after the closing prayer of Neila. He did not even go home at night. Not till Hoshana Rabbah, when it is believed that the verdict of man that was decided on Yom Kippur is sealed and sent out, did Grandfather Backenroth relax and feel reassured that all would be well with his family. In addition to the accepted mystical significance of the day, Hoshana

Rabbah had a special meaning for him, for it was the yahrzeit, the anniversary of the death of the Tchortkover Rebbe, Rabbi David Moshe (1824–1904), the son of Rabbi Israel of Rizhin. He was sure that the rebbe's merit would protect him and his family. After Simhat Torah and a big Kiddush in the house of Sarah and Leibele Backenroth, the family departed and returned to their homes across Europe, only to gather once more at the patriarch's Schodnica home the following spring for the holiday of Passover.

Passover was the holiday that set the pace for the rest of the year. Sometime during the previous summer, Grandfather Backenroth and his sons would drive out to the fields and reap a section of wheat grown under special supervision. Under the watchful eye of Grandfather Avrumche, the wheat was gathered, ground, and baked just before Passover into beautiful, thin, round matzot. During the baking of the matzot, all men were required to immerse themselves in the mikveh. The Hallel, hymns of praise, were sung as the matzot were placed swiftly in the oven and removed before they could rise and become leavened. No women were allowed in the bakery where the matzot were being baked. Grandmother did not mind. She had her hands full as early as Hanukkah, where preparations for Passover began with the rendering of large quantities of chicken fat, which was then stored in huge clay jars.

A few days prior to the holiday, the needy and the poor began to stream to the Backenroth home. Leibele Backenroth was in charge of the distribution of Maot Hittim money to buy wheat for matzot, and of clothes and shoes for the needy. A list was made up of items and sizes, and just before Passover everything would be delivered to the appropriate homes.

On Seder night, around the huge family table, thirteen pillows were set up for reclining in front of thirteen magnificent ceremonial Seder plates, one for each of the married male members of the family. Grandfather's pillow for reclining was known throughout the region. It had been made by Aunt Rivka out of satin, embroidered with gold and silver, and studded with rubies, diamonds, and pearls. The Seder began with Grandfather reciting the Kiddush, followed, according to seniority, by the other males. The Four Questions were asked by the Backenroth sons and addressed to their father. They, in turn, were asked the Four Questions by their own children. This ceremony alone lasted over an hour and a half. Each female member of the family had her prescribed role and function and performed it at the prescribed time. Food was served by the kitchen maids dressed in their festive uniforms. As on all other holidays and secular days, there was also a table for the needy, for Grandfather Backenroth never sat down to dine before making sure that the hungry were fed first.

In 1939 this way of life came to an abrupt end. The war broke out. The Russians occupied Schodnica and nationalized the oil wells. Leibele Backenroth, with many others, was arrested. He was released after three months due to the workers' intervention on his behalf. They signed a petition to the Russian commissar describing his kindness toward the workers and the poor. Although Leibele was released from prison, others were deported to Siberia. After his release, the family fled to Rumania, but sometime later returned once more to their beloved Schodnica. Slowly they became accustomed to the Russian occupation, hoping that this too would soon end and life in Schodnica would return to normal.

But instead came June 22, 1941. Germany invaded Russia and within a few days a world was to vanish forever.

On the night of July 4/5, 1941, Ukrainian peasants from the mountains and from the village of Mraznica, as well as next-door neighbors and many who had worked for the Backenroth family, surrounded the town. On July 4, Friday, all able-bodied Jewish men and young women were ordered to report to the town's main street; older women and children were to remain at home. They assembled as ordered. Leibele Backenroth and his daughter Stella were among them. The girls were ordered to scrub the cobblestones with toothbrushes; the men were marched off in small groups under heavy guard in the direction of the forest.

Nachman Pessach, the town's woodchopper, a simple Jew and a devout Hasid, wrapped himself in his prayer shawl and began to recite the Vidduy, the confession before one's death. Leibele Backenroth asked him, "What are you doing, Reb Nachman?" "We are on our last walk in this hallway called earth. We are about to enter eternity," replied Nachman and resumed the reciting of the Vidduy.

The pumps of the oil wells were still. From a distance shots were heard echoing in the mountains. It was late Friday afternoon. The girls were still scrubbing the cobblestones. More and more men were led off in the direction of the forest. Suddenly, as if driven by an impulse, Stella ran over to the Ukrainian commander of the pogrom from the nearby village of Mraznica. Stella knew him, for he, too, had been one of their workers. "I beg you, spare my father, my uncles, my cousins, I will give you all the money and the family possessions you want." He looked at her with a sarcastic smile. Only a while ago it would have been a great privilege for him even to speak to Stella Backenroth, an heiress to the Backenroth wealth. Now she was begging him to spare the Backenroth lives. The war indeed is a marvelous fortune wheel! "I can't talk to you here; follow me to your home." She did.

Once inside the house, Stella encouraged him to take all his heart desired. "It is not yours to give anymore, it all belongs to us," he told Stella in a matter-of-fact voice. He took a few bottles of vodka and promised that he would come for the rest later. "My father, my uncles, my cousins, would you spare their lives?" Stella continued to plead with him. "It is too late, they are all dead. Only your father is still alive; he is hiding in the house of one of your maids." He ordered Stella back to the street to scrub the cobblestones.

By Saturday, July 5, only girls were left on the main street of Schodnica. They were given shovels and ordered to march in the direction of the forest. The sight that appeared before their eyes was worse than their worst premonitions. The mutilated bodies of hundreds of their loved ones were lying on the forest ground. They had been shot with explosive bullets, stabbed with knives and pitchforks, cut with axes. The girls were ordered to bury the dead. Each began to search for her own loved ones, to assemble mutilated bodies of fathers, brothers, bridegrooms, uncles, cousins. Stella found the members of her family scattered throughout the killing grounds. She found them, her uncles, cousins, nephews. She hardly recognized one uncle. Only three days ago when she had last seen him alive, he was a young man with a shock of black hair. Now his hair was as white as a dove. Together with her relatives in the grave she dug, she also placed the body of a young man, a friend since childhood. Slowly she pulled out the kitchen knife from his heart as she put his lifeless body next to the others. *"Schnell! Schnell!"* she heard a command behind her back. Only then did she realize that the local Ukrainians had been joined by German soldiers. They were pointing their guns at the girls and shooting down the vultures and crows that were hovering above the graves. Stella never knew if the bullets were intended for her or for the birds of prey above the graves.

The burial was over. Most of the Schodnica men were covered by mounds of earth in a single corner of the forest that they had known so well in their brief lives. "The forest is filthy with Jewish blood," announced a German officer. "You will lick it with your tongues till it is spotlessly clean." They did.

Then, from among the trees, as if in a strange vision, appeared five living men. Among them was Stella's father. They asked permission to say the prayer for the dead. Their voices tried to overcome the German laughter, the drunken Ukrainian songs, the shrieks of the vultures. The Carpathian mountains, where the founders of Hasidism prayed and lived, echoed with the muffled sobs of the girls and the ancient prayer of the mourner's Kaddish: "Magnified and sanctified be his great Name in the world which he hath created according to his will."

The girls were ordered to return home. Stella left the forest not knowing if the Ukrainians would spare her father and the handful of other men who survived the pogrom. As she entered the house she met her mother and brother Zygus who had just returned from their hiding place. They had no need to ask for an explanation. Stella's blood-smeared clothes, face, and hands told it all. She washed; her mother prepared a cup of tea for her, and they sat near the huge family dining-room table. Sarah looked at her grown-up daughter, at her eleven-year-old son, and said, "Grandfather Backenroth was a lucky man to die before this terrible war. He was buried in the family plot at Drohobycz in a coffin made from his dining-room table, the table where the poor and the needy ate. Only the merciful God knows what fate awaits the handful of us still left among the living." Just then the door opened and Leibele Backenroth walked in. "I am the most fortunate woman in the world," said Sarah, as she and her children embraced the man who had just returned from the dead.

On the following day, the surviving Jews of Schodnica were marched on foot to the neighboring town of Drohobycz. Stella, her grandparents, her parents, and her brother were among them.

*Based on my interview with Stella Wieseltier, née Backenroth, June 17 and 22, 1981.*

# Rejoining the Human Race

IN DROHOBYCZ, STELLA AND HER FAMILY QUICKLY LEARNED THAT hunger does not discriminate even against a Backenroth. In the Drohobycz of 1941, a table such as Avrumche Backenroth's where the hungry were fed did not exist.

Stella soon realized that her father, Leibele Backenroth, the oil magnate, who returned that night from the pogrom in Schodnica, was a changed man. All his initiative, vigor, and drive were gone. He was a desperate man, unable to cope with the new order of things. Once when Stella scolded her brother for not addressing their father properly, Leibele Backenroth responded: "The child is right. A father is no longer a father if he cannot provide a slice of bread and a pair of shoes for his children. I do not deserve the respect accorded to a father."

The burden of the family's survival was now thrust upon Stella's young shoulders. Under the cover of night she and other young girls would sneak out of Drohobycz, make their way across forest and fields back to Schodnica, and pick vegetables from their own gardens. With loads of fifty pounds and more they would return to Drohobycz. Stella even managed to go back to Schodnica and, in broad daylight, bring to Drohobycz the family cow, parading her under the Gestapo windows! Three days later a decree was issued banning Jews from owning livestock. The cow was confiscated by the Gestapo. Stella did not rest. Nothing was too big, too small, or too difficult for her as long as it brought some food for her darling Zygus, her parents, and her mother's parents, the Tenzers, who had come with them. Conditions in the ghetto became more difficult with each passing day.[1] Stella's father was taken away to the labor camp of Dachufka. Aktions against the very young and the aged became more frequent. The lives of her brother, mother, and grandparents were in constant danger. And then it happened. In the summer of 1943, Stella's grandfather and grandmother were taken aboard trucks to Bronica.[2] In the evening the trucks returned to Drohobycz with the victims' clothing. On the fifth day of Sivan, May 8, 1943, her mother and brother were murdered in Bronica. On the twentieth day of Tamuz, July 23, 1943, her father was shot there too.

Stella was on one of the trucks going to Bronica but she was pulled down by a member of the Judenrat: "You are too young to die," he announced. "You can still serve the Third Reich." As she stood there in a daze, a Gestapo man by the name of Landau was practicing target shooting. Instinctively, she bent down. But Stella was not his target that day. He had a pocket full of lollipops. A group of children who were dragged out of hiding were standing around him. He asked them, one by one, if they would like lollipops, and if they wanted one, they should open their mouths. They did. One by one he shot them in their open mouths. Stella fainted. (Until today, she feels faint when she sees dolls. To her, they represent the little, lifeless bodies of the innocent children on that Drohobycz street.)

After the liquidation of the ghetto, Stella somehow made her way back to Schodnica and found refuge with Stanislav and Aniela

Nendza there in a cellar under a stable on the premises of the Backenroth oil wells. She lived with four more adults: her uncles, Leon and David Thorne,[3] Dr. Isidor Friedman, a lawyer, and Luisa Mahler. The cellar was six feet long, about four feet wide, and about five feet high. It was filled with water and rats. Above, in freedom and more spacious quarters, were a pig, a goat, rabbits, and chickens. Never did Avrumche Backenroth dream that his beloved granddaughter would use his oil fields in this manner!

On Tuesday, August 8, 1944, at 7:00 A.M., Benek, the sixteen-year-old son of Janiewski, opened the trapdoor to the cellar and brought them the message of freedom: Russian troops had just liberated Schodnica.[4] Stella, with the others, climbed out of the cellar. It was the first time in nine months that she had seen the sky and the sun.

With swollen feet, barely able to walk, Stella decided to see Schodnica once more. The big synagogue was a stable filled with horses. Her own home was occupied by three Ukrainian families. Around Grandfather Backenroth's huge dining-room table were sitting some drunken Ukrainians. Only the Carpathian mountains were as graceful as ever, and the Backenroth pumps were still bringing up oil from the blood-soaked earth of Schodnica. Stella vowed never to return to this cursed town that she had once loved. She left for Warsaw. There she met and married a young man named Mark Wieseltier, an officer in the Polish Army who had spent the war in Siberia. For some time they lived as Christians in a house filled with icons, fearing that they too would join the ever-growing list of Jewish casualties, Jews who survived the war only to be killed by hostile Poles.[5]

In the fall of 1945 there was a hanging of Nazi war criminals in Majdanek.[6] Stella decided to go there for the occasion. She wanted revenge, revenge for every Jew whom she had buried with her own hands, for each child shot in Drohobycz, for her mother, father, grandparents, for her beloved Zygus, for the world of her youth that was so brutally murdered. She traveled all night to assure herself a choice seat. The hanging began. The noose was placed around the neck of each criminal. The chairs were kicked out from underneath, the bodies dangled, the crowd cheered. Stella closed her eyes in horror. "My God! What am I doing here?" she mumbled to herself. "Cheering death? Death begets more death, hatred more hatred. It will never bring back Father, Mother, and Zygus." Her revenge was short-lived, it had lost all its sweetness. All she wanted was to get away, away from Majdanek, from Warsaw, from Poland, away from this accursed soil—once her ancestral home, now the graveyard of her people.

In that moment, Stella sensed that she had once more joined the human race that still must exist somewhere, someplace—a world like that she once knew in Schodnica.

*Based on my interviews with Stella Wieseltier, née Backenroth, on June 17 and 22, 1981.*

# Glossary

**Agudat Israel** Hebrew for Union or Association of Israel. World Orthodox Jewish movement, founded in 1912, seeking to preserve and institute Orthodoxy by adherence to Halakha as the principle governing Jewish life and society.

**Aktion** Ghetto operation in which Jews were rounded up and deported to death camps or killed on the spot or in the nearby vicinity.

**Appell** *See* ZEILAPPELL.

**Askari** Swahili for soldier, guard, policeman. Used in World War II for Ukrainians who had volunteered for service with the German S.S. Usage dates from German colonial days in East Africa.

**Baal Shem Tov** Israel ben Eliezer 1700–1760, founder and first leader of Hasidism.

**Bar Mitzvah** Aramaic for son, Hebrew for command or duty, thus "man of duty." Jewish boy who has reached thirteen, the age of religious duty and responsibility, and can now be counted as part of a MINYAN. Also the ceremony at which this is recognized.

**Beit midrash** Hebrew for house of study. Synagogue or place attached to a synagogue where Jews gather to study sacred books.

**Bevorzugenlager** Sector in a concentration camp for people with special privileges.

**Bimah** Platform of a synagogue on which stands the desk from which the Scriptures are read.

**Blockälteste, blokhova** Female inmate, supervisor of a barracks in a concentration camp. Her functions, title, and privileges varied from camp to camp. *See also* STUBHOVA.

**Bund** Jewish secular labor movement, founded in Vilna in 1897, supporting Jewish national rights. Originally Yiddishist and anti-Zionist.

**Diaspora** Originally the Greek term used by Hellenistic Jews for all Jewish settlements that were dispersed outside ERETZ YISRAEL; all lands of dispersion outside the land of Israel.

**Din Torah** Hebrew for judgment or law. Lawsuit presented before an individual or individuals well versed in Jewish law.

231

**Dybbuk** Hebrew for joining, sticking, clinging. Spirit of deceased that is believed to enter the body of a living person and possess it.

**Einsatzgruppen** Mobile killing units. After the German invasion of the Soviet Union on June 22, 1941, the Einsatzgruppen murdered an estimated million and a half Jews and also many other "dangerous" persons, including Communists.

**Eretz Yisrael** Hebrew for the Land of Israel.

**Final Solution** Or "Final Solution of the Jewish Question." *Endlosung der Judenfrage.* Nazi euphemism used in correspondence and other forms of communication, denoting the program relating to annihilation of the Jews.

**Four Questions** Passage in the Passover HAGGADAH customarily asked by the son or the youngest person present at the SEDER service. The father's reply is the Haggadah's narrative about the Exodus from Egypt and its importance in the history of the Jewish people.

**Gabbai** From the Hebrew verb *to collect.* Honorary official of a Jewish congregation who assists during the TORAH reading and at other functions. Originally, a collector of taxes or dues. In the Hasidic community, the rebbe's personal aide and attendant.

**Gemara,** *pl.* **Gemarot** Aramaic for learning. The traditions, discussions, and rulings of the Amoraim, supplementing the rabbinic scholars (the Tanaim) of the MISHNAH, forming part of the TALMUD. In common speech, a single volume of the Talmud.

**Gestapo** Acronym for *Ge*heime *Sta*atspolizei, the Secret State Police in the German Third Reich.

**Gut Shabbes** Yiddish for "Good Sabbath." Traditional Jewish Sabbath greeting.

**Haggadah** Hebrew for telling. Set form of benedictions, prayers, biblical quotations, Psalms, MIDRASHIC commentary, and songs recited at the SEDER during PASSOVER. It is based on the service prescribed in the MISHNAH (Pesachim 10).

**Halakha,** *pl.* **Halakhot** Hebrew, from the verb *to go.* An accepted decision in rabbinic law. Also used for purely legal matters in the Talmud, and for all Jewish lore collectively.

**Halatl** Yiddish for robe, diminutive form. Robe worn by Hasidim on festive occasions and ceremonies at synagogue and home.

**Hallah** Special, soft white bread, often in braided shape, eaten on the Sabbath and holidays.

**Hallel** Prayer of Praise (Psalms 113–18) recited on certain festivals and on days of the New Month (Rosh Hodesh).

**Hametz** Leavened foodstuffs that may not be eaten, found in the house, or owned during the Passover holiday. Hametz is disposed of in three ways: by burning, annulling, and selling. Since disposing of hametz may result in hardships, especially when large quantities are involved, as when it is needed for business, the hametz can be sold to a non-Jew for the duration of the holiday. The sale must be of a legal nature, carried out by means of a bill of sale. Any hametz which a Jew has kept over Passover may never be used by him.

**Hanukkah** Hebrew for dedication, consecration. The Feast of Lights, an eight-day celebration commemorating the victory of Judah Maccabee over the Syrian King Antiochus Epiphanes and the subsequent rededication of the Temple in 165 B.C.E.

**Hanukkiah** Candelabrum or oil lamp with eight branches or compartments, used in the celebration of HANUKKAH.

**Haroset** Mixture of apples, nuts, cinnamon, and wine consumed during the SEDER meal, symbolic of the mortar used by Jews to make bricks during their slavery in Egypt.

**Hasid,** *pl.* **Hasidim** Hebrew for pious, a follower of the religious movement founded by the BAAL SHEM TOV.

**Havdalah** Hebrew for differentiation, distinction. Ceremony marking the end of the Sabbath, and of biblical holidays.

**Hazan** Preceptor who intones the liturgy and leads the prayers in the synagogue.

**High Holidays** ROSH HASHANAH and YOM KIPPUR, a period in the autumn dedicated to spiritual regeneration and religious rehabilitation. Also known as The Days of Awe.

**Hoshanah Rabbah** The seventh day of SUKKOT, the harvest festival. Climax of the festival in the time of the Temple, when seven processions were made around the altar and verses of Hoshana (O Save) were sung.

**Jewish Agency** International nongovernmental body centered in Jerusalem, established under the League of Nations Mandate in 1922, whose aims were to assist and encourage Jews throughout the world to help in the development of the Land of Israel.

**Judenfrei, Judenrein** German adjective for an area whose Jews had all been killed or deported to ghettos or to concentration, labor, or death camps.

**Judenrat** German for Jewish council appointed by the occupation authorities to administer the ghetto, according to an order issued by Reinhard Heydrich, September 21, 1939.

**Kaddish** From the Aramaic for holy. Ancient prayer, originally used after the study period, now recited publicly at the death of parents and other close relatives for the first eleven months and on the anniversary of the death.

**Kapo** Nazi term, derived from the Italian *capo* (head), denoting a concentration camp inmate in charge of other inmates.

**Kapote** Long black coat once worn by Eastern European Jews and now worn by some Hasidic men.

**Kapparot** *pl.* of **Kapparah,** a symbolic ceremony taking place before YOM KIPPUR in which the sins of a person are symbolically transferred to a fowl, a white hen or rooster.

**Karpas** Bit of vegetable to be dipped in salt water during the SEDER service.

**Katzetnik** Camp inmate. From KZ, abbreviation for *Katzetlager* or KONZENTRATIONS LAGER.

**Kiddush** Hebrew for sanctification. Prayer recited over wine or bread before the evening and morning meals on the Sabbath and festivals. Also a festive meal on the Sabbath and holidays to which one invites friends.

**Kippah** *See* YARMULKE.

**Kittel** White robe worn on the HIGH HOLIDAYS and other occasions, symbolizing remembrance of death, also purity.

**Kol Nidrei** Literally, "all vows." Ancient prayer in Aramaic recited at sundown on the eve of YOM KIPPUR.

**Kommando** German for unit or group.

**Konzentrations Lager** German for concentration camp.

**Kvitl,** *pl.* **kvitlach** Yiddish for note or receipt. Folded note addressed to a ZADDIK, living or dead, containing a special request. The devout HASID believes that with the zaddik's intervention on his behalf, the written wish will materialize.

**Maror** Hebrew for bitter herb. Traditional accompaniment of the SEDER meal, which the children of Israel were commanded to eat both in Egypt (Exodus 12:8) and "throughout their generations."

**Matzah,** *pl.* **matzot** From the Hebrew verb *to squeeze*. Unleavened bread, eaten during PASSOVER as remembrance of the Israelites' hasty Exodus from Egypt.

**Melamed,** *pl.* **Melamdim** Hebrew for teacher. Generally applied to old-time tutor or preceptor.

**Messiah** Hebrew for anointed. Originally a king or priest anointed with holy oil and consecrated to carry out the purpose of God. Later the focus of a prophetic vision of the restoration of Israel and establishment of the just kingdom on earth. The yearning for the Messiah's coming is part of the Jewish tradition and psyche.

**Midrash** Hebrew for exposition. Homiletic commentary on the Scriptures elucidating legal points (Midrash HALAKHA) or bringing out lessons by stories and anecdotes (Midrash AGGADAH). Also a collection of such rabbinic interpretations.

**Mikveh** Hebrew for a collection of water. Ritual bath for purification. The ritual immersion of women in the mikveh seven days after the end of the menstrual flow is a fundamental HALAKHIC principle governing the traditional Jewish family.

**Minyan** The minimum number of adult men (ten) required for communal prayer. Quorum.

**Mishnah** Hebrew for teaching. Codification of Jewish oral law by Judah the Prince about 210 A.C.E. Consists of Six Orders. *See* TALMUD.

**Mitnagged,** *pl.* **Mitnaggedim** Hebrew for opponents. Originally Eastern European Jews, chiefly in Lithuania, opposed to Hasidism. Used as synonym for Lithuanian Jews.

**Mitzvah,** *pl.* **Mitzvot** Hebrew for command. A commandment, precept, or religious duty, either biblical or rabbinic. Also a meritorious act or good deed.

**Mizrach** Hebrew for Eastern. The wall in the synagogue facing east, toward Jerusalem, along which sat the most highly respected males, mainly scholars, notables, and well to-do individuals.

**Mizrachi** Religious Zionist movement, founded in 1904. United in 1957 with Hapoel Hamizrachi into a unified religious Zionist organization, both national and worldwide.

**Musselman** German for Muslim. Name given to an emaciated concentration-camp inmate who had lost the will to live.

**Neolog** Member of the Jewish Reform movement in Hungary.

**Niggun,** *pl.* **Niggunim** Melody or tune used traditionally for chanting specific prayers or on specific holidays. Hasidic dynasties are distinguished by their particular *niggunim*, some composed by the ZADDIK himself.

**Ninth of Av** *See* TISHAH BE'AV.

**Pan, Pania** Polish for Mr., Mrs.

**Parental blessing** Blessing of children by their parents on all important occasions, notably on the eve of Sabbath and festivals. There is a special blessing for boys and one for girls.

**Passover** Spring festival beginning on the fifteenth day of Nisan, continuing for seven days in the Land of Israel and eight days in the DIASPORA, that commemorates the Exodus from Egypt. No leaven may be eaten; MATZOT replace bread. The ceremonial commemorative meal, the SEDER, is conducted on the first night and in the Diaspora also on the second night.

**Payot** *See* SIDELOCKS.

**Pogrom** From the Russian for devastation, destruction. An organized massacre, especially of Jews.

**Prayer for Dew** On the first day of Passover a special prayer for dew is recited in the synagogue. It does not rain in Israel during the summer (May–October) and dew is of primary importance.

**Rabbin, Rabbiner** Polish and German, respectively, for rabbi.

**Reb** Honorary title like Mr., used when addressing an elderly Jew.

**Rebbe** Yiddish form for rabbi, applied usually to a teacher or Hasidic spiritual leader.

**Rebbetzin** The wife of a REBBE or RABBI.

**Rosh Hashanah** The Jewish New Year, beginning on the first day of the month of Tishrei, start of the HIGH HOLIDAYS. Since early times, a day of reflection and repentance, concerned with the individual and his relation to God and to his fellow men. A prominent feature is the sounding of the SHOFAR.

**Sanhedrin** Supreme judicial body in Palestine during the Roman period, consisting of seventy-one ordained scholars. Also a tractate in the TALMUD.

**Seder** Hebrew for order, sequence. Ceremony celebrated at table in the home on PASSOVER night, according to order prescribed in the HAGGADAH. During the ceremony four cups of wine are drunk, a meal is eaten, and adult male members sit in a reclining position to symbolize that they are free men.

**Selection** Concentration camp process of selecting inmates for death, forced labor, or other purposes.

**Shalom aleichem** Hebrew for "Peace be with you." Traditional Jewish greeting.

**Shavuot** The Feast of Weeks, completing seven weeks from the second day of PASSOVER, on which a measure of the new barley was brought to the Temple. Also commemorates the giving of the Ten Commandments.

**Shegetz,** *pl.* **shkotzim** A non-Jewish boy or youth.

**Shema Yisrael** Hebrew "Hear, O Israel." First words of confession of faith proclaiming the absolute unity of God. Recited at daily prayers and before death.

**Shemini Atzeret** The Eighth Day of Solemn Assembly, celebrated after the seventh day of the SUKKOT festival.

**Shikse** A non-Jewish girl or young woman.

**Shivah** Hebrew for seven. The seven days of mourning following burial.

**Shofar** Ram's horn sounded on ROSH HASHANAH, at the conclusion of YOM KIPPUR, and on other occasions.

**Shohet,** *pl.* **Shohatim** Ritual slaughterer of animals and poultry in accordance with Jewish dietary laws.

**Shtetl,** *pl.* **shtetlach** Yiddish for little-town. Jewish small-town communities in Eastern Europe.

**Shtibl,** *pl.* **shtiblach** Yiddish for little house. Prayerhouses, especially Hasidic.

**Shtraiml,** *pl.* **shtraimlach** Fur-edged hat worn by some Hasidic Jews on the Sabbath, holidays, and joyful occasions.

**Shul** Yiddish for synagogue, place of study. From the German *Schule* (school).

**Sidelocks** Unshorn sideburns worn by Orthodox Jewish males, according to Leviticus 19:27: "Ye shall not round the corners of your heads, neither shalt thou mar the corners of thy beard." PAYOT in Hebrew.

**Simhat Torah** Holiday of Rejoicing in the Torah. In the Diaspora, it follows SHEMINI ATZERET, when the reading of the Pentateuch is completed and begun anew for the coming year. In Israel, the two holidays are celebrated on the same day.

**Sonderkommando** A special KOMMANDO.

**Stubhova** Female inmate supervisor of a section of a barracks in a concentration camp, responsible to a BLOKHOVA. Varied from camp to camp.


**Tachrichim** Burial shroud (shrouds in Hebrew).

**Tallit** A prayer shawl, rectangular in form with fringes at the corners.

**Tallit Katan** *See* TZITZIT.

**Talmud** Hebrew for study, learning. The major body of Jewish teachings, consisting of the MISHNAH, in Hebrew, and the GEMARA, in Aramaic. Written by generations of scholars and jurists in two centers, Babylon and Palestine, in the third to fifth centuries, the Talmud concerns itself with every area of human activity and experience. It is to be found on the bookshelves of many Jewish homes and in every BEIT MIDRASH.

**Tefillin** Phylacteries, small leather cases containing passages from Scripture and affixed to the forehead and arm by male Jews during the recital of morning prayers on weekdays.

**Third Sabbath meal** Most spiritual and mystical of the three meals taken on the Sabbath. It is stated in the TALMUD that the obligation to eat three meals on the Sabbath is reflected in the threefold repetition of the word *today* in Exodus 16:25.

**Tishah Be'Av** The ninth day of the month of Av, a fast day commemorating the destruction of the First and Second Temples. Also a day on which other calamities came upon Israel.

**Torah** Hebrew for teaching, instruction. The first five books of the Bible, also known as the Five Books of Moses, or the Pentateuch. Also used for the Pentateuchal scroll for reading in synagogue, and for the entire body of traditional Jewish teaching and literature.

**Tzitzit** Rectangular garment of linen, cotton, or wool with woolen *tzitziot* (Hebrew for fringes) on its corners, worn during the day by observant Jews. The number of threads and knots in each fringe is prescribed (Numbers 15:37–41; Deuteronomy 22:12).

**Umschlagplatz** Assembly point from which mass deportations took place in the Warsaw ghetto.

**Untersturmführer** S.S. officer, equivalent in rank to second lieutenant.

**Vidduy** Hebrew for confession. Prayer recited on several occasions, as when a Jew realizes he is about to die. It must be recited while the person is fully conscious.

**WAGRO** Warsaw Ghetto Resistance Organization. Organized in the U.S.A. by Warsaw survivors. Holds annual memorial services to commemorate the ghetto uprising.

**Washing the hands** Obligatory before a meal, accompanied by a blessing.

**Wehrmacht** German for armed forces. Name by which the German armed forces were known in World War II.

**Yad Vashem** Israel's Martyrs and Heroes Remembrance Authority. National institute in Jerusalem dedicated to perpetuating the memory of the martyrs of the Holocaust through research, documentation, and publications. Origin of name Isaiah 56:5.

**Yahrzeit** Anniversary of a person's death, observed by reciting the KADDISH in the synagogue and by lighting a memorial candle.

**Yarmulke** Word of Slavic origin, used for the skullcap worn by observant Jews when not wearing a hat, to keep the head covered. Also called KIPPAH or *kappel*.

**Yeshivah,** *pl.* **yeshivot** Hebrew for sitting. Academy of higher Talmudic learning; the Yeshivot are the centers of traditional Jewish education and study of TORAH.

**Yeshivah bocher** Unmarried man student of YESHIVAH.

**Yom Kippur** The Day of Atonement, the holiest day on the Jewish calendar, a day of fasting and prayer. *See* HIGH HOLIDAYS.

**Zaddik,** *pl.* **zaddikim** Spiritual leader of a Hasidic community. Also used for a man of saintly behavior.

**Zeilappell** German for roll call. A call-up of camp inmates for the purpose of making a head count.

**Zemirot** Table songs sung during Sabbath meals. Composed by poets, mystics, scholars, and ZADDIKIM over a period of centuries; new ones are constantly being added.

**Zohar** The Book of Splendor, mystical commentary on the Pentateuch. Main text of the Kabbalah, or Cabala.

# Notes

## ONE: ANCESTORS AND FAITH

### Hovering above the Pit

1. The Janowska Road Camp was situated near the cemeteries and sand mountains outside the city of Lvov, in the Ukraine. It was established in October–November 1941 by Dr. Wechter, the governor of the District of Galicia, and S.S. Major General Katzman, police chief of Galicia. Officially a forced-labor camp, it was in reality a place of torture and death which was eventually taken over by the S.S. economic administrative main office (WVHA), the agency that controlled concentration camps. The camp was notorious for the cruelty of its German commanders and their Ukrainian and Russian collaborators. In many instances, inmates were brutally murdered for the entertainment of the camp officials. Tens of thousands of Jews, mainly from eastern Galicia, met their deaths there. The Germans, because of the threat of possible resistance, liquidated the camp in a surprise action on November 20, 1943. The "death brigade" was spared that liquidation and then given the task of erasing all traces of the murder. Bodies were exhumed from the mass graves, burned, and the ashes scattered in the fields and buried in the pits. Only a few individuals escaped and survived. For eyewitness accounts, see Leon Weliczker Wells, *The Death Brigade: The Janowska Road* (New York: Holocaust Library, 1978)—Wells was a member of the death brigade and kept a diary while in camp; Leon Thorne, *Out of the Ashes* (New York: Bloch Publishing Co., 1976) —Dr. Thorne wrote a diary while in hiding, after his escape from Janowska; and David Kahana, *Yoman Ghetto Lvov* (Jerusalem: Yad Vashem, 1978).

Kahana is another escapee from Janowska. His diary describes his experiences in the Lvov ghetto and Janowska in detail. Like the other diaries, it is a primary source, since it was written during the war while Kahana was in hiding in the monasteries of Metropolitan Andreas Scheptytzkyj, who deserves special mention as one of the few "righteous among the nations" in the bloody vicinity of Lvov. Scion of one of the most prominent Polish Catholic families, he left the Catholic Church in 1886 and joined the Uniate Eastern Church where he soon rose to the position of metropolitan. In 1906 he founded the Studite Order dedicated, among other goals, to social welfare projects. The Studite monasteries and convents, under Metropolitan Scheptytzkyj and his brother Clement's jurisdiction, served as a hiding place for a number of Jews, especially children, during the war. After Kahana escaped from Janowska, he hid in the metropolitan's private study. Of special interest is Scheptytzkyj's Pastoral Letter of June 1941, "Thou Shalt Not Kill"; see Kahana, pp. 135–85.

2. The vicinity of the Janowska Road Camp was scarred with bomb craters from World War I. The huge pits were used as torture sites and mass graves. See Lohamei Hagetaot, pictorial archives, photograph no. 19150.

## The Son of the Shohet of Medzhibozh

1. The Soviet–German nonaggression pact was signed on August 23, 1939. Among other items, it included an agreement on German and Russian spheres of influence, with the river Vistula as the border between the two spheres. On September 17, 1939, Soviet troops crossed into Poland and the western river Bug became the new border. On October 22, the Russians held elections in the newly acquired territories. On November 1, 1939, the Supreme Soviet of the USSR approved the new territories as part of the Soviet Republics of Belorussia and the Ukraine. Lvov became a Ukrainian city. On June 30, 1941, it was occupied by the Germans.
2. At that time he was still known as the Rabbi of Pruchnik, where he had been rabbi until 1932. Only after his arrival in the United States in 1946 did he assume the title Bluzhover Rabbi. His grandfather, Rabbi Zevi Elimelekh (1841–1924), was founder of the Bluzhov dynasty, of which Rabbi Israel Spira is the sole survivor. The Hasidic origins of the dynasty date back to Rabbi Zvi Elimelech of Dinov (1783–1841). His two brothers, Rabbi Eliezer of Ribatisch and Rabbi Meir of Bluzhov, and their families were murdered by the Nazis.
3. Rabbi Abraham Jacob Friedman of Boyan-Lvov (1886–1942) lived in Lvov and perished in the Holocaust with his wife Hannah. See Menashe Unger, *Admorim Shenispu Bashoah* (Jerusalem: Mossad Harav Kook, 1969), pp. 14–17. The same tale with slight variations is told there.
4. Medzhibozh is a small town in Podolia, today in the Ukrainian USSR. It is the cradle of Hasidism, associated with the founder of the movement, the Baal Shem Tov. He lived in Medzhibozh from 1740 until his death in 1760. The town remained a Hasidic center until the destruction of the Jewish community during the Holocaust.

## The Kiss

1. Jews with foreign passports enjoyed special privileges. For more on this subject, see Part Two, the tale "For the Sake of Friendship."
2. Lemberg is the German name for Lvov, now capital of the Lvov oblast, in the western Ukraine, USSR. It was occupied by German troops from 1941 to 1944, and most of its Jewish population of about 100,000 was massacred.
3. Sanhedrin 19/b; Megila 13/a.

## The Halatl of Rabbi Baruch of Medzhibozh

1. Baruch of Medzhibozh was one of the three sons of Edl, the daughter of the Baal Shem Tov (1700–1760), the founder of the Hasidic movement.
2. For eyewitness accounts of the Shpitalna bath-house experience of Janowska inmates, see Thorne, *Out of the Ashes*, pp. 57–63, and Kahana, *Yoman Ghetto Lvov*, pp. 111–13.

## Kindling the First Hanukkah Light in Bergen Belsen

1. Zishe Zamietchkowski (1921–1974), born to Bundist parents in Lodz, was educated near Warsaw. After World War II, he settled with his wife and mother in Brichbach, Lower Silesia, where he served as secretary of the Bund. In 1951, he emigrated to Israel where he was one of the Bund's leaders until his death on May 21, 1974. See *"Nishto mer unzer Zishe"* in *Lebens Fragn Socialistishe Chodes-Schrift far Politik Virtshaft un Cultur*, Tel Aviv, Israel, June 1974.
2. Sima, a Lithuanian Jewish woman, also conducted Hanukkah services at Bergen Belsen. Told by Leslie H. Hardman and written by Cecily Goodman, *The Survivors* (London: Valentine, Mitchell, 1958), pp. 27–28.

## Seder Night in Bergen Belsen: "Tonight We Have Only Matzah"

1. Bergen Belsen was established as an *Aufenthaltslager*, a transit camp. In the spring of 1943, an agreement was made between the German Foreign Office and the S.S. leadership to retain some 10,000 Jews with foreign passports and papers, who would be exchanged for Germans in English and American occupied territory. About 5,000 *Austauschjuden* (exchange Jews) were deported to Bergen Belsen between 1943 and 1945. Only 351 of them were actually exchanged. The Bochnia transport of "exchange Jews" arrived on July 11, 1943. According to directions from Heinrich Himmler, the S.S. head and later Minister of the Interior, the Bergen Belsen transit camp, while not given the status of an internment camp, was subordinated to the S.S. WVHA and thus integrated into the concentration-camp system. This proved to be a decision of disastrous consequences.
2. I discussed this incident with Dr. Eberhard Kolb on January 21, 1980. He explained that the commandant's reply was a figure of speech. To make such a decision was Haas's prerogative as camp commandant.
3. From the morning prayers for the Sabbath and Festivals.
4. Zechariah 14:7; Isaiah 9:1.

## The Berlin–Bucharest Express

1. The massacre of the Jews of Zhitomir was one of the killing operations by the Einsatzgruppen. For a description of this episode see Raul Hilberg, *Destruction of European Jewry* (New York: Harper Colophon Books, 1979), p. 197.

## The Vision of the Red Stars

1. Rabbi Shlomo Chanoch Rabinowitz of Radomsk (1882–1942) was one of Poland's most outstanding Hasidic rabbis. He established a network of thirty-six yeshivot, the Keter Torah, where thousands of young men studied. He was a successful businessman and among the financial supporters of his yeshivot. His library was second in size only to that of the Grand Rabbi of Gur. When World War II broke out, the Radomsk rabbi and his family fled from Sosnowiec to Lodz and from there to Warsaw. They were all murdered in the Warsaw ghetto on August 1, 1942. See Unger, *Admorim Shenispu Bashoah*, pp. 283–84.

## Honor Thy Mother

1. *Obozy Hitlerowskie na Ziemiach Polskich,* pp. 118–19.
2. In October 1938, the Gestapo rounded up and expelled about 15,000 Jews, Polish citizens residing in Germany. At first, Poland refused to admit them. They lived in appalling conditions on the Polish side of the border at Zbaszyn near Rosen, the Koczicki family among them.
3. The ghetto of Bochnia, in the Cracow district, was established on March 15, 1941, and liquidated in September 1943. It was populated by Jews from Bochnia and neighboring towns and by refugees from various other places, about 15,000 in all. See *Obozy Hitlerowskie na Ziemiach Polskich 1939–1945* (Warsaw: Panstwowe Wydawnictwo Naukowie, 1979), pp. 110–11.

## A Mother's Heart

1. *Obozy Hitlerowskie na Ziemiach Polskich,* p. 110.

## God Is Everywhere . . . But . . .

1. Jews working in the workshops of the Bochnia ghetto were issued special papers, which saved them for some time from deportation and starvation. The papers were the "magic charm ensuring life," without which one faced an immediate and certain death. See *The Black Book* (New York: Durrell, Sloan and Pearce, 1946), pp. 190–94.
2. Rabbi Moshe Friedman (1881–1943) of Boyan-Cracow, a Hasidic rabbi and outstanding scholar, was spiritual head of the famed Academy Yeshivat Chahmei Lublin. In 1941 he escaped to Tarnow. An attempt was made to secure papers of a foreign national for him. After great effort, Mr. Hayyim Eiss of Zurich, Switzerland, was able to obtain Paraguayan papers for the rabbi, but it was too late. He was deported to the gas chambers of Belzec where he perished on the second of Elul, 1943. See Unger, *Admorim Shenispu Bashoah,* p. 226. However, there are conflicting reports as to the rabbi's place of death. See Ber Mark, ed., *Megilat Auschwitz* (Tel Aviv: Tel Aviv University Press, 1978), pp. 221–22. A diary kept at the time by a member of the Sonderkommando states that Rabbi Moshe Friedman of Boyan perished in the Auschwitz gas chambers. Dr. Menachem M. Brayer, father of the present Boyaner Rebbe, Rabbi Nachum Dov Brayer, confirms the facts in the Unger source; see also Hillel Zeidman, "Harav Moshe Friedman Admor Mi-Boyan," in *Eleh Ezkera* (New York: Research Institute of Religious Jewry, 1957), vol. II, pp. 109–17.
3. Sanhedrin 37/a.
4. See Robert L. Hewitt, *Work Horse of the Western Front: The Story of the 30th Infantry Division* (Washington, D.C.: Infantry Journal Press, 1946), pp. 263–65.

## The Amulet of the Belzer Rabbi

1. *Obozy Hitlerowskie na Ziemiach Polskich,* p. 516.

## The Little Slave Girl from the Toy Factory

1. Among many workshops operating in the Bochnia ghetto were those for tailoring, underwear, shoemaking, brushes, locksmithing, box making, carpentry, handkerchiefs, toys, motorcars, and electrical apparatus. See *The Black Book*, p. 191.
2. Hewitt, *Work Horse of the Western Front*, pp. 263–65.

## The Zanzer Kiddush Goblet

1. Rabbi Hayyim ben Leibush Halberstam (1793–1876), founder of the Zanz dynasty, is usually referred to as the Divrei Hayyim, the name of his three books: *Divrei Hayyim* (Zolkiev, 1864), on ritual purity and divorce laws; responsa *Divrei Hayyim* (Lemberg, 1875); and *Divrei Hayyim* (Munkacz, 1877), Hasidic sermons, the Torah, and festivals.

## No Time for Advice

1. Genesis 32: 8–9.
2. Rabbi Yehuda Leib Alter (1847–1905) was the author of *Sefat Emet*, homiletics on the Torah for the Sabbath and holidays, written in the Hasidic spirit (Cracow: Pietrokov, 1905–1908).
3. Bava Kama 102/a.
4. Deuteronomy 28: 28–29.

## "The Messiah Is Already Here!"

1. Isaiah 35: 3–6.

## "Jew, Go Back to the Grave!"

1. Judges 16:30.
2. See Dr. Shaul Barkli and Peretz Alufi, eds., *Eisyshok-Korotea ve-Hurbana* (Jerusalem, 1950), pp. 57–66, 125–26.
3. Leon Kahn, *No Time to Mourn* (Vancouver, B.C.: Laurelton Press, 1978), pp. 17–45.
4. Jews were first mentioned in Eisysky in the year 1145. The tombstones in the old cemetery where the town's Jews were annihilated in September 1941 dated back to the thirteenth century. Eisysky was founded by the Lithuanian prince Eisys in 1070.

## God's Messenger, the Grandson of the Pnei Yehoshua

1. It is customary in Judaism to call the authors of religious books by the name of one of their books. Joshua Falk, author of *The Pnei Yehoshua*, was a famous scholar and the teacher of the great Hasidic leader Dov of Mezerichi, the successor of the Baal Shem Tov.
2. Each Jewish community had a guest house (*hahnasat orhim*), a place kept by the community, mainly by volunteer women, for people who passed through the town and had no relatives with whom to stay. They slept there free of charge and were

invited for meals by the townspeople. The invitations were usually extended Friday night in the synagogue after evening prayers.

3. The literal meaning of the term *eruv* is blending, amalgamating. According to Halakha (law) a Jew is prohibited on the Sabbath from carrying things from one domain to another, unless an *eruv* was prepared beforehand. There are various types of *eruvim*. The amalgamation of courtyards is one of them. It is prepared as follows: Each of the tenants of the particular courtyard joins in providing an article of food that is deposited in an appropriate place on Friday, as if to say "we are all associated together; we possess one and the same food and none of us holds a domain distinct from the domain of the other."

4. One of the tractates of the Talmud.

## Number 145053

1. Joseph Mengele was chief physician at Auschwitz, a specialist in what he called the "science of twins." He conducted many selections both on the arrival of prisoners at the platform of Auschwitz and afterwards. He was known as the Angel of Death.

2. Each Hebrew letter has a numerical value. The number 18 equals the Hebrew word *chai*, which means life. *Chai* is considered a lucky number endowed with mystical qualities. There are similar testimonies attaching great significance to the number assigned in concentration camps. In the Janowska Road Camp, David Kahana was given the number 2250. He was sure that he would survive the war since its sum equals 9, half of *chai*. See *Yoman Ghetto Lvov*, pp. 114–15.

## Save This One Grandchild

1. *Obozy Hitlerowskie na Ziemiach Polskich*, p. 386.

2. On the destruction of the gypsies, see Miriam Novitch, *Rezach Hazoanim Beyemei, Hashilton Hanazi* (Israel: Lohamei Hagetaot, August 1969); and "The Gypsies and the Third Reich," *The Wiener Library Bulletin*, vol. 8, 1949.

## A Pail of Potato Peels and Two Halberstams

1. Flossenburg was liberated by the 358th Infantry Regiment, 90th Infantry Division. There were 1,160 inmates in camp on the day of liberation.

## A Brother's Tefillin

1. A Jewish settlement in Rzeszow, capital of Rzeszow province, southeastern Poland, dates back to the fifteenth century. A center for Jewish culture, Hasidim, and Zionism, the Jewish community was destroyed during the Holocaust and not reconstituted after World War II. See *Obozy Hitlerowskie na Ziemiach Polskich*, pp. 441–42.

## The Rain

1. When the soldiers of the U.S. 102nd Infantry Division liberated Gardelegen on April 16, 1945, they found the mounds of charred bodies. The American commander ordered the German citizens of Gardelegen to bury the remains of the dead

men in individual graves with coffins for each that measured six feet long and three feet wide, and 1,016 male citizens were held responsible for the future care of the graves. See *After Action Report,* 102nd Infantry Division, May 12, 1945 (Washington, D.C.: National Archives, record group 407); and Edmund C. Hassett, ed., *701st Tank Battalion* (Nuremberg, Germany, 1945), pp. 28–29, 96–205.

## A Natural Victory: Churchill and the Rabbi of Gur

1. For a detailed account of the spectacular rescue of the Rabbi of Gur, see Moshe Yehezkeeli, *Nes ha-Hatzala shel ha-Rabbi mi-Gur* (Jerusalem: Yeshurun, 1959).
2. This story is also mentioned in *Notes from the Warsaw Ghetto, The Journal of Emmanuel Ringelblum* (New York: Schocken Books, 1974), p. 265.

## The Rebbetzin of Gur: Two Passports

1. Rabbi Israel Alter of Gur was the son of the world-renowned Rabbi Abraham Mordechai Alter. In 1948, Rabbi Israel became the world leader of the Gerer Hasidim, a post he held until his death in 1977. He arrived in Israel with his father in 1940, during the Holocaust. See A. M. Alter and I. M. Alter, eds., *Beit Gur* (Israel, 1977).
2. Rudolf Haas was one of the commandants of Bergen Belsen. After his portrait was painted by an inmate, he was sent to the eastern front.
3. After liberation, the Rabbi of Bluzhov, Rabbi Israel Spira, then an inmate in Bergen Belsen, wrote to the Rabbi of Gur in the Holy Land and informed him of the memorial day of his wife and son. For the arrival of the transport from Bergen Belsen at Auschwitz, see *From the History of K.L. Auschwitz—Chronology* (Krakow: Panstwowe Muzeum w Oswiecimiu, 1967), vol. I, p. 204. According to this source, a transport from Bergen Belsen with 1,700 Jews arrived in Auschwitz instead of Switzerland on October 23, 1943. Realizing that they had been deceived, women from the transport attacked S.S. guards on the way to the gas chambers. This episode, which includes the killings by S.S. Oberscharführer Schildinger, served as a basis for the novel by Arnost Lustig, *A Prayer for Katerina Horovitzova* (New York: Avon Books, 1975).

## The Shofar of the Rabbi of Radorzytz

1. Yitzhak Alfasi, *Hahasidut* (Tel Aviv: Maariv, 1977), pp. 155–56.
2. I am grateful to Ilana Guri at Yad Vashem, Israel, for locating the shofar and its accompanying testimony by Moshe Ben-Dov (Winterer), file no. 1530.

## The Keepers of the Holy Temple

1. Rabbi Feifush Ashkenazi was a native of Safad, Israel, and the scion of a prominent family of scholars. Years before the war, he went to visit the Rabbi of Satmar, who was very impressed with him and asked him to stay with him. This story appears in a slightly different version in Shlomo Rozman, *Sefer Rashei Golat Ariel* (Brooklyn, N.Y., 1975), vol. I, pp. 46–47.
2. First Chronicles 9:23.

3. Rabbi Ashkenazi was less fortunate than the book that saved his life. After the Rabbi of Satmar's escape to Klausenburg, he stayed behind to take care of a few details. He was caught by the Germans and deported to Auschwitz, where he was murdered on June 3, 1944. His son, Rabbi Yossl Ashkenazi, remained with the Satmar Rabbi throughout the war and until the rabbi's death on August 19, 1979.

## The Kasztner Transport and a Zionist Leader's Dream

1. Rozman, *Sefer Rashei Golat Ariel*, vol. I, pp. 60–61.
2. This episode supports the statement in the Zoltan Glatz report from Geneva, dated February 10, 1946, that Jozsef Fischer had input regarding the Klausenburg list.
3. Short for *Vaada Ezrah ve-Hazzalah* (Relief and Rescue Committee), established in Budapest in January 1943.
4. The role of Kasztner in his dealings with the Nazis and their collaborators remains controversial. In his report he wrote about the difficult—and positive—part he played in the rescue of some of Hungary's Jews.
5. Bitterness over the list, and the fact that relatives of the organizers were saved, is still alive. In 1957, Rudolf Kasztner was shot on a Tel Aviv street. For the Grunvald accusation against Kasztner, see Israel Supreme Court, *Piskei Din*, 1958, no. 12, pp. 317–2017. For the list of those who left for Budapest, and from there to Bergen Belsen, see Yad Vashem Archives, M 20/59 and M 20/68.
6. Andre Biss, *A Million Jews to Save* (London: New English Library, 1975), pp. 168–77.
7. Joel Brand (1906–1964) was a member of the Vaada who negotiated the rescue of Hungarian Jewry with Adolf Eichmann. Upon Eichmann's orders, Brand left for neutral Turkey on May 17, 1944. His mission was to present the Jewish Agency with the German proposition, the exchange of the lives of Hungarian Jews for a supply of trucks and other goods. This came to be known as the "blood for trucks" deal. Moshe Shertok (Sharett), then head of the political department of the Jewish Agency, was prevented by the British from traveling from Palestine to Turkey. Brand left Turkey for Palestine, and was arrested by the British in Aleppo, Syria, and taken to a Cairo prison. The British claimed that Brand was a German agent. The Germans viewed the arrest as Brand's defection. See Joel Brand, *Be-Shlihut Nidonim la-Mavet* (Tel Aviv: Ayanot, 1957); S. B. Beit-Zvi, *Post-Ugandian Zionism in the Crucible of the Holocaust* (Tel Aviv: Bronfman Publishers, 1977), pp. 127–29; and Yehuda Bauer, *The Holocaust in Historical Perspective* (Seattle: University of Washington Press, 1978), pp. 94 155.
8. For a detailed account, see Randolph L. Braham, *The Politics of Genocide* (New York: Columbia University Press, 1981), vol. II, pp. 965–66.
9. For a historical account of the events of December 7, 1944, see Braham, *The Politics of Genocide*, pp. 962–65.
10. In the course of conducting interviews for this tale, I asked a well-known Hasidic personality, "How did the Rabbi of Satmar agree to be rescued by a Zionist leader?" "This may be the only merit of the Zionist movement," he responded.

## A Holy Book

1. Biss, *A Million Jews to Save*, pp. 64–70.
2. Kasztner originally suggested that 100,000 Jews be "put on ice." He eventually agreed to pay a $100 minimum for every Jew who remained alive. See *Der Kastner Bericht* (Basel: 1946), pp. 113–14.
3. Biss, *A Million Jews to Save*, p. 70.

## The Yellow Bird

1. Since the interview for this tale took place, Livia Bitton Jackson has published her own memoirs, *Elli, Coming of Age in the Holocaust* (New York: Times Books, 1980). See pp. 39–40.
2. Jackson, *Elli*, pp. 28–29.

## A Bowl of Soup

1. The Auschwitz platform was the threshold between life and death. Upon arrival there, the initial selection took place. Men were separated from women, and women with young children, the old, the sick, and those unfit for work were sent to the left, directly to the gas chambers. See Primo Levi, *Survival in Auschwitz* (New York: Collier Books, 1961), pp. 15–17.
2. Jackson, *Elli*, pp. 67–68.
3. Amon Goeth was sentenced to death by the Supreme Tribunal in Cracow in 1946. United Nations War Crime Commission, *Law Reports of Trials of War Criminals*, vol. 7 (1948), pp. 1–10.
4. Jackson, *Elli*, pp. 110–14.
5. Women were employed by the S.S., were paid and wore a uniform, but were not members of the S.S. itself.
6. Jackson, *Elli*, pp. 147–48.

## Who Will Win This War?

1. The Second Hungarian Army was deployed after September 1941 on the eastern front. Jews were also mobilized by an order of the minister of defense. Jewish labor companies were utilized in the military operation zones, even if the men were above forty-two years of age, the limit by law for frontier service. Tens of thousands of Jews served along the front lines, under the most cruel conditions. See Braham, *The Politics of Genocide*, vol. I, pp. 307–12.
2. The Arrow Cross party, the Hungarian Nazi party, was headed by Ferenc Szalasi, who was executed for war crimes in 1946.
3. The Todt Organization was the labor corps, organized and headed by Fritz Todt. For more information on Todt and the Hungarian labor battalions, see Braham, *The Politics of Genocide*, vol. I, pp. 330–31; and Dietrich Orlow, *The History of the Nazi Party, 1933–1945* (Pittsburgh: University of Pittsburgh Press, 1973), pp. 376–77.
4. Braham, *The Politics of Genocide*, vol. I, p. 313.

5. *Ibid.*, pp. 306–307. The introduction of the yellow armbands was demanded by the general staff early in May 1941, after some Hungarians allegedly complained about seeing Jews wearing armbands with the national colors.

# TWO: FRIENDSHIP

## Good Morning, Herr Müller

1. After the German occupation of Poland, many *Volksdeutschen* were eager to serve the Nazi cause. They joined the Nazis and took revenge upon their Polish neighbors in reprisal for the alleged anti-*Volksdeutschen* pogroms that took place in Poland in the late 1930s. See Hans Schadeaaldt, comp., *Polish Acts of Atrocity against the German Minority in Poland: Documenting Evidence,* published for the German Foreign Office (Berlin/New York, 1940).

## Two Capsules of Cyanide

1. The departure and return of the inmates from and to the camp was also sometimes accompanied by music. A special piece of music, "Death Tango," was composed for the occasion. Professor Striks and the famous conductor Mund were forced to lead the musicians. The entire orchestra and its conductor were liquidated. See *The Black Book,* pp. 308–9.
2. Poison, cyanide in particular, was a precious commodity at the camps and ghettos. The prices fluctuated according to supply and demand. Prices rose before an Aktion and declined afterward. See Thorne, *Out of the Ashes,* pp. 115, 124–25; and Kahana, *Yoman Ghetto Lvov,* p. 82.

## On the Waiting Bench at the Gallows

1. The cruelty of the Janowska Road Camp officials knew no limits. Each S.S. officer had his own style of torture. A twenty-three-year-old officer named Schanbach, after beating his victims, tried to prolong their agony by reviving them with some food and water, then continued his torturing (*The Black Book,* pp. 308–9, 315–16). The camp commandant, Obersturmführer Wilhaus, was the brother-in-law of Major General Katzman of the S.S., and police chief of Galicia. Wilhaus lived in the camp in a beautiful villa furnished with looted goods and artwork. On his daughter's birthday, he took her out on the front porch, aimed his revolver, and one by one killed inmates of the "cripples brigade." The tiny tot Hydka clapped her hands with great joy. His wife, Otilia, particularly enjoyed the Aktions in the ghetto of Lvov. She had a specially designed lady's pistol which she constantly put to use. See an eyewitness account by a former Lvov resident and Janowska inmate, David Kahana, in *Yoman Ghetto Lvov,* pp. 107–8.
2. "Hot roll call" was the inmates' camp language for a day of many executions. See Thorne, *Out of the Ashes,* p. 54.

## A Sip of Coffee

1. *Obozy Hitlerowskie na Ziemiach Polskich,* pp. 93–94. An eyewitness report on a transport from Lvov that arrived in Belzec at the end of August 1942 states the 6,700 Jews were packed in a train of forty-five wagons; 1,450 arrived dead. See the Kurt Gerstein report quoted in Saul Friedlander, *Pius XII and the Third Reich* (New York: Alfred A. Knopf, 1966), pp. 125–28.
2. The Rabbi's wife, Perl, née Unger, was murdered in Belzec on October 18, 1942; see Tarnow, *Sefer Zikaron,* (Israel, 1968), vol. II, p. 229n.
3. The belongings and clothing of the approximately 600,000 Jews murdered at Belzec were transported in trucks to Janowska. The warehouse complex there was under the direction of a Nazi named Blum and three Jewish managers appointed by him. See Kahana, *Yoman Ghetto Lvov,* p. 109.
4. It was possible to purchase coffee and many other items in the camp. See Wells, *The Death Brigade,* pp. 133–34; and Thorne, *Out of the Ashes,* pp. 72–73.
5. Rabbi Meyer Landau settled in Israel after World War II.
6. Genesis 27:22.

## For the Sake of Friendship

1. Women endangered their lives by going to the camp's barbed-wire fences to maintain contact with relatives and friends. They brought letters and food. It was possible to send packages from the ghetto of Lvov to the Janowska Road Camp. See Kahana, *Yoman Ghetto Lvov,* p. 131; and Wells, *The Death Brigade,* pp. 63, 67–69.
2. There is a different version of this acquaintance between the Rabbi and a German; see Leon Thorne, *Out of the Ashes,* p. 69. Rabbi Israel Spira confirms the authenticity of the version as it appears here.
3. On Helmut Müller, see *Trials of War Criminals before the Nuernberg Military Tribunals, Nuernberg, October 1946–April 1949* (Washington, D.C.: U.S. Government Printing Office), vol. IV, pp. 864–66, Green Series.
4. There were other incidents of friendship and love between top Nazi officials and Jews in Janowska. Obersturmführer Fritz Gerbauer had a Jewish mistress; his wife's lover was her Jewish chauffeur. See Wells, *The Death Brigade,* pp. 87–88.

## Under the Blue Skies of Tel Aviv

1. *Obozy Hitlerowskie na Ziemiach Polskich,* p. 110.

## "What I Learned at My Father's Home"

1. After the war, when it became known that he was the only survivor of the Bluzhov dynasty, Rabbi Israel Spira, the Rabbi of Pruchnik, assumed the title of Rabbi of Bluzhov.

## The Yeshiva Student

1. Ezekiel 37:1–14.
2. Bava Kama 113/b.

## Stars

1. The Lodz ghetto was established in April 1940, six months earlier than the Warsaw ghetto. Its final liquidation took place in July and August 1944.
2. Camp near Ludwigslust was liberated the first week in May 1945, by the U.S. 82nd Airborne Division and the 8th Infantry Division.

## A Girl Called Estherke

1. Genesis 22:12.
2. On the fate of children in Auschwitz, see the notes written in Auschwitz, *Amidst a Nightmare of Crime* (Auschwitz: State Museum of Auschwitz, 1973), pp. 118–19; and Mark, *Megilat Auschwitz*, pp. 22, 226–27.
3. Beginning in November 1944, several large transports of women were transferred from Auschwitz-Birkenau to Bergen Belsen; see Bertha Ferderber-Salz, *And the Sun Kept Shining* . . . (New York: Holocaust Library, 1980), pp. 142–57.
4. Sanhedrin 19/b; Megila 3/a.

## In the Image of God

1. In March 1944, the status of Bergen Belsen was officially changed from a transit camp to a camp for the sick and exhausted. In the summer of 1944, it became a regular concentration camp and a women's camp was established. The population swelled rapidly with a constant influx of inmates from the east as a result of the German retreat. Inmates arrived after long death marches, lasting for weeks. Those who survived the marches were starved and disease-ridden.

## The Merit of a Young Priest

1. Mordechai Gebirtig was born in Cracow in 1877. The most famous song he wrote is *"Undzer Shtetl Brent"* ("Our Town Is Burning"), which appeared in 1938 after the pogrom in Przytyk. His prophetic vision of the doomed shtetl makes the poem a virtual hymn, often sung at Holocaust memorials. See Ferderber-Salz, *And the Sun Kept Shining* . . . , pp. 29–36.
2. The ghetto of Cracow had an active underground. For an eyewitness account, see Gusta Davidson, *Yomana Shel Yustina* (Israel: Ghetto Fighters House, 1978). To date, only parts of the handwritten diary have been discovered. Yustina and her husband were two of the most active members of the underground in Cracow. They did not survive.
3. *Obozy Hitlerowskie na Ziemiach Polskich*, p. 249; and Ferderber-Salz, *And the Sun Kept Shining* . . . , pp. 67–71.
4. The letter is reproduced in "Christian Woman, Priest and Congress Co-operate to Save Polish Orphan," *Congress Bulletin* (Montreal), August-September 1949, p. 8.
5. *Ibid.*
6. The *Montreal Daily Star*, July 4, 1949, printed Shachne Hiller's picture aboard the *Batory*. The caption reads: "Polish Boy to Live in Montreal."
7. See "Orphan who Escaped Nazis to Learn Thrill of Camp Life," *Montreal Daily Star*, July 6, 1949.

8. Dorothea Andrews, "Boy, 10, Orphaned by Nazis, Reaches Haven in District,"
   *The Washington Post*, February 9, 1951.

## THREE: THE SPIRIT ALONE

### Circumcision

1. Genesis 22:1–19.

### Slain with Hunger

1. One Gestapo official at Janowska, named Wepke, made a wager with the other
   camp executioners that he could chop a boy in half with one blow of an axe. When
   the others refused to get him one, he caught a ten-year-old boy, forced him to
   kneel, bent his head in his hands, took aim, adjusted the boy's head, and slit the
   child's body open with one blow. The onlooking Nazis congratulated Wepke and
   shook his hand. *The Black Book*, p. 309.
2. The daily ration in Janowska consisted of watery soup and a small slice of ersatz
   bread (bread substitute).
3. Lamentations 4:9.

### Even the Transgressors in Israel

1. In September and October there are several major Jewish holidays: Rosh
   Hashanah, the New Year; Yom Kippur, the Day of Atonement; Sukkot, the Festival of the Tabernacles; Hoshana Rabbah, the seventh day of Sukkot; Shemini
   Atzeret, the final feast day at the conclusion of Sukkot; and Simhat Torah, the rejoicing in the law.
2. Thirty-nine main categories of work are forbidden on the Sabbath and on Yom
   Kippur, the "Sabbath of Sabbaths." These tasks, and analogous ones, are related
   to the kinds of work performed by the children of Israel in building the Sanctuary
   during their sojourn in the desert in biblical days.
3. For an eyewitness account of the same event, written during World War II, see
   Thorne, *Out of the Ashes*, p. 69.
4. From the Morning Services.
5. The Germans deliberately used the verb *fressen*—to gorge oneself, to feed as animals
   do—rather than the polite *essen*, used for humans.
6. Erubin 19/a.

### Death of a Beloved Son

1. For more details on the life of the Rabbi of Belz during the Holocaust period, see
   Moshe Yehezkeeli, *Hazalat ha-Rabbi mi-Belz* (Jerusalem: Yeshurun, 1960).

### Satan's Altar

1. Leviticus 1:3.

## The Grandson of the Arugat Ha-Bosem

1. The Arugat Ha-Bosem, Rabbi Moshe Greenwald (1853–1911), was invited at the age of forty to assume the rabbinate of Chust, Hungary. He was known for his scholarship, leadership, and his books *Arugat Ha-Bosem, Responsa in Halakha*, and *Commentary on the Five Books of Moses.*
2. The same story appears in *Torah Umitzo* No. 64, no date printed.

## "He Hath Delivered Me out of All Trouble"

1. The geographic distribution of Soviet Jewry determined to a large extent the basic strategy of the Nazi mobile killing units designed to reach as many cities as quickly as possible. The Einsatzgruppen moved closely upon the heels of the advancing army, trapping the large Jewish population centers. The three cars of the Einsatzgruppen C followed the first tanks into Zhitomir and murdered the Jewish population. See Hilberg, *Destruction of European Jewry*, pp. 190–208.
2. Stinko's cruelty was not unique but rather the norm. The cruel and bizarre conditions under which the Jewish labor servicemen lived and worked in the Ukraine were primarily due to the viciously anti-Semitic attitude of most of the company commanders and guards. They acted not according to written regulations regarding the labor battalions but according to oral instructions given to the commanders. Major General Artur Horvay allegedly informed the commanders at an orientation session that Jews were not entitled to receive packages and their correspondence should be strictly censored. See Braham, *The Politics of Genocide*, vol. I, pp. 315–17.
3. *Ibid.*, p. 343.
4. The Swedish Red Cross, which enjoyed great prestige and influence in Hungary because of its services there during World War I, played a major role in the relief and rescue operations of Hungarian Jewry. The humanitarian activities of Raoul Wallenberg are an outstanding example. For more details see Braham, *The Politics of Genocide*, vol. II, pp. 757–58, 1083–91.
5. Gunskirchen was an *Aussenkommando* camp of Mauthausen, located six kilometers north of Lambach, Austria. See Yaffa Eliach and Brana Gurewitsch, eds. *The Liberators* (Brooklyn, N.Y.: Center for Holocaust Studies, 1981), pp. 48–49.

## A Prayer and a Dream

1. Since Bergen Belsen was deep inside Germany, it became a center for prisoners after the German defeat on the eastern front. There was a constant influx of prisoners from the east, and the camp population swelled rapidly. The new inmates arrived starved and riddled with disease after forced marches of many weeks. There was a breakdown of the camp's essential services, and typhoid and other epidemics broke out. The death rate was high in March 1945, when nearly 20,000 people died, including Anne Frank. Before liberation, on April 15, 1945, 17,000 more perished. After being freed, yet another 17,000 died while all the others were in need of medical care.

## The Third Sabbath Meal at Mauthausen

1. Franz Ziereis was camp commander of Mauthausen from February 1939 to May 1945, when the camp was liberated by the Americans. He was shot by a U.S. patrol when he tried to escape. He was known for his cruelty. According to an eyewitness account, he gave his son as a birthday present, fifty Jews for target practice. For more on Ziereis, see "The Confessions of the Former Camp Commander of Mauthausen, Franz Ziereis" (Brooklyn, N.Y.: Center for Holocaust Studies), Irving Fox Collection, RG 272, pp. 1–6. On general conditions in Mauthausen, see Jacob Presser, *The Destruction of Dutch Jews* (New York: E. P. Dutton, 1969).

2. Rabbi Asher Zelig Grunsweig, the last Rabbi of Dolha in Carpathian Russia, was known as a scholarly and saintly man. Together with his family, he was deported to Auschwitz and perished at the gas chambers. See Rozman, *Sefer Rashei Golat Ariel*, vol. I, pp. 274–83.

3. Shabbat 118/a.

## A Hill in Bergen Belsen

1. On the typhus epidemic in Bergen Belsen, see the description of a former inmate and doctor in the camp, Dr. Leo Fritz, quoted in Hardman, *The Survivors*, pp. 3–9.

2. When the British liberated Bergen Belsen on April 15, 1945, there were more than 40,000 inmates in the camp. Of these, 28,000 needed hospital care, and 17,000 subsequently died from typhus, tuberculosis, starvation, and dysentery. See articles by Brigadier General H. L. Glyn Hughes, "Belsen, April 1945," pp. 94–97, and Derick Sington, "The 15th of April, 1945," pp. 69–80, in *Belsen* (London: Narod Press, 1957). For a report on the medical state of the inmates on liberation day, written by a senior medical officer after twenty-four hours' contact with them, see W. R. F. Collis, M.D., "Belsen Camp, a Preliminary Report," *British Medical Journal*, June 9, 1945, pp. 814–16.

## A Father's Blessing

1. With the approach of the Red army, thousands of labor servicemen were killed in cold blood. The exhumations conducted after liberation disclosed in Hidegseg alone a mass grave of 790 bodies. See Braham, *The Politics of Genocide*, vol. I, pp. 342–43.

## A Sign from Heaven

1. The Stutthof concentration camp was located twenty-two and a half miles east of Danzig. It existed from September 2, 1939, until May 9, 1945. It was greatly enlarged in the spring of 1944 and became virtually a death camp. Beside the central camp a number of satellite camps were built. The greatest increase of Jewish prisoners occurred in June–October 1944, when more than 20,000 Jews, Elaine Seidenfeld among them, were shipped to Stutthof from Auschwitz. See Arolsen, 1969, pp. 221–40; *Obozy Hitlerowskie Na Ziemiach Polskich*, pp. 492–506.

## A Bobov Melody

1. Song and dance enjoy a unique place in the Hasidic movement. A Hasidic master once said, "If I could sing, I would force God to dwell among men."

## A Miracle in a Potato Field

1. A large group of inmates were taken under heavy guard to Kutno. On their arrival there, they were loaded onto a train and shipped to Dachau. They reached Dachau on August 9, 1944. About one-third of the inmates died on the death march.

# FOUR: AT THE GATES OF FREEDOM

## The Plague of Blood

1. Jeremiah 3:14.
2. Shemot Rabba 9/10.

## "I Envy You"

1. Yoreh-Deah, 376ff.

## "Pray for Us!"

1. Psalms, 20:9–10.

## The Grip of the Holy Letters

1. Buchenwald was liberated April 11, 1945, by the U.S. Army, 6th Armored Division, Combat Team A. See Eliach and Gurewitsch, *The Liberators*, pp. 16–25.
2. *Ibid.*, p. 20.
3. The Torah is read in the synagogue on Sabbath morning and afternoon as well as on Monday and Thursday (the market days in biblical times) and on holidays. It is now the custom to complete the public reading in an annual cycle. The Five Books of Moses are divided into fifty-four weekly portions. The text in a Sefer Torah, the parchment scroll, is written without vowel signs or cantillation (liturgical chanting) marks.

## To Marry a Baker

1. A group of European Jews, among them students of the Mir Yeshivah, found refuge in Shanghai during World War II. Rabbi Abraham Kalmanowitz (1881–1964), the Rosh Yeshivah of Mir, succeeded in emigrating to the United States in 1940. There he devoted himself to rescuing European rabbis, heads of yeshivot, and their students. Rabbi Kalmanowitz arranged for the transfer of the Mir Yeshivah from Vilna to Kobe, Japan, and later to Shanghai. In 1945 he arranged for its transfer to the United States and to Israel, and in 1946 he reopened it in Brooklyn. See David Kranzler, *Japanese, Nazis and Jews, the Jewish Refugee Community of Shanghai 1938–1945* (New York: Yeshiva University Press, 1976).

## "The Happiest Day of My Life"

1. My father is not a Hasidic Jew. His family, for generations, were Mitnaggedim, opponents of the Hasidic movement. In tribute to my father, a marvelous storyteller, I have included a few non-Hasidic tales in this collection.

## Hans and I at the Rema's Grave

1. In 1978, U.S. President Jimmy Carter established the President's Commission on the Holocaust. It was charged with recommending an appropriate memorial for the victims of the Holocaust. On September 27, 1979, at the White House Rose Garden, the commission presented its report to President Carter, suggesting the building of a museum in Washington, D.C.
2. Rema is the acronym of Moses Isserles (1525 or 1530–1572), one of the great scholars of Polish Jewry, a native of Cracow, a great scholar, codifier, and Halakhic authority. In 1552, his first wife died at the age of twenty. In her memory, he built a beautiful synagogue, now known as the Rema Synagogue.
3. Lamentations 1:1.

## Two Funerals

1. Rabbi Chaim Solovieitchick Brisker (b. 1853) was one of the great Talmudic scholars of Lithuania, head of the famed Academy of Wolozhin, and after its closing by tzarist authorities, Rabbi of Brisk. He died in Otwock near Warsaw in 1918.
2. For the activities of Rabbi Kahana Schapira in the Kovna ghetto, see Ephraim Oshry, *Mimaamakim* (Brooklyn: Modern Linotype Co., 1959–1975), 4 vols.

## Tipping the Scales of Justice

1. WAGRO stands for Warsaw Ghetto Resistance Organization.

## Grandfather Avrumche Backenroth's Table

1. It has become a custom in some places to light one candle for the souls of the living and another for the souls of the dead. See Abraham b. Nathan ha-Yarhi, "Hilkhot Zom Kippur," in *Sefer Hamanhig*, Yitzhak Rafael, ed. (Jerusalem: Mossad Harav Kook, 1978) vol. I, pp. 362–63; Efraim E. Urbach, ed., *Arugat ha-Bossem* of Abraham bar Azriel (Jerusalem: Mekize Nirdamim, 1963), vol. III, p. 572; *"Sefer ha-Minhagot* of Asher bar Saul of Lunel," in Simcha Assaf, *Sifran shel Rishonim* (Jerusalem: Mekize Nirdamim, 1935), pp. 152–53; and *Shulkhan Aruch, Orach Hayyim*, 610.

## Rejoining the Human Race

1. On life in the ghetto of Drohobycz, see Thorne, *Out of the Ashes*, pp. 100–194.
2. *Ibid.*, pp. 147–53.
3. Dr. Thorne wrote his book in that cellar. See pp. 13–15.
4. Thorne, *Out of the Ashes*, pp. 195–203.

5. There were many pogroms against Jews in Poland. The best-known pogrom took place in Kielce on July 4, 1946, when forty-two Jews were murdered. Others occurred as early as October 20, 1944. See Barkli and Alufi, *Eisyshok-Korotea ve-Hurbana*, pp. 67–70, 82–86.
6. *Obozy Hitlerowskie na Ziemiach Polskich*, pp. 302–12.

# Geographic Index

# Name Index

Agnon, S. Y., xvi, xvii, xxiv
Alter, Rabbi Abraham Mordechai (Rabbi of Gur), 79–80
Alter, Rabbi Israel, 80
  wife and son of, 80–84
Alter, Rabbi Mendel (Grand Rabbi of Pabianic), 49, 50
Anna (inmate at Bergen Belsen), 177–178
  father of, 177–178
Aron, Mr. and Mrs. H., 145, 146
Arrow Cross party, 101
Arugat Ha-Bosem, grandson of, 164–166
Ashkenazi, Rabbi, 9
Ashkenazi, Rabbi Feifush, 87
Ashkenazi, Rabbi Joseph, 88, 91

Baal Shem Tov (Israel ben Eliezer), xv, xvi, xix–xx, 11
Bachner, Abraham, 217–218
Backenroth, Avrumche, 219–223, 226, 227, 228, 229
Backenroth, Grandmother, 220, 222, 227, 228
Backenroth, Rivka, 222
Backenroth, Sarah (née Tenzer), 219, 222, 225–226, 227, 228–229
Backenroth, Stella. See Wieseltier, Stella
Backenroth, Yehuda Leib, 219, 222, 223–227, 228–229
Backenroth, Zygus, 219, 225, 227, 228–229
Backenroth family, 219–229
Baer, Baruch, 197
Baruch of Medzhibozh, Rabbi, 11, 12
Belz, Grand Rabbi of. See Rokeach, Rabbi Aaron
Benek (of Schodnica), 228
Ben-Zeev, Zahava, 50n.

Ben-Zion (of Janowska Road Camp), 157
Berger, Jenny, 143, 145, 146
Berger, Stanley. See Hiller, Shachne
Berkowitz family, 92–94
Bielgory, Rabbi of. See Mordecai, Rabbi of Beilgory
Biss, Andre, 91
Bitton, Emily, 95n., 99n.
Blakfein, Ellen, 132n.
Blascke, Mayor of Vienna, 92
Bluzhov, Rabbi of. See Spira, Rabbi Israel
Bobov, Grand Rabbi of. See Halberstam, Rabbi Ben-Zion
Borack, Hayyim, 42–43
Boyaner, Rebbe. See Friedman, Rabbi Abraham Jacob
Brand, Joel, 90
  family of, 90
Brecht, Bertolt, xxxiii
Brisker, Rabbi Chaim, 214
British Army, 138, 178
Buber, Martin, xvi–xvii

Carter, Jimmy, xxiii
  Commission of the Holocaust, 210, 212, 213–215
Chafetz Chayim. See HaCohen, Israel Meir
Chaim Yitzhak (shoemaker), 51
Chmielnicki, Bogdan, xv
Churchill, Winston, 79
Council of the Four Lands, xv

Dan, Yoseph, xx
David (grandson of Arugat Ha-Bosem), 164–166
David Moshe, Rabbi (Tchortkever Rebbe), 222
Dingott, Kalia, 178n.
Dora (of Bochnia ghetto), 121

262